YELLOW STAR, RED STAR

YELLOW STAR, RED STAR

Holocaust Remembrance after Communism

JELENA SUBOTIĆ

CORNELL UNIVERSITY PRESS
Ithaca and London

First published 2019 by Cornell University Press

Printed in the United States of America

Library of Congress Cataloging-in-Publication Data

Names: Subotic, Jelena, author.
Title: Yellow star, red star : Holocaust remembrance after communism / Jelena Subotić.
Description: Ithaca, [New York] : Cornell University Press, 2019. | Includes bibliographical references and index.
Identifiers: LCCN 2019019610 (print) | LCCN 2019020851 (ebook) | ISBN 9781501742408 (cloth ; alk. paper)
Subjects: LCSH: Holocaust, Jewish (1939–1945)—Europe, Eastern—Historiography. | Holocaust, Jewish (1939–1945)—Europe, Eastern—Influence. | Memorialization—Political aspects—Europe, Eastern. | Nationalism and collective memory—Europe, Eastern. | Post-communism—Europe, Eastern.
Classification: LCC D804.348 .S83 2019 (print) | LCC D804.348 (ebook) | DDC 940.53/1860947—dc23
LC record available at https://lccn.loc.gov/2019019610
LC ebook record available at https://lccn.loc.gov/2019020851

For Doug and Leo, always

Contents

Illustrations

Maps

Figures

Preface and Acknowledgments

Milivoje Jovanović was a career civil servant in Belgrade in the kingdom of Yugoslavia. After graduating from law school in 1934, he joined the Ministry of Internal Affairs and worked his way up to the rank of senior police inspector. In 1938, as an elite police commissioner, he became the chief of personal security of the Yugoslav prince regent Pavle Karađorđević. Steadily moving up the ranks of Yugoslav police, on the eve of occupation in April 1941, Jovanović was the chief of the Department of General Police in Belgrade.

In the early morning of April 6, 1941, an officer on duty telephoned Jovanović to inform him that German warplanes had taken off from Romania and were on their way toward Belgrade. Jovanović quickly made his way to the office and, together with a few gathered officers, burned the files the police kept on suspected communists. A few hours later the Axis bombing of Belgrade began. Jovanović was recruited by the Yugoslav army to fight against the Germans in the doomed "April war." After just a few days, the Yugoslav army collapsed and German troops marched into Belgrade on April 12. The next day, Jovanović reported back to duty.

His job, however, had changed. The German occupying administration moved quickly to set up a new apparatus of power. The Department of General Police was renamed the Special Police and Jovanović appointed as its head. The Germans immediately ordered a series of repressive measures—including specific discriminatory measures against the Jews, Roma, and communists. The Belgrade Special Police was in charge of implementing these measures and reporting back to the German authorities. This was Milivoje Jovanović's new job. He filled out his new personnel profile, and in response to question ten, "Nationality and race; do you have anyone in your family of Jewish or Gypsy origin," he answered, "Serb—pure Aryan."

As the head of Special Police, Jovanović reorganized his department to reflect its new priorities. For the first time, a special department for

Jewish affairs was established. In a May 1941 reorganization order, Jovanović instructed this new police unit:

> [The chief of this unit] will carry out general control over the Jews—register them, manage the database of Jews, organize the archives of Jews and Jewish businesses. In terms of dispatching Jews for communal service, issuing special permits, or excusing Jews from labor due to age or illness, [the unit] will monitor their complete compliance with the existing orders. [The unit] will especially control whether the Jews are complying with the order to wear the Jewish symbol, whether their business is allowed or prohibited, whether a special plaque is placed on Jewish stores, and whether a sign is posted if the store had been confiscated. It will make sure that all the orders regarding Jews are fully implemented, and so it will also carry out various administrative acts regarding the general control of the Jews. It will also implement orders regarding control of the Gypsies.[1]

He also sent regular reports to his superiors in Belgrade City Management, who then forwarded them on to the Germans. In a report from June 10, 1941, Jovanović writes, "There is daily control of the Jews and they are being arrested or searched according to German orders."[2] His report from July 10 says,

> Distinguished communists were arrested and a number of them sent to the concentration camp [in Banjica]. Until today, 9,435 Jews and 670 Jewish businesses have been registered, as well as 3,050 Gypsies. There is constant control of Jews and Gypsies and there were many cases where these individuals were handed over to the Gestapo for violating the orders.[3]

It is in these first few months of the occupation from April to July 1941 that the early measures of discrimination, isolation, and dispossession of the Jews were carried out. To monitor and implement these measures of "suppressing the Jewish-communist action," the Gestapo provided the Belgrade Special Police with 16,000 Yugoslav dinars each month. This money was collected from Serbian Jews and put to use for their own destruction.

In mid-July 1941 Jovanović was dismissed (or resigned, as he claimed) from his post as head of Special Police and moved to a lower tier position as a

1. Files regarding activities of the Special Police Unit 1941–1944, Historical Archive of Belgrade, Belgrade City Management, Special Police, box 589, translation by author.
2. Special Police Unit files, Report of June 10, 1941.
3. Special Police Unit files, Report of July 10, 1941.

regular inspector of Belgrade's Seventh Quarter. He was replaced with an ambitious appointee, Miodrag Petrović, who apparently was not up to the task either and was dismissed just two months later. From September 1941 until the end of the war, the head of Special Police was Ilija Paranos, who proved to be much more of a true and sustained believer in the German cause.

Even though he was no longer in a high-profile position, Jovanović did not completely lose the trust of the occupation authorities. He was appointed to a commission to categorize the inmates of the Banjica concentration camp, the first concentration camp in Serbia and a site of imprisonment and torture of almost twenty-four thousand communists, Jews and Roma, of whom four thousand were killed.

In March 1944, however, he fell out of favor with the occupation regime and was arrested by the Gestapo, presumably on suspicion that he was collaborating with the communist resistance. He was tortured with electric shocks. In April, he was transferred to Banjica—the very same camp the Special Police he worked for had helped to establish. In July, he was on the list of prisoners to be deported to Mauthausen. Through a combination of luck, intervention by friends, and the increasing disarray among the German occupation authorities, he missed the Mauthausen transport. The Germans decided to close the Banjica camp and kill the remaining prisoners. Jovanović was discharged instead, and the notoriously brutal Banjica camp commander Božidar Vujković told him on release, "We are not going to waste a bullet on you, Mr. Jovanović. You will eventually be shot by the communists."

In October 1944, Belgrade was liberated and Tito's communist army marched in. Jovanović was arrested by the new regime in December on charges of collaboration. The hearing focused less on his wartime activities and instead more on his "character" and how many members of his extended family had joined the partisans. He counted as many as he could remember, emphasizing as evidence that his nieces were "educated in the spirit of antifascism." He was released. Over the years, he was arrested by the communist regime for shorter or longer spells—the longest being nine months in prison in 1949–50. His postwar years were marked first by poverty and general distrust of the communist establishment and then by prolonged economic instability. He eventually rebuilt his legal practice and retired as a lawyer for a construction company. He died in 1984 at the age of seventy-nine.

Thirty years after his death, his family received a file that had been prepared by a Belgrade lawyer in Jovanović's defense. The file contained lists of distinguished communists Jovanović had apparently warned of pending arrests throughout the occupation and throughout his work in the Special Police. On another occasion, Jovanović's daughter was contacted by an old school friend who wanted her to know that her father saved his Jewish aunt's life during the war. Jovanović apparently procured false documents so the aunt did not have to wear the yellow armband. He also intervened to prevent two other members of the family from being deported to Germany. Many years after the war, this friend, now a medical doctor, recognized Jovanović in his office waiting room, introduced himself, and helped him get to the front of the long line. "This is all I could then do for him," he wrote in a letter to Jovanović's daughter.

This story reflects the complex nature of collaboration and rescue, responsibility and memory. Some people collaborated out of an ideological affinity with the fascist cause. Some collaborated out of careerism, others because they did not know how to get out of the situation they found themselves in, or out of fear, insecurity, or cowardice. Some—like Milivoje Jovanović—seem to have worked for the occupying regime, but also helped many people by sharing the information granted by their high positions. Jovanović likely worked for the Germans in the morning and worked against them in the afternoon. He was arrested by the Germans and then by the communists, and yet he somehow survived both.

He was also my grandfather.

I remember very fondly the many city walks he took me on when I was a small child. I remember our favorite game was guessing various car models—apparently my greatest interest when I was five. He was always very gentle, never raised his voice at me or anyone else, and was mostly quiet and somewhat reserved. I was too young to ask any questions about his past and I have a feeling he would have been reluctant to share.

The information I gathered about his work during the war is completely new information I discovered halfway through doing research for this book. Growing up, I had a vague idea that he worked for the police during the war, but not that he was the chief of Special Police for the first three months of the German occupation. As I researched specific anti-Jewish measures—yellow armbands, confiscation of property, prohibition of use of public fountains, or public transportation—and matched them with the months of April–July 1941 when he was at the head of the Special Police, I was overwhelmed by a growing sense of dread. I imagined my own husband and son with yellow stars on their coats, waiting in line to register their own fate, and my grandfather counting them as two out of nine thousand registered Jews he reported back to his German superiors. Or maybe they would have been the ones he helped? This is not a fair image and it does grave injustice to the experiences of both my families—but I can't get it out of my head. Halfway through writing this book, I began to feel that my own family history was inextricably linked to the history of the Holocaust in more ways than I had previously considered.

And yet, this was not how my family narrative had always been constructed. My family's narrative was mostly one of anticommunism—of the horrors of the Russian revolution my Russian grandmother experienced as a child, the many arrests and humiliations my grandfather suffered at the hands of Yugoslav communists after the war, and, for my parents, the censorship and one-party rule under Tito and the difficult life in the early years of communism. There were memories of abject poverty and insecurity and, for my father, memories of his childhood in a Croatian Ustasha concentration camp, a formative trauma that has, I believe, shaped the rest of his life. My family narrative, then, was one of our own suffering. It was overwhelming and pervasive—it was also all true—but it did not allow much room for the memory of suffering of others. This book came out of a deep need to reconstruct the memory of others and make these memories also, centrally, our own.

I owe a debt to many friends and colleagues for help with various aspects of the project and for many conversations over many years—Duška Anastasijević, Jessica Auchter, Christian Axboe Nielsen, Michael Barnett, Maria Birnbaum, Volha Charnysh, Michael Colborne, Patrick Cottrell, Denise Davidson, Ben Denison, Jelena Đureinović, Filip Ejdus, Aida Hozić, Juliet Johnson, Jeffrey Kopstein, Maria Mälksoo, Taylor McConnell, Ana Milošević, Valerie Morkevicius, Ana Muller, Dragana Nikolajević, Or Rosenboim, Jason Sharman, Ben Stanley, Brent Steele, Srđan Vučetić, Jason Wittenberg, and Ayşe Zarakol. I am grateful to Jovan Byford and Jasna Dragović Soso for sharing documents from their own archives, and to Vladimir Kulić and Vjeran Pavlaković for sharing their vast collections of memorial photographs. Elizaveta Gaufman, David Leheny, Nadya Nedelsky, and Sarah Wagner all read parts of this manuscript and helped immensely with comments and suggestions.

In Zagreb, I owe special gratitude to Andriana Benčić, Dario Čepo, Ivo Goldstein, Sanja Horvatinčić, Nataša Mataušić, Sven Milekić, and Vjeran Pavlaković; in Ljubljana, to Jovana Mihajlović Trbovc, Tamara Pavasović Trošt, and Kaja Širok; in Belgrade, to Olga Manojlović Pintar, Sanja Petrović Todosijević, Milovan Pisarri, and Dubravka Stojanović for extensive help with all aspects of this project; in Vilnius, to Dovid Katz, Andrius Kulikauskas, Andžej Pukšto, and Dovilė Rūkaitė. I am also very grateful to Daniel Newman of the US Holocaust Memorial Museum for his help with sources on Lithuania, as well as to the staff of the Museum of History of Yugoslavia, the Jewish Historical Museum, and the Center for Holocaust Research and Education—all in Belgrade; the Auschwitz Memorial Museum, and the Lithuanian Jewish Community in Vilnius. I am also indebted to Daniel and Gabriel Glid, sons of Nandor Glid, the great Yugoslav artist and Holocaust survivor, for providing context and information on their father's art discussed in the book. Many thanks also to Aleksandar Stanojlović for creating fantastic maps.

Emil Kerenji provided detailed comments on the manuscript with a historian's precision and knowledge that I lacked and guided me through the rich but overwhelming archival material at the US Holocaust Museum. I cannot thank him enough. Dovilė Budrytė taught me everything I know about Lithuania. We talked about this project many, many times in Atlanta. She helped introduce me to scholars in Vilnius and provided incredibly valuable feedback on the entire book, but especially the delicate chapter on Lithuania. She challenged me to see Lithuania in all its complexity—good and bad. I quite certainly would not have been able to do research on this fascinating country without her help.

Few words can do justice to how much this book owes to Evgeny Finkel. Not only was my book inspired by his own fantastic work on the Holocaust, but Evgeny must have fielded a thousand questions, over many years, about every single detail about the Holocaust that I was just discovering and that he already had encyclopedic knowledge of. He was an early and enthusiastic supporter of this book and I thank him so, so much.

The book has also benefited greatly from comments I received on various parts of the project presented at the University of North Carolina-Chapel Hill, the University of Utah, Linfield College, POLIN Museum in Warsaw, the 2017 International Studies Association conference in Baltimore, and a special workshop on ontological security and the European Union in Ystad, Sweden. I have learned much from participating in the weeklong Jack and Anita Hess Seminar for Faculty at the US Holocaust Memorial Museum in January 2017. I have also received generous financial support from the Scholarly Support Grant, the Provost Fellowship, and the Center for Human Rights and Democracy, all at Georgia State University, and have benefited from excellent research assistance by Georgia State University students Efe Can Coban, Rebekah Dowd, Michael Jablonski, and Michael Westberg. I also thank Taylor and Francis for granting permission to republish material from my articles "Political Memory, Ontological Security, and Holocaust Remembrance in Post-Communist Europe," *European Security*, 27, no. 3 (2018): 296–313, and "Political Memory after State Death: The Abandoned Yugoslav National Pavilion at Auschwitz," *Cambridge Review of International Affairs* (forthcoming, 2019).

Roger Haydon at Cornell University Press liked the idea of this book when it was no more than three sentences in an email. He saw its potential and encouraged me to pursue it, and was involved in its design and development every step of the way. What an amazing pleasure this process has been. This book was quite literally written with Roger's guidance in mind, and I would have not sent it anywhere else. Many thanks also to other members of the Cornell team—Julia Cook, Ellen Murphy, Susan Specter, and Carmen Torrado Gonzalez—for helping with many aspects of the project.

The greatest debt, as always, goes to my family. First, to my mother, Irina Subotić, who has taken on this project with extraordinary interest and dedication. She has done invaluable research for me—she went to the archives and the museums, she talked to the experts, she contacted anybody she thought could help with a particular detail I was interested in, she collected primary sources, and she shared her immense archive of literature on Yugoslav postwar art. In fact, it is her own deep expertise in twentieth-century art and architecture that has influenced how I began to think about the role of public art in Holocaust memory. I want to think that, however painful she may find it to read at times, she thinks of this book as—partly—her own.

My father, Gojko Subotić, has shown nothing but support and love throughout my life and my scholarly career. He has disagreed with my conclusions more often than not—but no matter. His support has always been unconditional and that is the measure of true love. My sister Ivana Subotić and her family welcomed me to their home in Rome—a beautiful refuge from my crisscrossing Europe in search of another Holocaust memorial. I looked forward to these trips so much and enjoyed every minute. My cousin Irina Ljubić is another unsung hero of this book—she has collected fantastic research materials for me and has discovered a whole world of online Holocaust remembrance in Serbia that I did not even know existed. As her daughters—my nieces—are growing to become Serbia's next tennis champions, I humbly ask that I be allowed to win at least one game next time we play. Just one.

Doug and Karol Ross, my wonderful, generous in-laws, were fascinated with my book subject and are already planning book parties. We had many conversations about my research and I know that it has touched them on a deep and very personal level.

And to Leo and Doug—thank you for making me laugh and bringing me daily joy during the years of researching and writing that were often so emotionally difficult for me that you saw me cry. I am not sure I quite understand where Doug finds the endless patience and humor to deal with everything I bring to the table, but somehow his reservoir has not dried up twenty years on. He is my biggest fan and has been confident in this book when I wavered, feared, and retreated, overwhelmed with the magnitude of both the topic and the material I was reading. There was no doubt in his mind I could do it.

Leo—if there ever has been a more amazing child, I yet have to meet him. I wrote my first book when he was just a baby. He has now grown into a remarkable young man, funny, smart, kind, so curious about the world, and about to start preparing for his own Bar Mitzvah. When he was ten I took him to the abandoned site of a former concentration camp outside Belgrade so I could take pictures. Taking all this in, he said, "I think it is very disrespectful to have a place that is so important look like this today"—displaying an intuitive understanding of what I took four years and three hundred pages to say. All I ever want is to continue to make him proud.

Abbreviations

CHRE	Center for Holocaust Research and Education
EP	European Parliament
EU	European Union
GDR	German Democratic Republic
GUE	Gauche unitaire européenne (European United Left)
HDZ	Hrvatska demokratska zajednica (Croatian Democratic Union)
HEH	House of European History
HNS	Hrvatska narodna stranka (Croatian People's Party)
HOS	Hrvatske obrambene snage (Croatian Defense Forces, 1991–1992)
HOS	Hrvatske oružane snage (Croatian Armed Forces, 1944–1945)
ICTY	International Criminal Tribunal for the former Yugoslavia
IHRA	International Holocaust Remembrance Alliance
ITF	Task Force for International Cooperation on Education about the Holocaust
KGB	Komitet gosudarstvennoy bezopasnosti (Committee for State Security)
LAF	Lietuvos Aktyvistų Frontas (Lithuanian Activist Front)
MP	Member of Parliament
NATO	North Atlantic Treaty Organization
NDH	Nezavisna država Hrvatska (Independent State of Croatia)
NGL	Nordic Green Left
NKVD	Narodnyy komissariat vnutrennikh del (People's Commissariat for Internal Affairs)
OECD	Organization for Economic Cooperation and Development
OSCE	Organization for Security and Cooperation in Europe
OUN	Orhanizatsiia ukrainskykh natsionalistiv (Organization of Ukrainian Nationalists)
PiS	Prawo i Sprawiedliwość (Law and Justice)
POW	Prisoner of war
SDSS	Samostalna demokratska srpska stranka (Independent Democratic Serb Party)

SNP	Srpska napredna stranka (Serbian Progressive Party)
SS	Schutzstaffel (Protection Squadron)
UN	United Nations
UPA	Ukrayins'ka povstans'ka armiya (Ukrainian Insurgent Army)
USSR	Union of Soviet Socialist Republics
WWII	World War II
YIVO	Yidisher Visnshaftlekher Institut (Yiddish Scientific Institute)
YLA	Youth Labor Actions

YELLOW STAR, RED STAR

The Big Gray Truck

Nada, my dear,

Tomorrow morning I leave for the camp. Nobody's forcing me to go and I'm not waiting to be summoned. I'm volunteering to join the first group that leaves from 23 George Washington Street tomorrow at 9 a.m. My family are against my decision, but I think that you at least will understand me; there are so many people in need of help that my conscience dictates to me that I should ignore any sentimental reasons connected with my home and family for not going and put myself wholly at the service of others. The [Jewish] hospital will remain in the town, and the director has promised that he will take me in again when the hospital moves to the camp. I am calm and composed and convinced that everything is going to turn out all right, perhaps even better than my optimistic expectations. I shall think of you often; you know—or perhaps you don't—what you have meant to me—and will always mean to me. You are my most beautiful memory from that most pleasant period of my life—from the [Literary] Society.

Nada, my dear, I love you very, very much.

Hilda

7 December 1941[1]

1. Hilda Dajč's letter is the property of the Jewish Historical Museum in Belgrade. It was translated into English by Timothy Byford, and is available at Jovan Byford, "Semlin Judelanger in Serbian Political Memory," accessed January 24, 2019, https://www.open.ac.uk/socialsciences/semlin/en/.

Hilda Dajč was a nineteen-year-old Jewish nurse from Belgrade, Serbia. She was interned in the Judenlager Semlin, one of the first extermination camps for Jews in Europe.[2] Semlin camp was created specifically for the internment of Jews in 1941 in Nazi occupied Serbia and was housed on the site of the former Belgrade Fairgrounds, an architectural wonder of the 1930s.[3] The inmates at Semlin were mostly women, children, and the elderly, as the male able-bodied Jews—some eight thousand of them—had by fall 1941 already been systematically shot in a wave of reprisal killings the Germans instituted as retribution for the casualties Yugoslav antifascist resistance was inflicting on the Wehrmacht. Hilda's letters to Serbian friends back in Belgrade described horrific conditions in the camp and the increasing desperation and fatalism of the inmates.

Semlin was not a site hidden from view. It sits right across the River Sava from downtown Belgrade, and many witness testimonies confirmed that citizens of Belgrade could see Semlin inmates crossing the frozen river during the winter to bury their dead in the Jewish cemetery. During one of these crossings, Hilda Dajč even arranged to see her friend Mirjana Petrović for a minute and exchange a few words. While life under the occupation in Belgrade continued with some degree of normalcy, the Semlin inmates "represented no more than small dots on the frozen surface of the river" to the citizens of Belgrade.[4]

Sometime between her last letter, written in early February 1942, and May 1942, Hilda Dajč stepped into a large, dark, gray truck. She was likely told that she was designated for transport to another camp, and that she needed to pack her belongings and label her suitcase, which was loaded onto another truck. The large gray truck, however, was a mobile gas van, which the Germans euphemistically called the "delousing truck" (*Entlausungswagen*). This was a retrofitted truck with a hermetically sealed compartment that pumped carbon monoxide from the exhaust pipe into the interior of the truck, turning it into a makeshift gas chamber. Hilda would have been one of

2. The Semlin camp is also known by its Serbian name Sajmište or Staro Sajmište. For consistency, I refer to the Nazi concentration camp as Semlin and to the location where it was housed as Sajmište. The account of the Semlin camp is based on Byford, "Semlin Judelanger"; Jovan Bajford (Byford), *Staro sajmište: Mesto sećanja, zaborava i sporenja* [Staro Sajmište: A site remembered, forgotten, contested] (Belgrade: Beogradski centar za ljudska prava, 2011); United States Holocaust Memorial Museum, "Axis Invasion of Yugoslavia," accessed January 24, 2019, https://www.ushmm.org/wlc/en/article.php?ModuleId=10005456. A powerful fictionalized account of the Semlin camp is in David Albahari, *Götz and Meyer* (London: Harvill Press, 2004).

3. The Belgrade Fairgrounds are also commonly refereed to as the Belgrade Exhibition Grounds. For consistency, I refer to the historic site as the Belgrade Fairgrounds throughout the book.

4. Aleksandar Ignjatović and Olga Manojlović Pintar, "Staro Sajmište i sećanja na II sv. rat" [Old Fairgrounds and memories of World War II], *Helsinška povelja* 117–18 (March–April 2008): 33–35, here 33.

between fifty and a hundred Jewish inmates from Semlin who were driven in this van through the center of Belgrade, in plain view of Belgrade passersby, for ten to fifteen minutes at a time which was how long was needed for the gas to take effect. The truck would then drive on to Jajinci, a killing site on the outskirts of Belgrade, where the prisoners from other camps would dump the bodies from the van into mass unmarked graves.

By May 10, 1942, the two SS officers in charge of the operation, Wilhelm Götz and Erwin Meyer, had taken between sixty-five and seventy trips in the van, killing around 6,300 Jews—almost every single inmate—detained at Semlin.[5] The Semlin camp was then transformed from a Jewish extermination camp into an *Anhaltelager*, a temporary detention camp for political prisoners, captured partisans, and forced laborers—the vast majority of whom were Serbs—on their way to labor camps in Germany and Norway. Out of around thirty thousand inmates in the newly repurposed camp, more than ten thousand died in the camp from disease, starvation, exposure, physical exhaustion, and savage guard beatings.[6]

In June 1942, Emanuel Schäfer, the head of the German Security Police in Serbia, reported back to his supervisors, "Serbien ist Judenfrei" (Serbia is free of Jews), as almost all of Jews in occupied Serbia had already been killed, less than a year since the beginning of the German occupation.[7] Belgrade was thus the first European city, and Serbia only the second Nazi occupied territory (after Estonia), to carry this macabre designation. The only Jews who remained alive were either in hiding, often in the countryside, or had joined the partisan resistance.

The Semlin camp is also a site of considerable importance for the larger historiography of the Holocaust, as it marks the period of particular intensification in the killing of European Jews.[8] Further, the systematic use of the mobile gas van points to the refinement and routinization of the Nazi killing techniques, soon to be expanded in the death camps across occupied Eastern Europe.[9] It is

5. While the Semlin camp also housed the detained Roma, those who survived the harsh winter of 1941–42 were subsequently released in 1942.

6. Milan Koljanin, *Nemački logor na beogradskom Sajmištu 1941–1944* [German camp at Belgrade's Sajmište 1941–1944] (Belgrade: Institut za savremenu istoriju, 1992).

7. Walter Manoschek, "The Extermination of the Jews in Serbia," in *National Socialist Extermination Policies: Contemporary German Perspectives and Controversies*, ed. Ulrich Herbert (New York: Berghahn Books, 2000), 163–85.

8. Christopher R. Browning, *The Origins of the Final Solution: The Evolution of Nazi Jewish Policy, September 1939–March 1942* (Lincoln: University of Nebraska Press, 2004).

9. After the killing at Semlin was completed, the van was sent for maintenance to Germany, and from there to Minsk, Belarus, where it was used in the gassing of the Minsk Jews. Manoschek, "The Extermination of the Jews in Serbia," 180. The gas van technology itself was first used in Nazi euthanasia killings within Germany. Its first use in extermination camps was in Chełmno, Poland in 1941, then followed by Belgrade's Semlin in 1942. See Christopher R. Browning, *Fateful Months: Essays on the Emergence of the Final Solution* (New York: Holmes & Meier, 1985), 57–67.

also the central site in the topography of the Holocaust in Serbia, as half of all Serbian Jews were killed there within a few short months in the spring of 1942.

And yet, as of 2019, the Semlin camp site is a grotesque "site of nonmemory."[10] At least five buildings—out of the total of thirteen that made the Sajmište complex—were partially or completely destroyed in the allied bombing of Belgrade in April 1944 and were demolished after the war. The remaining buildings have been taken over by overgrown foliage, dumped trash, stray animals, and wasp nests. The buildings are crumbling, some populated by indigent squatters, some by artists who repurposed the buildings into studios (and some also into ramshackle living quarters). Some have turned into small businesses—there is a car mechanic shop, a bodega, a storage facility of some kind, an abandoned, overgrown, and depressing looking children's playground. The shining new shopping center "Ušće" glitters through the treetops.

The most prominent building of what remains of the site, the Central Tower, is abandoned and in ruins. For many years, the former Spasić Pavilion, the architectural jewel of the 1930s Belgrade Fairgrounds, housed a nightclub, which hosted a number of rock concerts, including a high-profile performance by Boy George in 2006, followed by an international boxing match in 2007. The nightclub has since closed and the gym "Poseydon," which offers weightlifting, fitness, mini soccer, and martial arts, has taken its place. A small restaurant has opened outside. Another restaurant on the site, "So i biber" (Salt and pepper), occupies the former Turkish Pavilion, which served as the Semlin camp morgue.[11] The restaurant website advertises itself as located on a small street, tucked in foliage, with extremely generous portions, available parking, and free Wi-Fi. The story of the Semlin camp, as well as that of the larger Holocaust in Serbia, remains almost entirely outside of Serbian public memory.

And yet, the Holocaust imagery is everywhere. In 2014, the Historical Museum of Serbia put up a highly publicized exhibition titled *In the Name of the People—Political Repression in Serbia 1944–1953*, which promised to display new historical documents and evidence of communist crimes, ranging from assassinations, kidnappings, and detentions in camps to

---

10. Omer Bartov, "Eastern Europe as the Site of Genocide," *The Journal of Modern History* 80, no. 3 (2008): 557–93, here 557.

11. Asked by the media about the ethics of placing a restaurant in the former concentration camp, the restaurant owner replied, "If the state cares so much about this object, it should buy it from me. I have to live off something." B92, "Staro sajmište—ruganje prošlosti" [Old Fairgrounds—mocking the past], September 4, 2013, http://www.b92.net/info/vesti/index.php?yyyy=2013&mm=09&dd=04&nav_category=12&nav_id=74990.

FIGURE 1. Restaurant at the site of the former Semlin death camp, Belgrade, Serbia (photograph by author)

collectivization, political trials, and repression. What the exhibition actually showed, however, were random and completely decontextualized photographs of "victims of communism," which included innocent people but also many proven fascist collaborators, members of the quisling government, right wing militias, and the Axis-allied Chetnik movement. But the most stunning visual artifact was a well-known photograph of prisoners from the Buchenwald concentration camp, including Elie Wiesel, taken by US soldier Harry Miller at the camp's liberation in April 1945. In the Belgrade exhibition, this canonic image was displayed in the section devoted to a communist-era camp for political prisoners on the Adriatic island of Goli otok.[12] The exhibition describes the display as "the example of living conditions of Goli otok prisoners."[13]

12. That the Buchenwald concentration camp was for a while after the war used by the German Democratic Republic as an isolation camp for political prisoners of the East German regime is of some irony here, but none of this historical information was displayed in the Belgrade exhibit.

13. Even after this misrepresentation was exposed, the Buchenwald photograph remained on display when I visited the exhibition in May 2014. Sometime thereafter, in response to an outcry from Holocaust historians, a small note was taped underneath the display caption that read, "A photograph of prisoner boxed beds in Dachau camp." That nobody bothered to check that the

This equation of communism and fascism, and then the appropriation of Holocaust remembrance and imagery to delegitimize communism, is hardly an indigenous post-Yugoslav invention. This process has occurred throughout Eastern Europe, with much historical revisionism resulting from the attempts of Eastern European countries to deny or cloud their participation in fascist crimes, including the Holocaust, by elevating communist crimes to the level of the Holocaust, by delegitimizing antifascism, and in so doing legitimizing resurgent neofascism.

In Hungary, contemporary Holocaust revisionism is perhaps the most extreme and is officially endorsed by the government of Viktor Orbán and embraced by a surprising number of Hungarian intellectuals. For example, the House of Terror museum that opened in 2002 in Budapest narrates the story of Hungary's twentieth-century experience as a nation victim of the foreign communist and, to a much lesser extent, foreign fascist regime. The museum truncates Hungary's twentieth century to 1944–89, so that the fascist era begins with the German occupation in 1944, and not in 1940 when Hungary joined the Axis alliance. This shift therefore completely removes the history of the Holocaust in Hungary before 1944, the period that left sixty thousand Hungarian Jews killed as early as 1942, an extermination carried out not by Germans, but by Hungarian forces under the rule of the regent Miklós Horthy.[14] This chronology also presents communism as a much longer and far more damaging terror in Hungary than fascism ever was, while there is virtually no mention of antifascism and communist resistance in the museum's exhibition narrative.

Similarly, the Memorial to the Victims of the German Occupation erected in 2014 in Budapest memorializes Hungary—the country—as the main victim of the German occupation, in a not very subtle depiction of Germany's imperial eagle crushing Hungary, which is symbolized by the Archangel Gabriel. The important narrative of Hungary's House of Terror and the Memorial to the Victims of the German Occupation is not only equating fascism and communism, but also placing them completely outside of the linear progression of Hungary's history, by presenting them as alien, foreign intrusions into the Hungarian body politic, and therefore swiftly removing

---

photograph was, in fact, from Buchenwald and not Dachau, is symptomatic of the broad indifference with which the Holocaust is met in Serbia.

14. The local participation in the anti-Jewish drives was extensive, and included some two hundred thousand Hungarian policemen and "patriotic" volunteers. Randolph L. Braham, "Hungary: The Assault on the Historical Memory of the Holocaust," in *The Holocaust in Hungary: Seventy Years Later*, ed. Randolph L. Braham and András Kovács (Budapest: Central European University Press, 2016), 261–309, here 266.

any traces of Hungary's own, quite domestic, fascists and communists and their responsibility for both the Holocaust and the Gulag. At the same time, rehabilitation of the Horthy era provides postcommunist Hungary with a mythologized connection to its precommunist past, conveniently side stepping the forty-four years of communism and deriving contemporary state legitimacy from national continuity with an earlier, more "authentic" (and therefore more legitimate) Hungary. But the Holocaust in Hungary is not *denied* in the most literal sense of "Holocaust denial;" Viktor Orbán even declared 2014 a Year of Holocaust Commemoration. Rather, the Holocaust is *incorporated* into the larger contemporary political narrative about twentieth-century totalitarianism and used to condemn, for the Hungarian political elite, its worse variant, that of communism.[15]

In Poland, the government of the Law and Justice party has prevented the opening of a new museum of WWII in Gdansk, unsatisfied with the museum's focus on the global, and not just Polish, history of the war. For the government and allied intellectuals, the museum did not express "the Polish point of view," and it smacked of "pseudouniversalism."[16] After the museum was finally opened in March 2017 to great international acclaim, the government replaced the director with a political appointee and merged the museum with another institution, in order to project a more "Polish" history of WWII. These moves are all part of the new Polish politics of memory, the purpose of which is to highlight Polish heroism and sacrifice throughout history and not dwell on negative episodes such as, well, the Holocaust. This memory policy pushes Polish artists to create a more positive narrative of Poland. As part of the goal, the government objected to Polish filmmakers continuing to make Holocaust related films, such as the Oscar-winning *Ida* (the 2016 state television broadcast of which was preceded by a warning to the Polish public about its "historical inaccuracies"—presumably because the main plotline implicates Polish peasants in the killing of Jews they were once hiding) and urged them to create art that reflected more positively on the Polish past.[17]

---

15. At its most extreme and anti-Semitic, some contemporary Hungarian Holocaust revisionists argue that communism itself was a Jewish political regime and its brutality the result of the surviving Jews lashing out at Christians in revenge for the Holocaust. For a review of varieties of Holocaust revisionism in contemporary Hungary, see Braham, "Hungary."

16. Claudia Ciobanu, "Poland's WWII Museum under Political Bombardment," *Politico*, May 15, 2017, http://www.politico.eu/article/polands-wwii-museum-under-political-bombardment.

17. Andrew Pulver, "Polish TV Broadcaster Criticised for Its Treatment of Ida Screening," *Guardian*, March 4, 2016.

Poland has also used various tools of the law to pursue this new remembrance. In 2018, the government passed a law that criminalizes the use of the phrase "Polish death camps" to designate German Nazi death camps in occupied Poland, such as Auschwitz, Treblinka, and many others, but also criminalizes any insinuation that Poles may have committed anti-Jewish crimes during the Holocaust.[18] In 2017, Poland moved to demand reparations from Germany for damages caused in WWII, arguing that "the historic bills have not been settled"—a move clearly aimed at retaliating against the EU's increasingly harsh (but toothless) rhetoric of concern vis-à-vis Poland's democratic backsliding.[19]

The esteemed Princeton historian Jan Tomasz Gross was questioned by Polish authorities for "insulting the nation" with his research demonstrating direct Polish participation in the killing of the Jews, and his statements on the relatively tepid Polish resistance to the Germans.[20] His pathbreaking study on the Jedwabne massacre—where in 1941 Polish peasants rounded up their Jewish neighbors and burned them alive in a barn seemingly without any German orders or presence—continues to be deeply contested and even outright rejected by much of the Polish public.

And this is because it is not Jedwabne, but Katyń, where in 1940 twenty-two thousand Polish soldiers were shot by the Soviet army and dumped into death pits, that remains the event central to the Polish narrative of WWII. Katyń, the martyrdom of Poles at the hand of the communist army, is invoked frequently in conjunction with the memory of the Holocaust, as in 2009 when on the occasion of the sixtieth anniversary of the outbreak of WWII, then Polish president Lech Kaczyński claimed that the Red Army's "treacherous attack" in 1939 brought "the night of occupation, the essence of which was the Holocaust, Auschwitz, Katyń."[21] The message here is not only that Auschwitz and Katyń are one of the kind, but also that communism *caused* Auschwitz. There is hardly a better way to delegitimize communism than to blame it for the Holocaust.

---

18. The law was amended in June 2018 to make the offense civil and not criminal.

19. Marek Strzelecki, "Poland Ramps Up Case for World War II Reparations From Germany," *Bloomberg News*, August 8, 2017, https://www.bloomberg.com/news/articles/2017-08-08/poland-ramps-up-case-for-world-war-ii-reparations-from-germany. On EU concerns, see Gabriela Baczynska, "EU Grapples with Signs of Eroding Democracy in Poland, Hungary," *Reuters*, October 16, 2018, https://www.reuters.com/article/us-poland-eu/eu-grapples-with-signs-of-eroding-democracy-in-poland-hungary-idUSKCN1MQ27X.

20. Alex Duval Smith, "'Vindictive' Polish Leaders Using New War Museum to Rewrite History, Says Academic," *Guardian*, April 23, 2016.

21. Quoted in Rolf Fredheim, "The Memory of Katyn in Polish Political Discourse: A Quantitative Study," *Europe-Asia Studies* 66, no. 7 (2014): 1165–87, here 1165.

This appropriated memory of the Holocaust, what Kristen Ghodsee has memorably called "the blackwashing of history," has become a form of "screen memory" that filters out and obfuscates any serious addressing of one's own responsibility for mass atrocity in more recent wars, but also clouds the memories that don't fit the current political moment, such as those of extensive Nazi crimes against communists and partisans.[22]

This remembrance of the Holocaust, then, is not exactly denial—however problematic, it does not prominently feature voices that deny the Holocaust as a historical fact or challenge its most established realities. It is also not quite the same as trivialization—while the emphasis always is on the larger ethnic suffering, it is relatively rare to hear outright belittling of Jewish victimization.[23] A more nuanced way of understanding this type of Holocaust remembrance, I suggest, is as *memory appropriation*, where the memory of the Holocaust is used to memorialize a different kind of suffering, such as suffering under communism, or suffering from ethnic violence perpetrated by other groups. It is Holocaust remembrance turned inward, away from the actual victims of the Holocaust or the Holocaust itself, what Ewa Płonowska Ziarek calls the "narcissistic identification with Jewish suffering."[24]

As my book demonstrates, this process is not simply a byproduct of postcommunist transitions; it is in fact an integral part of the political strategy of postcommunist states, which are basing their contemporary legitimacy on a complete rejection of communism and a renewed connection to the precommunist, mythically nationally pure, and, above all, ethnic character of states. It is this rejection of communist supranationalism and its replacement with old-fashioned ethnic nationalism that colors how the Holocaust is remembered. In a global environment of anticommunism, this nationalized Holocaust remembrance has also completely erased the memory of communist antifascist resistance as its constitutive part, and this exclusion provides contemporary anticommunist regimes their legitimacy shields.

22. Kristen Ghodsee, "Blackwashing History," *Anthropology News*, March 16, 2013, http://scholar.harvard.edu/files/kristenghodsee/files/blackwashing_history.pdf. On screen memory, see Lindsey A Freeman, Benjamin Nienass, and Laliv Melamed, "Screen Memory," *International Journal of Politics, Culture, and Society* 26, no. 1 (2013): 1–7.

23. On routine trivialization of the Holocaust in Eastern Europe, see Michael Shafir, *Between Denial and "Comparative Trivialization": Holocaust Negationism in Post-Communist East Central Europe* (Jerusalem: Hebrew University of Jerusalem, Vidal Sassoon International Center for the Study of Antisemitism, 2002). For evidence of increasing trivialization of the Holocaust in Hungary, see Braham, "Hungary."

24. Ewa Płonowska Ziarek, "Melancholic Nationalism and the Pathologies of Commemorating the Holocaust in Poland," in *Imaginary Neighbors: Mediating Polish-Jewish Relations after the Holocaust*, ed. Dorota Glowacka and Joanna Zylinska (Lincoln: University of Nebraska Press, 2007), 301–26, here 320.

Holocaust remembrance, then, ceases to be about the Holocaust at all, and is instead about the very acute legitimacy needs of postcommunist states which are building their identity as fundamentally anticommunist, which then in turn makes them more legitimately European.

The Argument

To illuminate this process, my book explores ways in which states make strategic use of political memory in an effort to resolve their contemporary ontological insecurities—insecurities about their identities, about their status, and about their relationships with other international actors. My principal argument is that postcommunist states today are dealing with conflicting sources of insecurity. These states are anxious to be perceived as fully European by "core" Western European states, a status that remains fleeting, especially in the aftermath of the openly anti–Eastern European rhetoric of the Euro crisis and Brexit in which, for example, Polish migrants are routinely depicted in the British press as economic threats flooding the country to take British jobs away.[25] Being fully European, however, means sharing in the cosmopolitan European narratives of the twentieth century, perhaps the strongest being the narrative of the Holocaust.

The European narrative of the Holocaust has created stress and resentment in postcommunist states, which have been asked to accept and contribute to this primarily Western European account as members or candidate states of the European Union. The problem is that the cosmopolitan Holocaust memory as developed in the West does not fit narratively with the very different set of Holocaust memories in postcommunist Europe.[26] This lack of fit is evident primarily in the lack of centrality of the Holocaust as the defining memory of the twentieth-century experience across the postcommunist space. As Tony Judt put it, "The really uncomfortable truth about World War II was that what happened to the Jews between 1939 and 1945 was not nearly as important to most of the protagonists as later sensibilities might wish."[27] Eastern European states after communism constructed their

25. Ariel Spigelman, "The Depiction of Polish Migrants in the United Kingdom by the British Press after Poland's Accession to the European Union," *International Journal of Sociology and Social Policy* 33, no. 1/2 (2013): 98–113; Adrian Favell, "European Union Versus European Society: Sociologists on 'Brexit' and the 'Failure' of Europeanization," in *Brexit: Sociological Responses*, ed. William Outhwaite (London: Anthem Press, 2017), 193–200.

26. Daniel Levy and Natan Sznaider, "Memory Unbound: The Holocaust and the Formation of Cosmopolitan Memory," *European Journal of Social Theory* 5, no. 1 (2002): 87–106.

27. Tony Judt, "From the House of the Dead: On Modern European Memory," *New York Review of Books* 52, October 6, 2005.

national identities on the memory of Stalinism and Soviet occupation, as well as precommunist ethnic conflict with other states, rather than the memory of the Holocaust. The Western European narrative of the Holocaust, then, threatens to replace the centrality of communist and ethnic victimization as the dominant organizing narrative of postcommunist states, and is therefore destabilizing to these state identities.

My book documents how, influencing the European Union's own memory politics and legislation in the process, postcommunist states have attempted to resolve these insecurities by putting forward a new kind of Holocaust remembrance where the memory, symbols, and imagery of the Holocaust become appropriated to represent the crimes of communism. The criminal past is not fully denied, but the responsibility for it is misdirected. This accomplishes two things—first, it absolves the nation from acknowledging responsibility for its criminal past; at the same time, it makes communism as a political project criminal. There is also a further, significant consequence. By delegitimizing communism, postcommunist states have also removed antifascist resistance from the core memory of the Holocaust, which has allowed for a revival and ideological normalization of fascist ideological movements in the present.

The Balkans and the Baltics

To illustrate these arguments, the book analyzes contemporary Holocaust remembrance practices in two postcommunist regions: the former Yugoslavia and the Baltics. The countries in the two regions have different histories of the Holocaust as well as of communism, but their principal memory actors—museums, education institutions, cultural ministries—have all carried out remarkable and diverse projects of Holocaust memory appropriation and inversion. It is this diversity of responses that makes the comparison among these cases compelling.

The experience of communism in the Balkans and the Baltics was hardly the same. First, Yugoslav communism was, especially after the split from the Soviet Union in 1948, of a qualitatively different kind than was the case in the Soviet-occupied Baltics. It was less oppressive, less doctrinaire, and much more open toward the West. More important, the lived experience of Yugoslav citizens was considerably different than that of their Soviet counterparts, which meant that the political space for some dissent—especially of the less overtly political, but more artistic or literary kind—was much broader. Communist Yugoslavia certainly engaged in property confiscation, extrajudicial detentions, and forced deportations and had harsh camps for political prisoners, the most infamous being Goli otok. But this repression and the daily terror Yugoslav citizens faced was on a totally different scale than what Soviet citizens had to endure. Even more to the point, the postcommunist transition in Yugoslavia brought a brutal civil war, crimes against humanity, and genocide to the region. Yugoslav communism was thus replaced not by something better, but by something much more devastatingly violent. This difference in the variety of communism and postcommunist aftermath is yet to be fully appreciated by political science scholarship in Eastern Europe, which, as Milada Vachudova aptly remarked, still has "a Yugoslavia problem."[28] Yugoslavia was there, right in the middle of the communist experience, and yet its story does not fit the dominant narrative of communism and postcommunism shared in other parts of the region.

Second, the Jewish experience during WWII as well as during communism was significantly different in the two regions. Yugoslav partisans during WWII welcomed a high percentage of Yugoslav Jews who joined the resistance as a strategy of survival, but also because as an extremely vulnerable minority they were attracted to the non-ethnic, pan-national Yugoslav communist identity. And unlike in the Soviet Union, and certainly unlike in Poland and Hungary, anti-Semitism among Yugoslav communist leadership was not nearly as pronounced, if it was visible at all. Communist Yugoslavia had no experience of anti-Semitic Communist Party purges such as those in the USSR or Poland, and so the relationship between the memory of the Holocaust and communist doctrine was also different. Unlike in the rest of the communist world, Yugoslavia allowed—especially in the early years right after the war—for a modest Jewish remembrance of the Holocaust, and even supported Jewish memorials to the victims, which the Soviet doctrine never permitted.

Finally, the most obvious difference between the two regions is that Yugoslavia was sovereign and increasingly independent from the Soviet Union, even creating a global third way, the Non-Aligned Movement, in the 1960s, further elevating its international status. The Baltic states, on the other hand, were occupied by the Soviet Union, their cultural and national identity crushed, their populations deported and abused, and their ability to remember either the Holocaust or communist atrocities governed directly from Moscow.

More recent experiences in the former Yugoslavia and the Baltics have been different as well. Of particular importance for my argument is the

28. Remarks at the workshop "Whither Eastern Europe? Changing Political Science Perspectives on the Region," University of Florida-Gainesville, January 9–11, 2014.

different timeline for accession to the European Union, and therefore different levels of pressure applied by the EU on candidate states regarding how to properly remember the Holocaust. The Baltic states joined in the first wave of EU Eastern enlargement in 2004 and had to develop a response to EU expectations more quickly. Once safely in the EU, however, they developed a whole new repertoire of remembrance practices, which their political representatives then promoted further through the EU's own political institutions.

States of the former Yugoslavia had a rougher go of European Union accession. Only Slovenia joined early in 2004, and since then Croatia has been the only former Yugoslavian state to successfully join the EU, in 2013. Serbia has been on a seemingly never-ending winding path to Brussels, with an uncertain membership date. Bosnia-Herzegovina, Montenegro, Macedonia, and Kosovo are even further down the road, with increasingly slim chances of membership as the EU itself reaches a point of enlargement saturation and fatigue. These different experiences, then, have clearly colored how the two regions processed the end of communism and how remembrance of both the Holocaust and communism developed over time.[29]

My book places Holocaust remembrance in comparison across the two poles of postcommunist Europe to demonstrate the power that ontological insecurity—insecurity over identity—holds over societies in the long aftermath of traumatic historical events. In the context of Holocaust remembrance, putting the countries on the "periphery" of the Holocaust (the former Yugoslavia) in dialogue with the "core" (former Soviet Union) provides for a much richer understanding of what contemporary anxieties about Holocaust memory are really about, and what strategies countries use to resolve them.

To get at this diversity, I sifted through hundreds of primary archival and secondary literature sources on the Holocaust and its remembrance in the two regions, including newspaper coverage of commemorations, museum exhibitions and catalogs, oral testimonies, history textbooks, public speeches, and theater, film, and literature sources. Over the course of four years (2014–18), I conducted dozens of interviews as well as museum and memorial site visits in Auschwitz, Belgrade, Berlin, Krakow, Ljubljana, London, Nuremberg, Prague, Terezin, Vilnius, Warsaw, Zagreb, St. Petersburg, FL, and Washington, DC.

---

29. For an attempt to map the diverse memory of communism in East Central Europe, see Michael H. Bernhard and Jan Kubik, *Twenty Years after Communism: The Politics of Memory and Commemoration* (Oxford: Oxford University Press, 2014).

Plan of the Book

This book has two main goals. The first is to provide a framework for understanding how political memory, such as the memory of the Holocaust, shapes the way in which states build their contemporary identities and to what political effect. It challenges the established scholarly consensus that calls for a full repudiation of Eastern European communist past, and instead points to the dangers of criminalizing communism and equating crimes of communism with those of fascism.

The second goal is to shed light on both the history of the Holocaust and its contemporary remembrance in postcommunist countries that are often seen as being on the periphery of this story. As Timothy Snyder claims, "Practically everyone who dies in the Holocaust either called Poland or the Soviet Union home before the war or was sent to German-occupied Poland or German-occupied lands of the USSR to be murdered."[30] Because of this overwhelming concentration of atrocity in one part of Eastern Europe, the Holocaust and its aftermath outside of these "bloodlands" often remains outside of scholarly focus. My book aims to bring the Holocaust from the periphery—especially the Yugoslav periphery, where most of the victims died right there, in Yugoslavia, before the death camps in the East were at full speed—and link it to the larger arc of the Holocaust and the broader European Holocaust remembrance.

Chapter 1 presents the theoretical argument about state responses to various ontological insecurities they face in the aftermath of a great political transformation—the end of communism—and links this framework to the issue of political memory. Rethinking the concepts of cosmopolitan vs. national memory, especially as they relate to Holocaust remembrance, the chapter introduces the notion of memory appropriation to more precisely capture the dynamics described later in the book. I outline the major historical junctures in the development of a "European" cosmopolitan memory of the Holocaust and discuss ways in which this remembrance is in conflict with the postcommunist, Eastern European narrative of WWII, the Holocaust being far from the central element of this story. The chapter describes various strategies of political resistance postcommunist states engaged in during this narrative dialogue with the West. But it was not only Eastern European states that changed their remembrance to appear more "European." The postcommunist states also successfully changed the European Union

30. Timothy Snyder, "Poland vs. History," *New York Review of Books*, May 3, 2016, http://www.nybooks.com/daily/2016/05/03/poland-vs-history-museum-gdansk.

approach to memory by pushing the EU to adopt the Eastern European position on the twentieth century's "two totalitarianisms."

Chapters 2 and 3 explore Holocaust remembrance in the former Yugoslavia by focusing on the two deeply interlinked narratives in Serbia and Croatia, respectively. These two states sit at the center of the narrative battle over the histories of WWII and communist Yugoslavia and these narratives are mutually reinforced and challenged in a constant dialogue. While one does not exist without the other—Serbia's entire repertoire of Holocaust remembrance is focused on Croatia's mass murder of ethnic Serbs—these two state responses to memory after communism are also quite different. While in Serbia the contemporary Holocaust remembrance is focused most directly on *inversion*—appropriating crimes of the Holocaust for discussion of crimes of communism—the Croatian response is a peculiar memory *divergence* and decoupling of the Holocaust from the fascist mass murder of the Serbs. In Croatia, this divergence has become so pronounced that the national memory includes the Holocaust with much ceremonial commemoration, while it almost completely excludes the mass extermination of the Serbs—both murderous plans carried out simultaneously by the same regime, the fascist Independent State of Croatia.

The two chapters each present a brief background on the Holocaust in Yugoslavia, especially as it occurred in the two major states, and an overview of the communist-era Holocaust remembrance, which the two states shared in the joint federation. The chapters then diverge to each tell a story of unique responses to communist collapse and new nation building through the analysis of contemporary Holocaust remembrance in the two countries.

Chapter 4 moves into the Baltics and anchors the discussion of this region on the case of Lithuania, the country with the highest numbers of both prewar Jewish populations and Jewish victims in the Holocaust in the Baltic region. It is also the country that has most aggressively pursued a strategy of memory *conflation*, by which the Holocaust and the Soviet occupation of Lithuania are considered, together, as a "double genocide" and not as distinct historical events with their own tragic trajectories and consequences. Lithuania has also been at the helm of a creative use of post-WWII architecture of international justice, where the state is prosecuting individuals for genocide—not for the Holocaust, but for the "genocide" of Soviet occupation. This chapter begins with the overview of the Holocaust in the Baltic states, then describes Holocaust remembrance practices in the Baltics during Soviet communism, and finally analyzes postcommunist strategies aimed at explicitly using the legal and political structure designed to deal with crimes of the Holocaust to instead criminalize the Soviet past.

The book's conclusion takes a broader view of the importance of Holocaust remembrance after communism and looks at how other states in the region have adopted their political memories to fit the new political environment. The conclusion also opens up a discussion about the larger implications of this variety of Holocaust remembrance practices, especially practices aimed at memory inversion and repurposing of fascist crimes into crimes of communism. Specifically, I discuss the relationship between Holocaust remembrance and the rise of the far-right movements in Europe, and the danger that inverted Holocaust remembrance presents in relegitimizing fascist movements in the present. I end with a call for memory solidarity—for groups to acknowledge, remember, and care for the memory of others as a foundation for building a more just society.

Implications for Scholarship

Why the Holocaust, why now? The memory of the Holocaust has been debated and revisited and debated again, so why does all this still matter? My principal argument is that, while the historical and moral importance of Holocaust remembrance should be self-evident, Holocaust remembrance is also important for global politics. As my book documents, the tremendous variety of remembrance practices across postcommunist Europe indicates that there is a lot going on under the European Union cloak. As the alarming turns to illiberalism in Poland and Hungary show, joining the EU was not the "end of history" its architects imagined, and in fact EU accession has allowed these states to embark on radical projects of historical inversion that do violence to the historical record of WWII for very contemporary political purposes. The great delegitimation of communism that has swept Europe since 1991 has also produced a legitimation of fascism, which is repackaged, retold, and reinterpreted to look more palatable and polite in the twenty-first century.[31] The great tragedy of the anticommunist moment is that it has weakened and made less imperative our collective antifascist moment. My book, therefore, points to the many ways in which the memory of the Holocaust continues to be unsettled, contested, and instrumentalized, more than seventy-five years after Hilda Dajč stepped into the big, dark, gray truck.

---

31. Hungary's turn under Viktor Orbán, especially the systematic glorification of Hungarian WWII fascists, may be the most obvious case of contemporary fascist normalization in postcommunist Europe. For an overview of Hungary's turn toward far right illiberalism, see Péter Krasztev and Jon Van Til, *The Hungarian Patient: Social Opposition to an Illiberal Democracy* (Budapest: Central European University Press, 2015).

CHAPTER 1

The Politics of Holocaust Remembrance after Communism

The Holocaust holds a central place in the global public memory of the twentieth century, especially in the West.[1] It is the paradigmatic trauma of that century, and a formative event and one of the foundational stories of the European Union.[2]

This was not always the case. What we today refer to as "the Holocaust" did not exist as a concept or as a marker in global collective memory prior to the early 1960s.[3] Holocaust memory has developed over time, and has gone through various phases in various countries and over various periods. The Holocaust we understand today is not the Holocaust as it was understood in the immediate aftermath of WWII, and it is certainly not understood in the same way across different countries—especially in Germany, Israel, and

1. The literature on the meaning of the Holocaust for the twentieth century is vast and cannot be fully summarized here. Some of the critical texts that discuss the role of the Holocaust in public memory in Europe and beyond are Peter Novick, *The Holocaust in American Life* (Boston: Houghton Mifflin, 1999); Jeffrey C Alexander, "On the Social Construction of Moral Universals: The Holocaust from War Crime to Trauma Drama," *European Journal of Social Theory* 5, no. 1 (2002): 5–85; James Edward Young, *The Texture of Memory: Holocaust Memorials and Meaning* (New Haven: Yale University Press, 1993).

2. Aleida Assmann, "Transnational Memories," *European Review* 22, no. 4 (2014): 546–56.

3. Daniel Levy and Natan Sznaider, "The Politics of Commemoration: The Holocaust, Memory and Trauma," in *Handbook of Contemporary European Social Theory*, ed. Gerard Delanty (London: Routledge, 2006), 289–97, here 292.

the United States, perhaps the most critical countries for the development of Holocaust memory in the West. The concept of "the Holocaust," therefore, did not really *exist* for at least a decade after the end of WWII.[4]

The development and transformation of Holocaust memory is often grouped into three phases: the immediate post-WWII period, the rising awareness since the 1960s, and the consolidation of a global memory of the Holocaust since the early 1990s. In the immediate aftermath of WWII, the Holocaust was not recognized as a unique event with its own trajectory, meaning, and consequence, but was subsumed under the broad understanding of WWII, and as one of many examples of Nazi cruelty and extensive war crimes.[5] This was the case in the West, which memorialized its victory over fascism and resistance to the occupation, the victory of democracy over totalitarianism, and above all else, the military triumph of the Allied forces. The Nuremberg trials, clearly the most important "memory event" of this period, presented abundant documentary evidence of Nazi extermination policies, but this evidence was universalized to all Nazi victims without focusing on particularly Jewish suffering.[6]

But this was also the case in the Soviet-dominated East, which placed events of the WWII within a larger narrative of communist revolutionary triumph and antifascist heroism.[7] Communist memory was hegemonic memory, not open to alternative or particular claims on suffering, such as the suffering of the Jews. In fact, communist regimes in the immediate aftermath of the war had a very clear understanding of who constituted a "victim of fascism" and who was not included and, thus, did not deserve such remembrance. In a July 1945 statement by the German Communist Party (in the Soviet Occupied Zone), this categorization was made very explicit:

> There are millions of people who are victims of fascism, who have lost their home, their apartment, their belongings. Victims of fascism are the men who had to become soldiers and were deployed in Hitler's battalions, those who had to give their lives for Hitler's criminal war. Victims of fascism are the Jews who were persecuted and murdered as

4. Levy and Sznaider, "Politics of Commemoration," 292.

5. Daniel Levy and Natan Sznaider, "Memory Unbound: The Holocaust and the Formation of Cosmopolitan Memory," *European Journal of Social Theory* 5, no. 1 (2002): 87–106, here 93.

6. For conceptualization of "memory events," see Alexander Etkind, Rory Finnin, Uilleam Blacker, Julie Fedor, Simon Lewis, Maria Mälksoo, and Matilda Mroz, *Remembering Katyn* (Cambridge: Polity, 2013).

7. Alon Confino, "Remembering the Second World War, 1945–1965: Narratives of Victimhood and Genocide," *Cultural Analysis* 4 (2005): 46–75.

victims of racial mania, the Jehovah's Witnesses, and the work-shy. But we cannot stretch the term "victims of fascism" to include them. They have all endured much and suffered greatly, *but they did not fight.*[8]

Starting with the 1960s, a more discreet narrative of the Holocaust emerges in the West, in large part due to major Holocaust trials—of Adolf Eichmann in Jerusalem in 1961 and the Auschwitz Trials in Frankfurt in 1964. These trials and their media coverage provided detailed accounts of the horrors of the Holocaust and began to build a narrative of the Holocaust as a uniquely catastrophic historical event, spatially and temporarily located within the larger context of WWII, but in its meaning and significance for the predominantly Jewish victims, now placed outside of the war, standing on its own. Another significant memory event in this period was the 1978 American TV show *Holocaust* and especially its broadcast in Germany in 1979, which then further solidified the main narrative arc of the Holocaust, popularized it for mass audiences, and created a visual representation of the Holocaust that has since remained mostly stable.[9]

At the same time, in communist Eastern Europe, Holocaust remembrance was exclusively produced through the framework of antifascism because this link established the communist regime with its new postwar identity and provided it with ongoing political legitimacy. Communist Holocaust remembrance, as Jeffrey Herf notes, was built on "Marxist orthodoxy which placed the Jewish question on the margins of the class struggle, viewed anti-Semitism primarily as a tool to divide the working class (rather than as a belief system with autonomous and widespread impact) and fascism as a product of capitalism."[10]

More broadly, throughout Soviet-controlled communist Europe, the memory of WWII was reduced to the memory of the victory of the Soviet Union over fascist forces.[11] The communist focus on antifascism as a military

8. Quoted in Peter Monteath, "Holocaust Remembrance in the German Democratic Republic—and Beyond," in *Bringing the Dark Past to Light: The Reception of the Holocaust in Postcommunist Europe*, ed. John-Paul Himka and Joanna B Michlic (Lincoln: University of Nebraska Press, 2013), 223–60, here 227–28, emphasis added.

9. For the role of atrocity photographs in affixing a visual collective memory of the Holocaust, see Barbie Zelizer, *Remembering to Forget: Holocaust Memory through the Camera's Eye* (Chicago: University of Chicago Press, 1998).

10. Jeffrey Herf, "The Emergence and Legacies of Divided Memory: Germany and the Holocaust after 1945," in *Memory and Power in Post-War Europe: Studies in the Presence of the Past*, ed. Jan-Werner Muller (Cambridge: Cambridge University Press, 2002), 184–205, here 192; also see John-Paul Himka and Joanna B. Michlic, eds., *Bringing the Dark Past to Light: The Reception of the Holocaust in Postcommunist Europe* (Lincoln: University of Nebraska Press, 2013).

11. Herf, "Emergence and Legacies."

and ideological battle with the ultimate triumph of the communist idea, therefore, completely effaced the unique experience of the Jews during WWII. For example, while Buchenwald concentration camp was a central site of memory in the GDR throughout the communist period, its presence in the East German narrative of WWII was about fascist persecution of communists and, ultimately, communist revolt and liberation—a narrative that completely marginalized the Jews who were killed at Buchenwald and ignored the role of the US troops in camp liberation while glorifying and embellishing communist resistance in the camp.[12]

This effacing of the Jewish experience under communism also continued after the war, as the Jewish identity—especially its religious element—was drowned out by the new construction of the supranational, de-ethnicized, and secular subject. The two ways of remembering, East and West, therefore, diverged almost immediately after the war and developed in quite different directions throughout the postwar period.

Holocaust as Universal Memory

Since the 1990s, as part of the larger global shifts after the Cold War, yet another narrative of the Holocaust has developed, which anchors the Holocaust to the emerging narrative of global human rights after the collapse of communism. Holocaust memory in this period began to solidify as an issue of human rights, the foundational event in the growing architecture of international justice, institutionalized in the establishment of international criminal tribunals for the former Yugoslavia, Rwanda, and the permanent International Criminal Court, all within one decade. Invoked as a warning that the promise of "never again" has been unfulfilled in the aftermath of genocides in Rwanda and Bosnia, the Holocaust becomes a narrative of atrocity prevention, forward- as much as backward-looking. Steven Spielberg's massively successful film *Schindler's List* (1993) presented the visual narration of the Holocaust but also this period's particularly appealing messages of rescue and survival. The opening of the United States Holocaust Memorial Museum in Washington, DC, that same year provided a physical place for Holocaust memory and a historical account that removes the stories of the Holocaust from their immediate locations (the memorials at former concentration camps or ghetto sites, for example), and makes them denationalized and universal. A "cosmopolitan memory" of the Holocaust was born.[13]

12. Monteath, "Holocaust Remembrance."
13. Levy and Sznaider, "Memory Unbound."

Holocaust remembrance since the 1990s, then, has contributed to the formation of a common European cultural memory. It is so central to European identity that it has become a "contemporary European entry ticket," where joining, contributing, and participating in a shared memory of the Holocaust defines what a European state is, especially for late Eastern European entrants to the EU.[14]

While this cosmopolitan memory of the Holocaust has global reach, its main storylines are canonized in the West.[15] As Maria Mälksoo argues, "The centrality of this event in the political consciousness of contemporary Western society has dictated the tuning and hierarchical organization of the overall public remembrance of WWII, totalitarian crimes and modern mass death."[16] From the perspective of the East, even the scholarly field of memory studies has developed within the context of this Western imperialist blind spot and has ignored Eastern European contributions.[17]

European Holocaust memory, in other words, has taken on a particular mnemonic code—a way of remembering—of its own. The memory of Jewish suffering was a critical element of this code, as, in the poignant words of Tony Judt, "the recovered memory of Europe's dead Jews has become the very definition and guarantee of the continent's restored humanity. It wasn't always so."[18]

The new universal memory of the Holocaust has over time expanded beyond the centrality of the Jewish experience to also include the victimization of the Roma and Sinti ethnic groups, homosexuals, and the disabled, with some of the first historical work on these victims published in the 1970s.[19] Parallel to the narrative of Holocaust victims, a central element of the cosmopolitan Holocaust memory is memory of resistance—both Jewish

14. Tony Judt, *Postwar: A History of Europe since 1945* (New York: Penguin Press, 2005), 803. Also, Maria Mälksoo, "The Memory Politics of Becoming European: The East European Subalterns and the Collective Memory of Europe," *European Journal of International Relations* 15, no. 4 (2009): 653–80.

15. This is not to say that there is no diversity of repertoires of Holocaust remembrance in the West. For some attempts at mapping this diversity, see Rebecca Clifford, *Commemorating the Holocaust: The Dilemmas of Remembrance in France and Italy* (Oxford: Oxford University Press, 2013); Dan Diner, "Restitution and Memory: The Holocaust in European Political Cultures," *New German Critique* 90 (Autumn 2003): 36–44; Małgorzata Pakier and Bo Stråth, *A European Memory?: Contested Histories and Politics of Remembrance* (New York: Berghahn Books, 2010).

16. Maria Mälksoo, "'Memory Must be Defended': Beyond the Politics of Mnemonical Security," *Security Dialogue* 46, no. 3 (2015): 221–37, here 226.

17. Joanna Wawrzyniak and Małgorzata Pakier, "Memory Studies in Eastern Europe: Key Issues and Future Perspectives," *Polish Sociological Review* 183, no. 3 (2013): 257–79.

18. Judt, *Postwar*, 805.

19. Some of the earliest accounts of the Roma Holocaust are Donald Kenrick and Grattan Puxon, *The Destiny of Europe's Gypsies* (London: Sussex University Press, 1972); Gabrielle Tyrnauer, *The Fate of the Gypsies during the Holocaust: Report to the United States Holocaust Memorial Council*

resistance and broader antifascist resistance to the Nazi regime. Much of this resistance, of course, was resistance by communists, which is a particularly problematic "memory knot" for the postcommunist Holocaust narrative, as I describe in detail later in the book.[20]

Over time, however, the Western, cosmopolitan memory of the Holocaust also began to subtly efface the Jews. In its focus on universal lessons of the Holocaust, on broader issues of racism, human rights abuses, crimes against humanity, mass atrocity, and education for tolerance, equality, and democracy, this narrative pushed aside the uniqueness of the Jewish experience of the Holocaust. The mission of the Anne Frank House, for example, is increasingly to educate the youth about the perils of discrimination and broader issues of social justice, and less on the specifically *Jewish* experience of Anne Frank herself. More bluntly, when it was first unveiled in Ottawa in 2017, the Canadian National Holocaust Memorial failed to mention the Jews at all, but instead commemorated "millions of men, women and children murdered during the Holocaust."[21] As Holocaust memory in the West developed from a particular story about the tragedy of the Jews into a universal lesson about inhumanity, the Jews have partly disappeared from this memory.[22]

The cosmopolitan memory approach to Holocaust remembrance, further, overlooks the fundamental cleavage in European memory, which is that the memory of the Holocaust in postcommunist Europe is qualitatively different from the memory of the Holocaust as developed in the West. This is because the Holocaust simply does not signify the central "good vs. evil" narrative in the East in the same manner it does in the West. The role of evil in postcommunist Europe is, instead, reserved for communism, as the more recent and immediate source of oppression and victimization. The encroaching (Western) European centrality of the Holocaust is therefore threatening and destabilizing to these state identities. That is the principal problem that this book takes on.

(Vt.?: G. Tyrnauer, 1985); for an early survivor account of the extermination of homosexuals see Heinz Heger, *The Men with the Pink Triangle* (Boston: Alyson Publications, 1980).

20. For the conceptualization of "memory knots," see Michael Rothberg, "Introduction: Between Memory and Memory: From Lieux de mémoire to Noeuds de mémoire," *Yale French Studies*, no. 118/119 (2010): 3–12.

21. Dan Bilefsky, "Canadian Holocaust Memorial Neglects to Mention Jews," *New York Times*, October 5, 2017.

22. I thank an anonymous reviewer for bringing up this very insightful point.

Auschwitz vs. the Gulag

The narrative of Stalinism was just as much constructed as was the narrative of the Holocaust. The construction of what we today understand as the Stalinist gulag owes much to literary sensations, such as the *Gulag Archipelago* by Aleksandar Solzhenitsyn, published in English in 1973, and since translated into more than thirty languages, which provided the first detailed survivor account of the network of Stalin's prison and torture camps. Another important literary work was *Life and Fate,* a semi-fictionalized memoir of the Holocaust and of subsequent communist oppression in the Soviet Union, written by Vasily Grossman and published posthumously in Switzerland in 1980.

But these two early accounts themselves arose out of very different political motivations. Solzhenitsyn, a Russian nationalist, from the beginning pitted the memory of Stalinism against that of the Holocaust. Grossman, in contrast, turned against Soviet ideology in large part in revulsion against Stalin's censorship of the *Black Book* project, a comprehensive and first of its kind report on the Holocaust in the Soviet Union written by Grossman and another famous Jewish communist writer, Ilya Ehrenburg, immediately after the end of the war.[23]

In communist Europe, there was obviously very limited political space to discuss the crimes of Stalinism, even many decades after its worst horrors subsided. A rare window was provided by Nikita Khrushchev in 1956 with his attempt at "de-Stalinization" and publication of the "secret" report to the Soviet Communist Party Congress, which denounced Stalin and his campaign of mass terror. But this effort was sidelined when Khrushchev was deposed in 1964. Instead, memories retreated to the private sphere and remained almost exclusively in the domain of victims of terror and their families, creating a very inward looking "victimhood nationalism."[24]

The collapse of communism provided an opportunity to completely revisit the history of Eastern Europe's twentieth century and the histories of both the Holocaust and Stalinism. Many archives opened for the first time, and historical research could proceed under seemingly little ideological control. Among many important postcommunist memory events, it was

23. As the concept of "the Holocaust" did not exist in 1946, this project had the long and meandering title of *The Black Book: The Ruthless Murder of Jews by German-Fascist Invaders Throughout the Temporarily-Occupied Regions of the Soviet Union and in the German Nazi Death Camps Established on Occupied Polish Soil during the War 1941–1945.*

24. Jie-Hyun Lim, "Victimhood Nationalism in Contested Memories: National Mourning and Global Accountability," in *Memory in a Global Age: Discourses, Practices and Trajectories*, ed. Aleida Assmann and Sebastian Conrad (London: Palgrave Macmillan, 2010), 138–62.

perhaps the 1997 publication of the *Black Book of Communism* (first published in France, then translated into English and other languages) that marked a specific moment in which the memory of communism was flattened to represent one unitary evil akin to Nazism and not a collection of disparate regimes over a long period of time, each with unique features and degrees of repression.[25] Again, the memory of communism was constructed against the memory of the Holocaust—the authors of the *Black Book of Communism* chose this title precisely to mirror Grossman's and Ehrenburg's *Black Book* of the Holocaust. The two memories, in other words, were in conflict from the beginning. Europe's divided memory is not a recent invention.

The postcommunist historical moment was quickly politicized, and it became the moment to reject all legacies of communism in the pursuit of a completely new system of meaning that provided new postcommunist regimes political and popular legitimacy.[26] To be fully rejected, communism needed to be fundamentally discredited, delegitimized, and criminalized. Thus it became symbolized by the gulag. The postcommunist narrative of Stalinism—a discrete historical period associated with Joseph Stalin's personality cult and reign of terror—came to represent *all* of communism, including its later, less systematically murderous manifestations after Stalin's death. It also came to represent the communist experience in countries with no history of brutality to mirror Stalinist crimes, and countries that developed a very different, more open brand of communism, such as socialist Yugoslavia.

Of course, by subsuming all varieties of communism under Stalinism, all previous regimes were equally delegitimized and various national narratives of crimes of communism spread across the postcommunist memoryscape, regardless of whether this interpretation fit the historical record of real, everyday experience of life under communism. References to communist history disappeared, replaced by increasing references to an imaginary precommunist national golden age (often imperial or at least monarchic, often very Christian) and a narrative that connected this mythical national past with enduring national values of righteousness, honor, sacrifice, and heroic suffering.[27] This nationalist narrative left very little space for minorities, and almost no space whatsoever for the millions of Jews who were also, once,

25. Stéphane Courtois, *Le Livre noir du communisme: Crimes, terreur, répression* (Paris: Robert Laffont, 1997).

26. Kristen Ghodsee, "A Tale of 'Two Totalitarianisms': The Crisis of Capitalism and the Historical Memory of Communism," *History of the Present* 4, no. 2 (2014): 115–42.

27. Aleida Assmann, "Europe's Divided Memory," in *Memory and Theory in Eastern Europe*, ed. Uilleam Blacker, Aleksandr Ėtkind, and Julie Fedor (New York: Palgrave, 2013), 25–41.

citizens of these countries. And because communism elevated the heroism of communists, partisans, and antifascists in resisting Nazism, the postcommunist narrative completely erased them.

The end of communism and the "return to Europe" of its East, then, brought the memory of Auschwitz and the memory of the gulag to a head. New states emerging after communism were expected to participate in and contribute to the already established and canonized Holocaust remembrance as developed in the West. But that was a difficult and often impossible demand to meet. This Holocaust remembrance was not central to these states' identities, it was overpowering the remembrance of communism which *was* central to their identities, and it asked for a reckoning with past crimes that was threatening, unwanted, and offensive to the newly constructed postcommunist nationalist narratives. However, to participate in the one joint Europe, postcommunist states could not just reject Holocaust remembrance outright. They needed a way to participate in the larger European memory space, but on their own terms.

Strategies of Memory Appropriation

To overcome these threats to their identities, postcommunist states pursued a variety of strategies to transpose their specific memory of communism onto the symbolic memory architecture of the broader Europe and institutionalize a completely new transnational memory of communism. But instead of crudely naming postcommunist Holocaust remembrance a form of Holocaust denial, it is more productive to talk about *memory appropriation*, where the Holocaust is remembered as a proxy for remembering something else—in this case for remembering communism. And while some form of memory appropriation has occurred in all of postcommunist Europe (with Russia remaining most tightly attached to the dogmatic Soviet-era Holocaust remembrance), there is still considerable diversity in individual state responses.

Some states—such as Serbia—have pursued *memory inversion*, where the Holocaust, its crimes, and its images are directly appropriated in order to make space for the discussion of crimes of communism. The Holocaust is not denied—it is not even obviously trivialized—but it is only remembered heuristically, as a vehicle for remembering the crimes of communism. It is used to invert the suffering and victimization of the Holocaust's principal victims—the Jews—and instead represent other victims—the ethnic majority—as its primary targets. The consequence of this strategy is that Holocaust remembrance and memorialization is no longer about the

Holocaust at all, but about the nationalist needs of an ethnically homogenous society that is using the existing narratives—textual and visual—of Jewish extermination to pursue its own political needs in the present.[28]

Other states—such as Croatia—have engaged in *memory divergence*. Here, the Holocaust is decoupled from other genocidal crimes committed during WWII in order to make the Holocaust a uniquely Nazi (that is, German) problem and absolve the local political community from participation in it. With this strategy, the ethnic majority is also absolved from carrying out other racial and ethnic crimes against non-Jews that occurred under the shadow of the Holocaust. The implication of this narrative intervention is also that fascism, anti-Semitism, and racialized ideologies that justified violence against the Jews and other "undesirables" are foreign imports with no indigenous roots. This outsourcing of ideology then also allows for the outsourcing of communism, which is treated as a foreign imposition with no local resonance or commitment. This narrative opens up space for a connection with an imagined precommunist past—the true home of the national state, unpolluted by external forces of violence and terror. The national self remains pure.

Finally, some states—such as Lithuania—have used *memory conflation*, where the Holocaust is directly combined with other atrocities, such as Stalinism. This historical narrative recognizes only one dimension of terror, tallies the victims of the Holocaust and Stalinism together, and obfuscates the understanding of the Holocaust as a distinct historical event with its own trajectory, consequences, and victims. This process has further led to the application of the legal infrastructure developed to prosecute crimes of the Holocaust (the Nuremberg principles) to now prosecute crimes of communism.

Memory studies scholarship has already pointed out that Europe's memory is "at war," and there have been studies detailing postcommunist responses to Holocaust memory.[29] But to fully understand this memory conflict, we need to actually analyze why it has come to be and why it has taken

28. While not the focus of my book, this kind of appropriation of Holocaust remembrance for contemporary nationalist needs is certainly highly visible in Israel. See Idith Zertal, *Israel's Holocaust and the Politics of Nationhood* (Cambridge: Cambridge University Press, 2005).

29. The most comprehensive academic project on this topic was the international collaboration "Memory at War," which resulted in a detailed website, http://www.memoryatwar.org, and an edited volume, *Memory and Theory in Eastern Europe*, edited by Uilleam Blacker, Aleksandr Ėtkind, and Julie Fedor (New York: Palgrave Macmillan, 2013). For comparative studies of postcommunist Holocaust remembrance, see Alejandro Baer and Natan Sznaider, *Memory and Forgetting in the Post-Holocaust Era: The Ethics of Never Again* (Milton Park: Routledge, 2017); Himka and Michlic, *Bringing the Dark Past to Light*.

this particular shape. To this end, it is useful to apply insights from the ontological security theoretical framework, and it is there that I turn next.

Political Memory and Ontological Security

As applied to states, the concept of ontological security is based on the assumption that states care as much about their ontological security—the security of their identity—as about material, physical security.[30] To continue being secure, states need predictability and order; they strive for routine and stable relationships with other states in the international system.[31] They also need stable narratives about their pasts, which form the basis of their identities.

While this stability is desirable, it is, however, fleeting. Crises or "critical situations" create stress, anxiety, and ontological insecurity.[32] Whether the critical situation truly is a crisis is beside the point—what is significant is how meaningful it is to the states themselves and what actions it produces.[33] Critical situations not only create ruptures in routines; they also lead to the questioning of state identity and, most important, the questioning of foundational state narratives on which this identity is built.

All states face ontological insecurities, but the nature of these insecurities varies depending on the sources of state identities and anxieties. In the United States, for example, the loss of international hegemonic status and perceived decline in power is creating a sense of ontological insecurity.[34] A sense of insecurity in a state's identity may develop over very different moments of crisis in very different ways. Without a full understanding of the

30. The concept of ontological security was first developed in psychoanalysis in R. D. Laing, *The Divided Self: A Study of Sanity and Madness* (London: Tavistock Publications, 1960), and applied to sociology in Anthony Giddens, *The Consequences of Modernity* (Cambridge: Polity Press, 1990). Applications in the field of international relations to explain the behavior of states include Catarina Kinnvall, *Globalization and Religious Nationalism in India: The Search for Ontological Security* (New York: Routledge, 2006); Jennifer Mitzen, "Ontological Security in World Politics: State Identity and the Security Dilemma," *European Journal of International Relations* 12, no. 3 (2006): 341–70; Brent J. Steele, *Ontological Security in International Relations: Self-Identity and the IR State* (London: Routledge, 2008); and Ayşe Zarakol, "Ontological (In)security and State Denial of Historical Crimes: Turkey and Japan," *International Relations* 24, no. 1 (2010): 3–23.

31. Bill McSweeney, *Security, Identity, and Interests: A Sociology of International Relations* (Cambridge: Cambridge University Press, 1999); Jef Huysmans, "Security! What Do You Mean?: From Concept to Thick Signifier," *European Journal of International Relations* 4, no. 2 (1998): 226–55.

32. Filip Ejdus, "Critical Situations, Fundamental Questions and Ontological Insecurity in World Politics," *Journal of International Relations and Development* 21, no. 4 (2018): 883–908.

33. Steele, *Ontological Security*.

34. Jelena Subotic and Brent J Steele, "Moral Injury in International Relations," *Journal of Global Security Studies* 3, no. 4 (2018): 387–401.

significance and impact of this type of state insecurity, our analysis of state behavior is incomplete. And while ontological insecurity is a feature of all states, it is especially states with unresolved or uncertain identities or states with internalized feelings of stigmatization and peripheral status that will experience this anxiety most acutely.[35]

It is here that I want to propose that conflict over political memory can be seen as an example of a critical situation that destabilizes both state identity and its relationships with other states. Memory is critical to ontological security. Just as our own individual memory constitutes our identity, political memory is what constitutes state identities.[36] Political memory helps create and sustain a particular biographical narrative through the use of historical signposts and careful curating of select events, setbacks and triumphs, myths, and symbols.[37] Political memory, therefore, is never just about the past but is also very much about a particular political project in the present that it supports and maintains, which of course was the principal insight of Maurice Halbwachs.[38]

Securing a desirable memory, one that presents the state and the nation as heroes rather than villains of some commonly shared and recognizable international story (of a global war, for example) is necessary both for the state's continuing sense of stability and for its status seeking—for membership in prestigious international clubs (such as the European Union) and for securing all sorts of international reputational benefits. In fact, national memories of violent pasts almost exclusively operate within one of three normatively acceptable frames: nation as victorious over evil, nation as resister of evil, and nation as victim of evil.[39] A desirable memory of the Holocaust, then, is an example of a type of memory that is important for states to maintain and promote in order to belong to the international society of liberal European states.

---

35. Ayşe Zarakol, *After Defeat: How the East Learned to Live with the West* (New York: Cambridge University Press, 2011).

36. Jeffrey K Olick and Joyce Robbins, "Social Memory Studies: From 'Collective Memory' to the Historical Sociology of Mnemonic Practices," *Annual Review of Sociology* (1998): 105–40.

37. Felix Berenskoetter, "Parameters of a National Biography," *European Journal of International Relations* 20, no. 1 (2014): 262–88; Catarina Kinnvall, "Globalization and Religious Nationalism: Self, Identity, and the Search for Ontological Security," *Political Psychology* 25, no. 5 (2004): 741–67; Vamik D. Volkan, *Bloodlines: From Ethnic Pride to Ethnic Terrorism* (New York: Farrar, Straus and Giroux, 1997).

38. Maurice Halbwachs, *On Collective Memory* (Chicago: University of Chicago Press, 1992); also Pierre Nora, "Between Memory and History: Les lieux de mémoire," *Representations* 26 (1989): 7–24.

39. Assmann, "Transnational Memories," 553.

The memory of the Holocaust is a clear example of a type of public memory that can lead to cultural, collective trauma—as it is often not events themselves that are traumatic but rather their consequent social remembrance that creates trauma.[40] The collective consciousness of a trauma is then institutionalized through routinized practices of remembrance such as museum exhibits, memorial sites, days of commemoration, history textbooks, or even inscribed law.[41] As we shall see in the discussion of postcommunist Holocaust representation in museums across and beyond Eastern Europe, historical museums are especially important memory actors as they are the main sites where historical narratives are being reproduced.[42]

The opening of the discussion about the Holocaust after communism in Eastern Europe can then be seen as a form of trauma, a flood of repressed, unwanted memories that the group does not know how to deal with but is unable to continue to avoid. We can understand contemporary postcommunist Holocaust remembrance practices as a way of dealing with this cultural trauma, changing the identities of these societies in the process. As I argue in the next section of this chapter, the attempt to introduce a "European," cosmopolitan, pan-national memory of the Holocaust into postcommunist states in Europe has created an especially acute case of ontological insecurity not only in these states themselves but also in the larger European Union. In other words, the ontological stress of having to confront the Holocaust after communism is a manifestation of the stress of reconciling history with memory.

Holocaust Remembrance and Ontological Insecurity in Postcommunist Europe

The stunningly rapid collapse of communism over only two years (1989–91) created a feeling of profound ontological insecurity across Eastern Europe. Since a coherent, stable, and hegemonic system of meaning basically vanished overnight, all of the routine relationships these states had established and maintained with other international actors became immediately disrupted, and new ones needed to be built from scratch. Political memory of

---

40. Jeffrey C Alexander, "Toward a Theory of Cultural Trauma," in *Cultural Trauma and Collective Identity*, ed. Jeffrey C. Alexander et al. (Berkeley: University of California Press, 2004), 1–30, here 1.

41. Levy and Sznaider, "Politics of Commemoration"

42. Ljiljana Radonić, "Post-communist Invocation of Europe: Memorial Museums' Narratives and the Europeanization of Memory," *National Identities* 19, no. 2 (2017): 269–88, here 271.

the old state no longer served its legitimizing purpose; new histories needed to be constructed to make sense to the new polities.[43]

This moment of insecurity was also driven by internalized feelings of backwardness and inferiority vis-à-vis the West.[44] This anxiety over being seen as backward was especially acute during the EU's period of Eastern enlargement, when the organization expressed some dismay at candidate states' reluctance to discuss the Holocaust and viewed them "as lagging behind and thus in need of re-education where the remembrance of Shoah is concerned."[45] The EU saw this Holocaust avoidance as a "moral failing or as a sign of backwardness" that needed to be rectified.[46] This position, however, conveniently overlooked the deep wells of social complicity in the Holocaust and profound reluctance to deal with it in the Western European "core"—in France, the Netherlands, Italy, or Belgium, a problem not lost on Eastern European critics.

From the perspective of postcommunist states, however, while Holocaust memory was not central to their identity, it proved useful for the larger project of bringing East Central Europe "back to Europe." Without directly challenging the Western memory of the Holocaust, the "new Europeans" instead pursued a form of memory reconciliation by promoting the idea that twentieth-century Europe experienced two totalitarianisms and two genocides—Nazism and Stalinism. The argument here is that the new, enlarged Europe after communism cannot be united unless it has a shared memory, which means adding Stalinism into the core European memory of the twentieth century. At the heart of this project was a profound sense of ontological insecurity and a feeling of being abandoned by Western Europe throughout much of the post-WWII period. This desire to belong to the European mnemonic and cultural center is clearly elaborated, for example, in this introduction to the Museum of the Occupation in Riga, Latvia:

> Fifty-one years of occupation took a heavy toll on Latvia. About a third of the population perished or were exiled as a result of political murders and genocide, war action and inhuman treatment in the Gulag, or became refugees at the end of World War II to escape the return

43. Richard J. Evans, "Redesigning the Past: History in Political Transitions," *Journal of Contemporary History* 38, no. 1 (2003): 5–12.

44. Julie Mostov, "The Use and Abuse of History in Eastern Europe: A Challenge for the 90s," *Constellations* 4, no. 3 (1998): 376–86.

45. Ewa Stańczyk, "Transnational, Transborder, Antinational? The Memory of the Jewish Past in Poland," *Nationalities Papers* 44, no. 3 (2016): 416–29, here 418.

46. James Mark, *The Unfinished Revolution: Making Sense of the Communist Past in Central-Eastern Europe* (New Haven: Yale University Press, 2010), xvi.

> of the Soviet regime. In their place, settlers from other parts of the Soviet Union were brought in. They did not speak the Latvian language and were strangers to Latvian culture and traditions. From the very first, both occupation powers tried to deprive the Latvian nation of its national pride and to deny, falsify or distort the history of Latvia and Latvia's historical ties to Europe. Latvia was estranged from the cultural foundations of Western culture. After war's end, the political economic and social life in the Western world thrived; at the same time, all progress in Latvia stopped. The Western world forgot Latvia. The name of Latvia disappeared from books of history, as though it never had existed. The borders of the Baltic states disappeared from maps.[47]

What is striking in this narrative is the almost exclusive focus on the Soviet occupation and especially the erasure of Latvian national identity through Sovietization. The one ambiguous reference to Nazism under "both occupation powers" is also presented as catastrophic for Latvian nation and culture and detrimental to its ties to Europe; ninety-four thousand Latvian Jews (5 percent of Latvia's prewar population) and their annihilation in the Holocaust—by Germans but with the help of their Latvian collaborators—are completely absent in this narrative of occupation.[48] They are not an important part of Latvian state identity, and not a constitutive element of this state's national biography.

This is not a careless omission. In fact, I would suggest that the centrality of the Holocaust as a foundational European narrative is soundly rejected across postcommunist Europe because of its perceived elevation of Jewish victimhood above victimhood of other regional majority ethnic groups, a move that is increasingly openly resented.[49] In the absence of almost any Jews across vast swaths of the East, postcommunist national identities were built on a rejection of the communist pan-national identity project (where the organizing narrative was loyalty to the socialist and not the ethnic subject) in favor of narratives based on ethnic majoritarianism, a very homogeneous basis that left almost no room for the incorporation of minority narratives. As Antonin Weiss-Wendt explained in his study of Estonia, Holocaust

47. Main print catalogue of the Museum of the Occupation in Riga, Latvia, quoted in Kevin M. E. Platt, "Occupation versus Colonization: Post-Soviet Latvia and the Provincialization of Europe," in *Memory and Theory in Eastern Europe*, ed. Uilleam Blacker, Alexander Etkind, and Julie Fedor (New York: Palgrave Macmillan, 2013), 125–48, here 136.

48. United States Holocaust Memorial Museum, "Latvia," accessed January 31, 2019, https://www.ushmm.org/wlc/en/article.php?ModuleId=10005443.

49. Baer and Sznaider, *Memory and Forgetting*.

remembrance there was linked exclusively to the Jewish minority and was referred to as "the Jewish issue." Since the Jewish minority in Estonia is very small, Holocaust remembrance simply does not matter for the majority ethnic population and, when brought up, brings about ethnic resentment and often new waves of anti-Semitism.[50] It challenges the security of a nation's identity because it problematizes the very biography on which this identity was founded.

But I would go further in suggesting that the Western European Holocaust memory's focus on Jewish suffering is also rejected in much of postcommunist Europe because it brings about debates about extensive and deep local complicity in the Holocaust and the material and political benefits for majority populations across Eastern Europe of the complete Jewish absence. This is an issue of great historical importance, and while carefully documented it is profoundly and persistently resisted by much of the Eastern European public.[51]

Eastern Europe is not only the main site of the Holocaust, but it is also the main witness to and the main beneficiary of the Holocaust. The extermination of the European Jewry was not only carried out behind the barbed wires of concentration camps, hidden from plain sight. It was also carried out in public view of non-Jewish citizens of these countries, on streets, squares, and farms across Eastern Europe. Non-Jews benefited from this Jewish erasure, often for generations after the Holocaust.[52] Jewish businesses, homes, and property have over decades of looting followed by communist seizures slowly been distributed within the general economy, with difficult and sporadic attempts at restitution. It is certainly not in the majority's interest to dig up whose apartments the new tenants now live in, whose dental practices they inherited, whose family heirloom brooch is in their jewelry box.

This is why much of post-Holocaust Eastern Europe has been described as a purposeful "site of nonmemory," a "landscape of erasure."[53] Ewa Płonowska Ziarek wrote of Poland, but her description is apt for the entire postcommunist political space when she describes "the erasure of collective

---

50. Anton Weiss-Wendt, "Why the Holocaust Does not Matter to Estonians," *Journal of Baltic Studies* 39, no. 4 (2008): 475–97.

51. John-Paul Himka, "Obstacles to the Integration of the Holocaust into Post-communist East European Historical Narratives," *Canadian Slavonic Papers* 50, nos. 3–4 (2008): 359–72.

52. Volha Charnysh and Evgeny Finkel, "The Death Camp Eldorado: Political and Economic Effects of Mass Violence," *American Political Science Review* 111, no. 4 (2017): 801–18.

53. Omer Bartov, "Eastern Europe as the Site of Genocide," *The Journal of Modern History* 80, no. 3 (2008): 557–93, here 557; Jennifer A. Jordan "A Matter of Time: Examining Collective Memory in Historical Perspective in Postwar Berlin," *Journal of Historical Sociology* 18, no. 1–2 (2005): 37–71, here 39; Baer and Sznaider, *Memory and Forgetting*, 105.

and individual memories of Jewish life . . ., the lack of mourning for the Jewish tragedy, and the overwhelming loss of awareness of the absence of Jews and Jewish culture."[54]

The fact that post-WWII Jewish communities in these countries are negligible in numbers and have limited political clout is not incidental to this condition.[55] These countries were once multicultural societies with large Jewish minorities, but today most are ethnically homogeneous, making Eastern Europe a site of "dismembered multiethnicity."[56] This very fact of postwar ethnic homogeneity is a problem of "cultural intimacy"—an issue of domestic identity building, the thing that builds the nation together—but simultaneously also an issue of international embarrassment and sometimes even shame.[57]

This argument builds on the already well-developed social psychology literature that emphasizes the need for cognitive consistency in the face of moral transgressions. People who have carried out an act that is inconsistent with their core beliefs or with their own self-identity (as "good," "victim," or "innocent") seek to reduce this cognitive dissonance and restore their self-esteem either by deflecting blame onto the victims of their actions, by flat denial, or by attributing the wrongdoing to external circumstances outside of their immediate control.[58]

---

54. Ewa Płonowska Ziarek, "Melancholic Nationalism and the Pathologies of Commemorating the Holocaust in Poland," in *Imaginary Neighbors: Mediating Polish-Jewish Relations after the Holocaust*, ed. Dorota Glowacka and Joanna Zylinska (Lincoln: University of Nebraska Press, 2007), 301–26, here 302.

55. For example, Jews made up almost 10 percent of the prewar population of Poland, and at least 30 percent in the major cities of Warsaw, Krakow, and Vilna. Hungary's capital, Budapest, was 23 percent Jewish before the Holocaust. Today, Hungary is the only country in the region with a sizeable Jewish population (one hundred thousand). Jewish communities in the rest of postcommunist Europe are largely non-existent. Michael Shafir, *Between Denial and "Comparative Trivialization": Holocaust Negationism in Post-Communist East Central Europe* (Jerusalem: Hebrew University of Jerusalem, Vidal Sassoon International Center for the Study of Antisemitism, 2002).

56. Karolina S. Follis, *Building Fortress Europe: The Polish-Ukrainian Frontier* (Philadelphia: University of Pennsylvania Press, 2012).

57. Michael Herzfeld, *Cultural Intimacy: Social Poetics in the Nation-State* (New York: Routledge, 2005); Jelena Subotić and Ayşe Zarakol, "Cultural Intimacy in International Relations," *European Journal of International Relations* 19, no. 4 (2013): 915–38.

58. Aarti Iyer, Colin Wayne Leach, and Faye J Crosby, "White Guilt and Racial Compensation: The Benefits and Limits of Self-Focus," *Personality and Social Psychology Bulletin* 29, no. 1 (2003): 117–29; Emanuele Castano and Roger Giner-Sorolla, "Not Quite Human: Infrahumanization in Response to Collective Responsibility for Intergroup Killing," *Journal of Personality and Social Psychology* 90, no. 5 (2006): 804; Miroslaw Kofta and Patrycja Slawuta, "Thou Shall Not Kill . . . Your Brother: Victim–Perpetrator Cultural Closeness and Moral Disapproval of Polish Atrocities against Jews after the Holocaust," *Journal of Social Issues* 69, no. 1 (2013): 54–73.

Of particular interest for my argument is research that shows that it is not only direct perpetrators but also their descendants and even much larger social groups to which perpetrators have belonged that react in anger and defiance, even engaging in further victimization of minority groups when confronted with the wrongdoings of their in-group members in the past.[59] The classic and very relevant example of this is so-called secondary anti-Semitism, where reminders of the crimes of the Holocaust and the long-term impact on Jewish suffering induce guilt and further strengthen anti-Semitism among contemporary Germans—even the youth, who are generations removed from the events of WWII.[60]

It is against this background that the destabilizing effects of Holocaust memory in both postcommunist Europe and the larger European Union can be best understood. Holocaust memory, as institutionalized in the Western mnemonic cannon, created significant stress and anxiety in postcommunist states. It challenged these states' biographies, their narratives about themselves and their past. It brought up undesirable memories that were contrary to their identities of victimization at the hands of German and Soviet occupiers. These memories needed to be challenged and confronted straight on.

Constructing Holocaust Remembrance after Communism

Communism strictly regulated Holocaust remembrance, primarily by absorbing it as just one event within the much larger story of WWII. Also, due to the region's international political and social isolation, communist Holocaust memory developed and solidified in almost complete marginalization from the cohering European Holocaust narrative in the West.

Postcommunist European states first encountered the European push for a unified cosmopolitan memory of the Holocaust as they tried to join various European organizations after 1991—foremost in their applications for European Union membership, but also in attempts to gain membership in other European institutions such as the Council of Europe. In 1995, the European Parliament passed the Resolution on the Return of Plundered

59. Katie N Rotella and Jennifer A Richeson, "Motivated to "Forget" the Effects of In-group Wrongdoing on Memory and Collective Guilt," *Social Psychological and Personality Science* 4, no. 6 (2013): 730–37; Nyla R Branscombe, Michael T Schmitt, and Kristin Schiffhauer, "Racial Attitudes in Response to Thoughts of White Privilege," *European Journal of Social Psychology* 37, no. 2 (2007): 203–15.

60. Roland Imhoff and Rainer Banse, "Ongoing Victim Suffering Increases Prejudice: The Case of Secondary Anti-Semitism," *Psychological Science* 20, no. 12 (2009): 1443–47.

Property to Jewish Communities, which contained explicit demands for Eastern European states to return property looted in the Holocaust, but also "welcome[d] the fact that certain Central and Eastern European countries have apologized publicly for the crimes committed against Jews during the Second World War and have recognized their responsibilities in respect of these crimes."[61] Implied in this statement was that the rest of the Eastern European states should do the same.[62]

Of course, the fact that none of the European Parliament documents have ever issued a similar demand for an apology for local complicity in the Holocaust from any Western European government—France, Belgium, Italy, Austria, and the Netherlands are obvious candidates—has further fueled the Eastern Europeans' sense of resentment and injustice. Eastern European elites are keenly aware that there is continuing denial of the extent of complicity in the Holocaust by the governments of these Western countries, which have anchored their memory of the Holocaust on glorifying anti-Nazi resistance and downplaying—if not flatly ignoring—pervasive local collaboration.[63]

Further infuriating Eastern European states has been Western Europe's lack of acknowledgment of its role in carving up the post-WWII East, making a deal with the Soviet Union that effectively handed over these states to Stalin's control. This issue would come up repeatedly in the discussions about appropriate Holocaust remembrance. Many Eastern European politicians have explicitly asked Western European governments to acknowledge that they had historically betrayed the East before any further debate was to occur regarding Eastern European complicity in the Holocaust. What post-communist states asked of the West was to admit that they "morally capitulated to the Soviets," as a Lithuanian Member of the European Parliament remarked.[64]

In January 2000, in a major European institutional push to regulate Holocaust remembrance across the continent, Sweden convened the Stockholm

61. European Parliament, Resolution on the Return of Plundered Property to Jewish Communities, December 14, 1995, Brussels.

62. Marek Kucia, "The Europeanization of Holocaust Memory and Eastern Europe," *East European Politics and Societies* 30, no. 1 (2016): 97–119.

63. These denials occasionally pop up to the surface, and produce much international embarrassment—such, as, for example, the statement by the French far-right presidential candidate Marine Le Pen in 2017 that "France wasn't responsible for Vel d'Hiv," referring to the largest round-up of French Jews by the French police in 1942, most of whom were then transported to Auschwitz. Adam Nossiter, "Marine Le Pen Denies French Guilt for Rounding Up Jews," *New York Times*, April 10, 2017.

64. Quoted in Alina Hogea, "European Conscience and Totalitarianism: Contested Memory in the European Union," *Revista Româna de Jurnalism si Comunicare* 7, no. 3/4 (2012): 59–71, here 66.

Forum on the Holocaust to define a common framework for European Holocaust remembrance, research, and education.[65] The forum established the International Task Force on Holocaust Education, Remembrance and Research, renamed International Holocaust Remembrance Alliance (IHRA) in 2012. It remains the international organization that most explicitly "constructs, institutionalizes and diffuses" transnational Holocaust memory in Europe.[66] In 2005, the European Parliament adopted its most complete resolution on the Holocaust, the Resolution on Remembrance of the Holocaust, Anti-Semitism and Racism, which established January 27 (the day of the liberation of Auschwitz in 1945) as "European Holocaust Memorial Day across the whole of the EU."[67]

And while postcommunist states accepted this new regulation, signed documents, and adopted major parameters of the memory framework, presumably not wanting to jeopardize the delicate process of EU accession, they also demanded a thorough renegotiation of European memory politics.[68] To respond to this reconfigured memory setting after communism, and to resolve the ontological insecurity it had brought, newly emerged East Central European states developed a memory strategy that presented a competing memory to that of the Holocaust—the memory of Stalinism. The memory of Auschwitz was now in competition with the memory of the gulag.

This new remembrance of communist crimes, however, was not a completely organic development. It did not emerge solely out of a collection of private and public memories that gathered, unrecognized and repressed during communism. Instead, communist remembrance in East Central Europe was constructed after 1989 using the already existing model of Holocaust remembrance.[69] Engaging in active historical knowledge production, various

65. Being at the forefront of European Holocaust remembrance effort was also important for Sweden's own sense of political identity as a "rescuer state" during the Holocaust. Karl Christian Lammers, "The Holocaust and Collective Memory in Scandinavia: The Danish Case," *Scandinavian Journal of History* 36, no. 5 (2011): 570–86. For the history of the Stockholm Forum, see Larissa Allwork, *Holocaust Remembrance between the National and the Transnational: The Stockholm International Forum and the First Decade of the International Task Force* (London: Bloomsbury, 2015).

66. Kucia, "Europeanization of Holocaust Memory," 105.

67. European Parliament, Resolution on Remembrance of the Holocaust, Anti-Semitism and Racism, January 27, 2005. The European Parliament was very active on this front. Between 1989 and 2014, the parliament adopted twelve separate documents on Holocaust remembrance. Kucia, "Europeanization of Holocaust Memory," 102.

68. Mälksoo, "Memory Politics"; Annabelle Littoz-Monnet, "Explaining Policy Conflict across Institutional Venues: European Union-Level Struggles over the Memory of the Holocaust," *JCMS: Journal of Common Market Studies* 51, no. 3 (2013): 489–504.

69. Máté Zombory, "The Birth of the Memory of Communism: Memorial Museums in Europe," *Nationalities Papers* 45, no. 6 (2017): 1028–46.

memory actors—historical commissions, institutes of national memory, and newly established museums of communism—used the Holocaust remembrance template, with a stratification of the victims, perpetrators, modes of terror, suffering, and death that already made epistemological sense to Western European audiences.[70]

These institutions performed memory events in the narrative language of Holocaust remembrance. This included the already existing repertoire of Holocaust imagery, such as concentration camps, slave labor, death marches, deportations, forced hunger, and deprivation, as well as visual cues of abandoned suitcases and boxcars—tropes of Holocaust remembrance that had now been repurposed to represent crimes of communism.[71] Holocaust memory was thus reclaimed to represent the memory of communism in quite a direct way. Communist crimes began to be referred to as the "Red Holocaust" or "the other Holocaust."

It is not a coincidence, then, that the founders of the Romanian Sighet Memorial Museum of Communism claimed to have come to the idea of creating such a museum after visiting Auschwitz in 1996, or that in 2000 Slovakia decided to revamp its national Museum of the Slovak National Uprising "to fill empty areas in the historical memory so as to be able to correspond to a European standard."[72] In fact, most of the museums of communism that sprung up after 1991 in some form instrumentalize already existing aesthetics of Holocaust remembrance, often for quite overt nation-building purposes, with narrative frames that used to be reserved for stories of fascism now used to narrate communism.[73] Universalization of the Holocaust, therefore, allowed for the Holocaust to be a "'container' for remembering different victims."[74]

This new communist remembrance was also to a large extent built on already existing communist remembrance in the West. For example, the already discussed, hugely influential *Black Book of Communism* quite explicitly built the case for the horrors of Stalinism on the existing Holocaust memory template. As Máté Zombory documents, the authors of the *Black Book of*

70. On the network of historical memory institutes and their efforts to change European Union policies and legislation on remembrance, see Laure Neumayer, "Advocating for the Cause of the 'Victims of Communism' in the European Political Space: Memory Entrepreneurs in Interstitial Fields," *Nationalities Papers* 45, no. 6 (2017): 992–1012.

71. For an exploration of ways in which the Holocaust was visualized, see Barbie Zelizer, *Visual Culture and the Holocaust* (New Brunswick: Rutgers University Press, 2001).

72. Radonić, "Post-communist Invocation," 273.

73. Radonić, "Post-communist Invocation," 271.

74. Ljiljana Radonic, "Conflicting Memories in 'Unified Europe'—Standards of Remembrance in the Center and at the Periphery," *Der Donauraum* 50, no. 3–4 (2010): 213–24, here 219.

Communism directly influenced subsequent debates in East Central Europe, including the establishment of the House of Terror museum in Budapest, as members of its founding board. This new construction of communist remembrance, then, "was the cooperative effort of a pan-European network of activists, scholars, and politicians engaged in the struggle for a legitimate anti-Communist revision of history."[75] Significantly, Eastern European states forged alliances with the Western European right, most directly the European People's Party in the European Parliament, in pushing for EU resolutions and proclamations that would decentralize the Holocaust from pan-European memory and add crimes of communism as the second and equal part of this memory project.[76] These campaigns then gave the "new Europeans" the opportunity and platform to elevate their presence in the European Parliament on issues of great importance.[77]

The first in a series of EU resolutions on crimes of communism came in 2005—The Future of Europe Sixty Years after the Second World War. Ironically, this expansion of totalitarianism to include all of communism—not only its most totalitarian Stalinist expression—also led to the return to a communist-era interpretation of the Holocaust, which deemphasized the uniqueness of Jewish suffering. The European Parliament's 2005 resolution on the sixtieth anniversary of the end of the Second World War in Europe on May 8, 1945, thus no longer referred to Jews as the Holocaust's principal victims, but instead to "all the victims of Nazi tyranny," thereby elevating the victimization of non-Jewish ethnic majorities in Eastern Europe.[78]

This demand to commemorate side by side—as consequentially the same—the "two twentieth-century totalitarianisms" culminated in two European Union documents, the 2008 Declaration on the Proclamation of 23 August as European Day of Remembrance for Victims of Stalinism and Nazism and the Resolution on European Conscience and Totalitarianism, which built on the 2008 Prague Declaration of the same name.[79]

---

75. Zombory, "Birth of the Memory," 1034.

76. Annabelle Littoz-Monnet, "The EU Politics of Remembrance: Can Europeans Remember Together?," *West European Politics* 35, no. 5 (2012): 1182–1202; Laure Neumayer, "Integrating the Central European Past into a Common Narrative: The Mobilizations Around the 'Crimes of Communism' in the European Parliament," *Journal of Contemporary European Studies* 23, no. 3 (2015): 344–63.

77. Neumayer, "Integrating the Central European Past."

78. European Parliament, Resolution on the 60th Anniversary of the End of the Second World War in Europe on 8 May 1945, May 12, 2005, Brussels.

79. European Parliament, Declaration on the Proclamation of 23 August as European Day of Remembrance for Victims of Stalinism and Nazism, September 23, 2008, Brussels; European Parliament, Resolution on European Conscience and Totalitarianism, April 2, 2009, Brussels. The equation of two totalitarianisms was also institutionalized by the Organization for Security and Cooperation in Europe (OSCE) in its 2009 Vilnius Declaration, available at the OSCE website, accessed January 31, 2019,

The Prague Declaration explicitly lays out the ideological framework postcommunist European states have used regarding the place of the Holocaust and communist memory. The rhetorical move of referring to "communist crimes" instead of "Stalinist crimes" is critical here as it implies that terror was communism's central organizing feature, which then makes it easy to equate it narratively with fascism. Indeed, while the first article states, "Both the Nazi and the Communist totalitarian regimes [should] each be judged by their own terrible merits," the declaration then goes on to claim that "exterminating and deporting whole nations and groups of population were indivisible parts of the ideologies they availed themselves with," which explicitly takes the specifically genocidal aspect of Nazism—extermination of whole nations—and attributes it to communism. This equation of the two regimes as being structurally the same even led one member of the European Parliament to declare, "I ask the European Parliament to stand in solidarity with the victims of *Fascist Communism.*"[80]

Acting on the 2008 Prague Declaration's invitation to treat communism similarly to the Holocaust, a group of East-Central European politicians and civil society actors—mostly from the right—organized another conference in Prague in 2010, which produced the Declaration on Crimes of Communism. This document explicitly demands that communism be retroactively criminalized and a special international tribunal be established "in a similar way as the Nazi crimes were condemned and sentenced by the Nuremberg tribunal."[81]

While the political purchase for postcommunist states of equating Nazism and communism is clear, a further implication of this mnemonic practice is that by appropriating the Holocaust to criminalize communism, postcommunist countries have also succeeded in removing the memory of antifascist resistance and its instrumental role in defeating Nazism from the memory of WWII. Here I do not only mean the obvious role of the Soviet Red Army in defeating the Wehrmacht and liberating concentration camps in the East, but even more so the role that hundreds of thousands of partisans across occupied Europe played in sabotaging, disrupting, distracting, and also directly fighting the Nazis and their local collaborators throughout the war.[82]

https://www.oscepa.org/documents/all-documents/annual-sessions/2009-vilnius/declaration-6/261-2009-vilnius-declaration-eng/file.

80. Neumayer, "Integrating the Central European Past," 353, emphasis added.

81. "Declaration on the Crimes of Communism," in *International Conference: "Crimes of the Communist Regimes"* (Prague: Institute for the Study of Totalitarian Regimes, 2011), 454–55, here 454.

82. United States Holocaust Memorial Museum, "Non-Jewish Resistance," https://www.ushmm.org/wlc/en/article.php?ModuleId=10005420.

It was the surviving socialists and communists of the Buchenwald concentration camp (many of them Jews themselves) who gathered in the first few days after camp liberation on April 19, 1945, and took an oath to "destroy Nazism from its roots . . . as our responsibility to our murdered comrades and their relatives."[83] The Buchenwald Oath, and its decidedly antifascist narrative, is probably the earliest public act of Holocaust memorialization. Removing this resistance from the memory of the Holocaust is not only a move in selective historical narration, but it also denies the very foundation of Holocaust memory. Of all the victims of Nazism and Stalinism, these resistance fighters seem to be left without anybody to advocate for their remembrance and increasingly, as the next three chapters of the book demonstrate, are facing retroactive criminalization themselves.

It is precisely this concern that some on the European left have expressed in the European Parliament. In a rebuttal to the 2013 Parliament proposal for a program titled Europe for Citizens, which adopted the two totalitarianisms narrative, a group of European United Left/Nordic Green Left (GUE/NGL) EP members dissented, on the grounds that "that future generations should [not] be told the historical lie that seeks to put Communists on a par with Nazis, nor should they be encouraged to forget both the fascist dictatorships that once held sway in southern Europe and the colonial past."[84] Similarly, Glyn Ford, the representative of the Party of European Socialists pleaded, "While I am in favour of the maximum objectivity in analyzing Europe's history, and while I recognize the horrific nature of the crimes of Stalinist Russia . . . I am not willing to equate the crimes of the Nazis, the Holocaust and the genocide that saw six million Jews, along with Communists, Trade Unionists and disabled, die, with those of Stalinist Russia. This political relativism threatens to dilute the unique nature of the Nazi crimes, and in doing so provides an intellectual underpinning to the ideologies of today's neo-Nazis and fascists."[85]

New European Memory from East to West

Postcommunist Holocaust remembrance and the elevation of communist crimes to the central historical narrative of the twentieth century has not

83. Baer and Sznaider, *Memory and Forgetting*, 9.

84. European Parliament, *Report on the Proposal for a Council Regulation Establishing for the Period 2014–2020 the Programme "Europe for Citizens"* (Brussels: European Parliament, 2013), 49.

85. Quoted in Aleksandra Gliszczyńska-Grabias, "Communism Equals or Versus Nazism? Europe's Unwholesome Legacy in Strasbourg," *East European Politics and Societies* 30, no. 1 (2016): 74–96, here 75.

remained an exclusively Eastern European phenomenon. Instead, through tremendous entrepreneurship by Eastern European memory actors including politicians allied with right-wing European political parties, this new European memory has now become a full feature of *all* European memory projects, East and West.

The full equation of fascism and communism and their leveling as two European totalitarianisms has gotten perhaps its clearest physical manifestation in the new House of European History (HEH), which after decades of delays—some political, some administrative—finally opened in Brussels in May 2017.[86] HEH was a key EU project aimed at shoring up the cultural foundation for integration, strengthening European identity and building EU legitimacy across the continent.[87] This is why the museum makes both the Holocaust and communist terror integral to the history of Europe, one that leads, teleologically, toward European integration.

HEH specifically avoids singling out the experience of the European Jewry and has no separate remembrance of their annihilation—a curating decision agreed upon early in the development of the museum.[88] Instead, the Holocaust is woven through other narratives of WWII and post-WWII remembrance, leading one scholar to wonder "to what extent history politics and remembrance policies of EU institutions more generally have become East Europeanized."[89]

There is a vibrant scholarship that looks at this outcome approvingly. As Maria Mälksoo has argued, postcommunist European memory projects were simultaneously about seeking recognition from and status in Europe while at the same time rejecting the dominant European narrative of its past, including the centrality of the Holocaust to European postwar identity.[90] Mälksoo sees this postcommunist move as a form of Eastern European

---

86. House of European History website, accessed January 31, 2019, https://historia-europa.ep.eu/en.

87. Wolfram Kaiser, "Limits of Cultural Engineering: Actors and Narratives in the European Parliament's House of European History Project," *JCMS: Journal of Common Market Studies* 55, no. 3 (2017): 518–34, here 518.

88. The purposeful marginalization of the Holocaust is evident in the extremely problematic composition of the Museum's Academic Committee, which includes Maria Schmidt, the director of the House of Terror in Budapest. Schmidt is a prominent Hungarian revisionist historian whose controversial views on the Holocaust have been notable for decades. Michael Shafir, "Hungarian Politics and the Post-1989 Legacy of the Holocaust," in *Holocaust in Hungary: Sixty Years Later*, ed. Randolph L Braham and Brewster S. Chamberlin (New York: Rosenthal Institute for Holocaust Studies, Graduate Center of the City University of New York, 2006), 257–90, here 275. Also, Kaiser, "Limits of Cultural Engineering," 529.

89. Kaiser, "Limits of Cultural Engineering," 531.

90. Mälksoo, "Memory Politics."

emancipatory decolonization, where postcommunist states rejected both Western European and Soviet hegemony over memory.[91] This is similar to Jay Winter's call to shift the European memory center of gravity "from Paris to Warsaw."[92]

The problem, however, is that this Eastern European desire to jump historically over the illegitimate communist period and find national legitimacy in the precommunist past finds itself immediately confronted with the collaborationist and often murderous quality of many of these past regimes, including fully homegrown fascist regimes in Slovakia, Croatia, Hungary, and Romania and many collaborationist forces across all other Eastern European states, a normative problem that the decolonization thesis often ignores. The search for the buried memory, then, also further stigmatizes the national body politic. Looking for good memories, only worse ones are found. Because it is difficult to erase or deny these memories, an easier path is to invert them—and claim that crimes of Nazism and their local collaborators were in fact crimes of communism. The criminal past is not fully denied, but the responsibility for it is misdirected, accomplishing two things: the absolution of the national criminal past and the criminalization of communism.

What this process has produced, however, are new ruptures within states and within the EU, where Holocaust memory is still pan-European and cosmopolitan and where nationalized, particularized memories are threatening. Postcommunist memory politics therefore has had a boomerang quality to it: the European push for cosmopolitan Holocaust memory created a national particularistic backlash, which then created further insecurities both in the states themselves and between the postcommunist states and the larger European Union.

To sum up, because the Holocaust is a "constitutive element of the European polity," removing the centrality of the Holocaust from European memory destabilizes the core of the European Union, which was built on the memory of WWII—no WWII, no European Union.[93] What postcommunist European remembrance demonstrates, however, is that it is not only postcommunist states that are facing narrative crises. It is also the EU itself—by

---

91. Mälksoo, "Memory Politics." For an even stronger elaboration of this thesis, see Maria Mälksoo, "Nesting Orientalisms at War," in *Orientalism and War*, ed. Tarak Barkawi and Keith Stanski (New York: Columbia University Press, 2012), 177–96.

92. Quoted in Michael Rothberg, "Between Paris and Warsaw: Multidirectional Memory, Ethics, and Historical Responsibility," in *Memory and Theory in Eastern Europe*, ed. Uilleam Blacker, Alexander Etkind, and Julie Fedor (New York: Palgrave Macmillan, 2013), 81–102, here 81.

93. Littoz-Monnet, "Explaining Policy Conflict," 490.

being confronted with the fact that, first, its foundational narrative of the Holocaust is no longer the central unifying narrative in Europe and, second, its foundational mission of peace is also on the verge of collapse after the EU so thoroughly failed to prevent war and genocide in Europe in the 1990s. Postcommunist remembrance, then, causes self-doubt within core European states, destabilizes relationships with the "new Europeans" in the East, and produces conditions that can contribute to old and new types of Holocaust revisionism, denial, and neofascist resurgence.

The Eastern Europeanization of Holocaust remembrance also destabilizes the "old" EU because it deconstructs the solidified narrative of primarily German responsibility and opens up a variety of new narratives about multiple responsibilities for the Holocaust in the West. It can bring, for example, a new reevaluation of Italy's fascism and its inadequate postwar repudiation, or focus new attention on the extent of collaboration and meeker resistance in occupied France, Belgium, and the Netherlands than has been maintained over the past decades.

This new European memory also endangers another of the EU's foundational narratives: that of post-WWII integration and progress as contrasts to the darkness of the Holocaust. By deconstructing these narratives, it also destroys the shield that has absolved the contemporary EU from reckoning with its problems of continuing racism or broader human rights deficits today. Finally, if the Holocaust and WWII are not "time zero" for the EU, this starts to bring up extremely uncomfortable memories of Europe's colonial crimes that in many ways foreshadowed the Holocaust.[94] The renegotiation of the official European memory of the twentieth century, then, can open up space for the renegotiation of Europe's more distant imperial past and thus situate WWII not as an aberration but a continuation of European history and the technology of violence, cutting at the core of the EU's contemporary identity.

The European Union as a whole and EU member states as its constitutive parts are in crisis—uncertain about their identities, the cohesion of their union, the strength of their mutual commitments, and about each other. This crisis can best be understood as a feeling of profound ontological insecurity—an insecurity of identity. I argued in this chapter that an additional contributing factor to this sense of general unease within the EU is its contested political memory, especially memory of the Holocaust and

94. Benjamin Meiches, The Politics of Annihilation: A Genealogy of Genocide (Minneapolis: University of Minnesota Press, 2019).

memory of communism. As the EU has enlarged to the East, a completely new set of memories and mnemonic practices was introduced to the European narrative. This process has been neither easy nor smooth, and it is far from resolved. It has also produced tremendous narrative rewriting, relaxing some of the most established mnemonic canons of the twentieth century (the memory of the Holocaust), which has in turn created a political environment fertile for memory challenges, disruptions, and revisions.

Encouraged by the European Union's declarations equating crimes of Nazism with crimes of communism under the umbrella of crimes of totalitarianism, many Eastern European states have appropriated Holocaust memory and even imagery to talk about crimes of previous communist regimes. Holocaust remembrance, then, is no longer about the Holocaust at all, but is about very acute ontological security needs of new states that are building their identity as fundamentally anticommunist, which then in turn makes them more legitimately European and capitalist.[95] Holocaust remembrance does not only provide a state its mnemonic security needs, but it secures its ideological legitimacy as well.

Political memory, therefore, can be both a source and a product of state ontological insecurity. It can destabilize identities within states themselves, by radically changing accepted state biographies and biographical narratives, but it often also destabilizes state relationships with other states and international actors, relationships that gave the state a sense of routine, familiarity, and calm. At the same time, new versions of political memory can be a result of state ontological insecurities. When states feel insecure, they may try to affix a certain memory in place, or try to replace bad memories with those more favorable to the state view of self. These radical mnemonic ruptures, however, can then further destabilize state internal and external relationships, to significant international political effect.

95. Ghodsee, "Tale of 'Two Totalitarianisms.'"

Chapter 2

At the Belgrade Fairgrounds

On the eve of World War II, there were around 33,500 Jews living in Serbia—eleven thousand in Belgrade.[1] By most accounts, Serbia's Jews integrated into the Serbian society quite well, with "political anti-Semitism virtually non-existent."[2] These good relations were in large part the result of Jewish participation in Serbia's Balkan Wars (1912–13) and World War I, where they served as high-ranking officers and suffered massive casualties alongside their Serbian compatriots.

In the 1930s, as fascist ideology began to diffuse across Europe and the anti-Semitic pamphlet *The Protocols of the Elders of Zion* was published, first in Split, Croatia, in 1929 and then in Belgrade, a quasi-intellectual narrative of European anti-Semitism began to emerge in Serbia. Anti-Semitic newspapers, such as *Balkan*, began to pop up, and anti-Semitic language became increasingly present even on the pages of mainstream publications such as

1. The number of seventeen thousand Serbian Jews that is frequently found in the literature includes only Jews in German-occupied Serbia, but not large Jewish populations in northern Serbia, which during WWII was under Hungarian control, and parts of western Serbia, under control of the Independent State of Croatia, as well as smaller Jewish populations in southern and eastern Serbia, who came under Italian and Bulgarian control. For the purposes of memorialization, it makes more sense to include all victims on the territory of what is today Serbia.

2. Emil Kerenji, "Jewish Citizens of Socialist Yugoslavia: Politics of Jewish Identity in a Socialist State, 1944–1974" (PhD Thesis, University of Michigan, 2008), 41.

Vreme. A society for eugenics, the Central Hygiene Office, was created, with an accompanying magazine, *Ideas*.[3]

The most prominent homegrown anti-Semitic organization was Zbor (Rally), established by Dimitrije Ljotić in 1935. Ljotić's anti-Semitism was deep and well documented. He claimed that every major historical event since the French Revolution in 1789 was brought on by the Jews and the Freemasons, whom he called the "Jewish Continental Comintern." He praised Hitler for discovering the conspiracy of the "World Jewry," and argued that eliminating "the influence of Masons, Jews, and every other spiritual progeny of Jews" was the only way of preventing war.[4] Ljotić was deeply religious and had close ties with the anti-Semitic Serbian Orthodox bishop Nikolaj Velimirović.[5]

While anti-Semitism was on the rise, it was however still limited to a narrow circle of anti-Semitic intellectuals and not to the general population. Ljotić's Zbor, for example, won only 1 percent of the vote in the 1938 elections, insufficient to gain any seats in Parliament.

In 1940, Serbian Jews' lives began to change dramatically. In July 1940, thirty-nine Jewish employees were summarily fired from the Serbian Banking Society, simply because they were Jewish.[6] In October, in an attempt to cozy up to Nazi Germany, the Yugoslav government passed two specifically anti-Jewish decrees. The first was *numerus clausus*, which instituted a quota system for Jewish students in schools and universities, limiting Jewish participation to no more than half of one percent. The second law was a ban on Jews working with food and produce. These laws seriously hampered Jewish education and commerce and were foreboding of what was to come.

On March 25, 1941, Yugoslavia signed the Tripartite Pact accession. This was followed by an attempted military coup on March 27. A few days later, on April 6, 1941, Germany attacked Yugoslavia, first with a devastating bombing of Belgrade, and then with a ground invasion. Yugoslavia was occupied and dismembered, its various regions controlled by either Germany or by its satellites and allies in Croatia, Italy, Bulgaria, and Hungary. Most of Serbia

---

3. Olga Manojlović Pintar, "Anti-Semitism in the Yugoslav State," in Milan Koljanin et al, *Final Destination Auschwitz* (Belgrade: Historical Museum of Serbia, 2015), 88–89.

4. Jovan Byford, "The Willing Bystanders: Dimitrije Ljotić, 'Shield Collaboration' and the Destruction of Serbia's Jews," in *In the Shadow of Hitler: Personalities of the Right in Central and Eastern Europe*, ed. Rebecca Haynes and Martyn Rady (London: IB Tauris, 2011), 298.

5. Byford, "Willing Bystanders," 298.

6. Vesna S. Aleksić, *Banka i moć: socijalno-finansijska istorija Opšteg jugoslovenskog bankarskog društva 1928–1945* [Bank and power: Social and financial history of the General Yugoslav Banking Society 1928–1945] (Belgrade: Stubovi kulture, 2002).

came under direct German occupation, but with local administration carried out by a Nazi-controlled Serbian government.

Jewish life in Serbia unraveled overnight.[7] German troops entered Serbia on April 12, looting and destroying property and particularly targeting Jewish property and assets. On April 15, Germany established a military occupation administration for Serbia, including a special police department for Jewish affairs. The following day, the German Operative Police group ordered all Jews to report to the occupation authorities and receive yellow armbands. As of April 20, Jews were no longer allowed to hold public employment and were forced to clear rubble debris from the air raids and dig out human remains. On April 25, a new proclamation decreed that Jews could only use public water fountains after 10:30 AM and only after "Aryans" had first secured their water. All retailers were now prohibited from selling any goods and services to Jews, violations punishable by imprisonment or deportation to concentration camps. Beginning April 28, Jews were no longer allowed to ride city trams and were ordered to officially register at a site at Kalemegdan Park in Belgrade. The Council of Commissioners, the first Serbian collaborationist administration led by Milan Aćimović, was formed on April 30, and on May 7 it established a Special Department "Management Belgrade" led by Dragi Jovanović, which, together with the Belgrade Special Police, was in charge of implementing anti-Jewish and anti-Roma laws.[8] On May 24, Jews were prohibited from using telephones; three days later, from using cameras and refrigerators.

Resistance and Collaboration

In June 1941, the Communist Party of Yugoslavia started to organize an armed resistance to the occupation. Many partisan units from across Serbia began a series of highly effective actions, including blowing up the main railroads used for German transport, disrupting radio signals, and attacking

7. The following timeline of the Holocaust in Serbia is based mostly on Milan Koljanin, "Camps in Serbia (German-occupied Territory)," in Koljanin et al, *Final Destination Auschwitz*, 97–99; Milan Ristović, "Jews in Serbia during World War Two: Between 'the Final Solution to the Jewish question' and 'the Righteous among Nations,'" in *Righteous Among the Nations: Serbia*, ed. Milan Fogel, Milan Ristović, and Milan Koljanin (Zemun: Jewish Community Zemun, 2010), 260–85.

8. For the role of the Serbian special police under the occupation, see Rade Ristanović, "Uloga i mesto Odeljenja specijalne policije u okupacionom aparatu, 1941–1944" [The role and place of the Special police unit in the apparatus of occupation, 1941–1944], in *Escalating into Holocaust*, ed. Vjeran Pavlaković (Belgrade: Historical Archives of Belgrade, 2017), 118–22. Also, Branislav Božović, *Specijalna policija u Beogradu: 1941–1944* [Special police in Belgrade: 1941–1944] (Belgrade: Srpska školska knjiga, 2003).

German troops. The Party called for a general uprising on July 4. Five days later, the first concentration camp in Serbia was opened in Banjica, a Belgrade suburb.[9]

The communist resistance movement under the leadership of Josip Broz Tito was committed to the multiethnic and multinational socialist ideology, which is why it included members from all Yugoslav ethnic groups, including a large number of Yugoslav Jews.[10] As in many other Nazi-occupied countries, joining the resistance in Yugoslavia significantly increased chances of Jewish survival as opposed to staying in hiding or living in the ghettos. During the war, Yugoslav partisans carried a daring action specifically aimed at liberating some 2,500 Jews from the Italian concentration camp on the Adriatic island of Rab, one of the largest single operations of Jewish rescue in WWII.[11] Jewish partisans also quickly rose to important positions in wartime leadership and later occupied some of the leading government roles after liberation.

The partisans also attracted a huge number of women who served in non-traditional gender roles in the resistance, including more than a hundred thousand frontline women fighters.[12] The heroism and the loss of life among the partisans were astonishing. Out of around eight hundred thousand enlisted Yugoslav partisans, two hundred fifty thousand were killed in the war.[13] In its strength and expanse of activities, it was probably the largest organized armed resistance movement in occupied Europe.

Throughout the summer of 1941, as the partisan resistance engaged in increasingly successful missions, including briefly creating a liberated zone around the Serbian city of Užice, the Germans retaliated with mass shootings and public hangings of communists, Jews, and other resisters.[14] The

9. The camp was divided into the German-run section and a section run by Serbian collaborationist administration, and it soon became a site of mass shootings of prisoners, Jews and partisans alike.

10. Between 4,500 and 5,000 Jews joined the partisan movement, of whom some 1,300 were killed in combat. United States Holocaust Memorial Museum, "Axis Invasion of Yugoslavia," accessed February 5, 2019, https://www.ushmm.org/wlc/en/article.php?ModuleId=10005456.

11. Jewish inmates at Rab camp even formed a Jewish partisan battalion, which then joined mainland partisans in the rescue operation. Emil Kerenji, "'Your Salvation is the Struggle against Fascism': Yugoslav Communists and the Rescue of Jews, 1941–1945," *Contemporary European History* 25, no. 1 (2016): 57–74.

12. Jelena Batinić, *Women and Yugoslav Partisans: A History of World War II Resistance* (New York: Cambridge University Press, 2015).

13. Vladimir Žerjavić, *Yugoslavia—Manipulations with the Number of Second World War Victims* (Zagreb: Croatian Information Centre, 1993).

14. Significantly for the larger historiography of the Holocaust, these retaliatory shootings were mostly carried out by the regular German army the Wehrmacht, and not by SS troops. Milan Koljanin, "Istorijska pozadina holokausta u Srbiji i koncentracionog logora na Beogradskom sajmištu"

Serbian collaborationist government and its special police and gendarmerie aided in these raids, confiscating Jewish property, monitoring compulsory wearing of armbands, enforcing a curfew and limiting freedom of movement, prohibiting Jews access to food and supplies, and searching for Jews who were in hiding. These policies all helped isolate and marginalize the increasingly vulnerable Jewish population, making the path to their extermination that much easier for the Nazis to accomplish.[15]

As the partisan resistance increased, so did the German reprisal killings. The Serbian government used this escalation to appeal to the Serbian public to help find the resistance fighters and any remaining Jews—so as to stop German collective punishment for the actions of a few "misled communists."[16] The problem for the Germans was that the partisan resistance swelled with time, undeterred, and if anything, it was further incited by German retaliation. From what initially was a communist movement, the partisan resistance grew to attract huge numbers of Yugoslav citizens, mostly peasants, many of whom had no particular ideological leaning other than a commitment to fight the occupation.

While the partisan movement was blossoming, the Yugoslav Army in the Homeland (more commonly referred to as the Chetniks, under the leadership of Dragoljub Draža Mihailović) represented the exiled Yugoslav government in London and formally fought on the side of the Allies until 1943, when they officially claimed loyalty to the Axis. On the ground, however, they had already started to collaborate with the Wehrmacht as early as the fall of 1941. It is because of the Chetniks' reluctance to fight against the German occupation, followed by their outright collaboration and attacks on the partisans, as well as their brutal violence against non-Serb civilians, that the Allies withdrew their support and fully backed the partisans instead.[17] Throughout the war, the Chetniks' primary ideological enemies were the

[Historical background of the Holocaust in Serbia and the concentration camp at the Belgrade Fairgrounds], in *Escalating into Holocaust*, ed. Vjeran Pavlaković (Belgrade: Historical Archives of Belgrade, 2017), 89–97.

15. Jovan Byford, "Between Marginalization and Instrumentalization: Holocaust Memory in Serbia since the Late 1980s," in *Bringing the Dark Past to Light: The Reception of the Holocaust in Postcommunist Europe*, ed. John-Paul Himka and Joanna B. Michlic (Lincoln: University of Nebraska Press, 2013), 516–48.

16. Manojlović Pintar, "Uprising."

17. Jelena Djureinovic, "Serbian Courts Reinterpret History to Forgive Chetniks' Crimes," *Balkan Insight*, June 6, 2017, http://www.balkaninsight.com/en/article/serbian-courts-reinterpret-history-to-forgive-chetniks-crimes-06-06-2017.

partisans, whom they fought on two grounds: anticommunism and Serbian nationalism (anti-Yugoslavism).[18]

Due to their inefficiency in curbing partisan resistance, by August 1941 the Council of Commissioners was replaced by the German occupation administration with the Government of National Salvation led by Milan Nedić. The Serbian government was placed completely under the auspices of the German occupying power and it fully assisted Germany in its genocidal project in Serbia. The new government issued notices to Jewish and Romani employees; administered their registration, arrest, and imprisonment; and co-ran the Banjica concentration camp. In September 1941, the German administration allowed Dimitrije Ljotić to establish a three thousand- to four thousand-member-strong Volunteer Corps, a paramilitary group that began to fight the partisan insurgency alongside Wehrmacht troops, but that was especially important in rounding up the remaining Jews.[19] Members of Ljotić's fascist Zbor movement were heavily represented in the Nedić government, and Nedić and Ljotić were personally close, as they were cousins.[20] Nedić's commitment to anti-Semitism was no less pronounced than was Ljotić's. A big priority of the Nedić government from 1941–45 was renaming city streets as a form of pushback against the ever-increasing "international spirit" brought on by "cunning Israelites," for because of "these activities of the Jews and their assistants among our nation, the Serbian people lost their state and their freedom."[21] As part of this "cleansing," all streets names after Jewish public figures were replaced with names of distinguished Serbs.

Extermination

In August and September 1941, all Jews from the northern region of Banat were deported to Belgrade. On August 22, a concentration camp for Jewish

18. Milivoj Bešlin, "Četnički pokret Draže Mihailovića: najfrekventniji objekat istorijskog revizionizma u Srbiji" [The Chetnik movement of Draža Mihailović: The most frequent object of historical revisionism in Serbia] in *Politička upotreba prošlosti: O istorijskom revizionizmu na postjugoslovenskom prostoru*, ed. Momir Samardžić, Milovoj Bešlin, and Srđan Milošević (Novi Sad: AKO, 2013), 83–142.

19. Byford, "Willing Bystanders." Ljotić's troops also participated in the mass shooting of 2,300 civilians in Kragujevac in 1941. See Jovan Byford, "The Collaborationist Administration and the Treatment of the Jews in Nazi-occupied Serbia," in *Serbia and the Serbs in World War Two*, ed. Sabrina P Ramet and Ola Listhaug (New York: Palgrave Macmillan, 2011), 109–27.

20. Byford, "Willing Bystanders," 300.

21. Olga Manojlović, "Kulturni život u Beogradu za vreme nemačke okupacije 1941–1945" [Cultural life in Belgrade during the German occupation 1941–1945], *Godišnjak za društvenu istoriju* 1, no. 1 (1994), cited in Nebojša Dragosavac, "'Prepakivanje istorije' masovnim preimenovanjem beogradskih ulica" ["Repackaging history" through mass renaming of Belgrade streets], in *Politička upotreba prošlosti*, ed. Momir Samardžić, Milivoj Bešlin and Srđan Milošević (Novi Sad: AKO, 2013): 333–51, here 340.

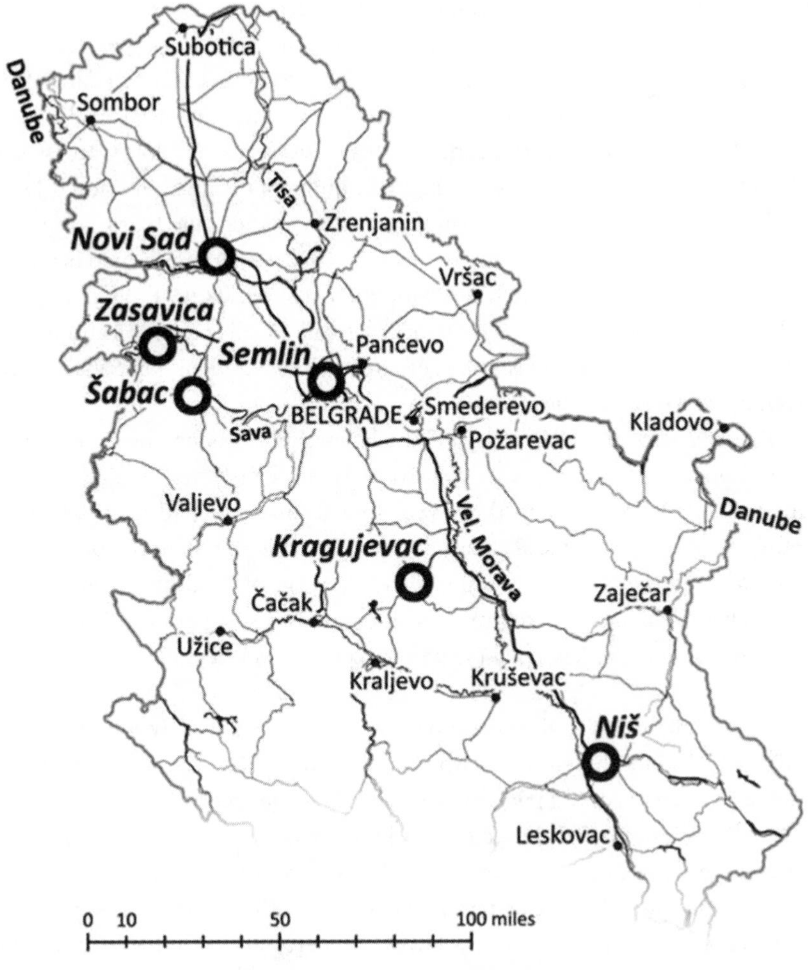

Map 1. Camps and execution sites in Serbia (map by Aleksandar Stanojlović)

men was set up at Topovske šupe, very close to Belgrade's city center. For the remainder of the Holocaust in Serbia, Topovske šupe remained a "reservoir" of Jewish hostages to be shot in increasingly frequent German retaliation shooting sprees. The camp was guarded by the Serbian gendarmerie. Throughout the camp's operation, citizens of Belgrade routinely passed by the camp on their commute downtown. Students went to schools nearby, football fans went to Sunday games, and the neighborhood cafes and restaurants remained full.[22]

---

22. Milovan Pisarri, *Stradanje Roma u Srbiji za vreme Holokausta* [The suffering of the Roma in Serbia during the Holocaust] (Belgrade: Forum za primenjenu istoriju, 2014), 104.

In September, an order was issued for the arrest of *all* Jews, Roma, and Serbian military officers resisting the occupation, who were then taken to Topovske šupe and Banjica camps. Another large camp was formed in October 1941 in the city of Niš ("Crveni krst"), and another one in Šabac. As the partisan resistance spread across Serbia, new German orders were issued for a hundred Serbs (and then, when this quota was filled, a hundred Jews and communists) to be shot for every German soldier killed, fifty for every wounded.[23] A few days after the order was issued, 2,200 Jewish men brought in from Topovske šupe and Šabac camps were shot, mostly at the killing site Jabuka, north of Belgrade. On October 12 and 13, all male Jews and Roma from Šabac, as well as Jewish refugees from elsewhere living in Šabac, were shot in the village of Zasavica.

By the end of the year, almost all male Jews in Serbia had been shot, and the Topovske šupe camp was dissolved. Many Jewish men had also been interned at Banjica, where they were shot in mass, or had been taken to other Belgrade locations, such as Ledine, to be shot. In a Report Concerning Jews and Gypsies from November 4, 1941, Sergeant Walther, commander of Wehrmacht Infantry Regiment 433, wrote to his superiors, "It must be recognized that the Jews [. . .] kept very quiet," "very calmly staring death in the eye."[24]

In December 1941, all remaining Jews—by this time only women, children, and the elderly—were transported to Semlin. The order of deportation stated that Jews "should take only as much luggage and bedding as they can carry themselves," and they could include "one plate setting, one blanket, and one day's meal."[25] As Jews were moved from other camps to Semlin, a consolidated *Judenlager*, German authorities and their Serbian government helpers assessed and sold seized Jewish property and administered Jewish apartments. A new proclamation was issued threatening death to anyone caught hiding or assisting the Jews.

During the harsh winter of 1941–42, an average of one hundred Semlin inmates died daily from exposure. On March 15, 1942, a mobile gas van, previously used at the death camp Chełmno in occupied Poland, arrived at

---

23. Christopher R. Browning, *Fateful Months: Essays on the Emergence of the Final Solution* (New York: Holmes & Meier, 1985), 47–48; Ben Shepherd, "Bloodier than Boehme: The 342nd Infantry Division in Serbia, 1941," in *War in a Twilight World: Partisan and Anti-Partisan Warfare in Eastern Europe, 1939–45*, ed. Ben Shepherd and Juliette Pattinson (Palgrave Macmillan: London, 2010), 189–209, here 194.

24. Document displayed at the Museum of the Banjica Concentration Camp, Belgrade, Serbia.

25. Jovan Byford, "Holokaust u Srbiji—Staro sajmište" [Holocaust in Serbia—The old fairgrounds], *Peščanik*, December 12, 2011, http://pescanik.net/holokaust-u-srbiji-staro-sajmiste/.

Semlin. The Jews interned at the camp were then systematically killed in the mobile van, fifty to a hundred at a time, over the course of the spring of 1942. By May 10, 1942, all Jews at Semlin had been killed.[26] On August 29, Harald Turner, the head of Nazi administration in Belgrade, proudly announced to his supervisors, "The Jewish question and the Gypsy question" in Serbia had been solved.[27] That this mission was fully endorsed by the quisling Serbian government is evident in this report by then prime minister Milan Nedić in 1942: "Owing to the occupier, we have freed ourselves of Jews, and it is now up to us to rid ourselves of other immoral elements standing in the way of Serbia's spiritual and national unity."[28]

At the same time, the Holocaust was being carried out in full force in the Serbian territories controlled by German satellites and allies. The region of Srem, which after occupation came under the control of the Independent State of Croatia, saw 2,515 out of 2,800 Jews killed by May 1943, many transported to Jasenovac, the major Ustasha-run concentration camp in Croatia.[29] In northern Serbia, a particularly deadly pogrom by Hungarian troops and gendarmerie occurred in January 1942 in Novi Sad, when four thousand people were killed, including more than a thousand Jews.[30] After Germany entered Hungary in March 1944, Hungarian authorities deported almost all of their remaining Jews, including fourteen thousand Jews from the region of Bačka in occupied northern Serbia, mostly to Auschwitz. Almost no one survived. Bulgarian authorities deported Jews on their occupied territory in southeastern Serbia to Treblinka, where they were all killed. After Italy capitulated in September 1943, previously Italian-occupied Albania and Kosovo came under German control. Albanian and Kosovo Jews were deported to camps in Belgrade, and from there to Bergen-Belsen, where almost all of them died.[31]

Of the 33,500 Jews who lived on the territory of pre-occupation Serbia, twenty-seven thousand (80 percent) were killed in the Holocaust.[32] In addition to Serbian Jews, among the Jews killed in Serbia were one thousand

26. On July 2, Germans wrapped up the extermination by killing all Jewish patients in treatment at two Belgrade hospitals.

27. Byford, "Between Marginalization and Instrumentalization," 519.

28. Quoted in Ristović, "Jews in Serbia," 16.

29. The Independent State of Croatia (Nezavisna država Hrvatska, NDH) was a Croatian fascist state during WWII. Chapter 3 covers in detail the establishment and crimes of the NDH, as well as the Holocaust in Croatia.

30. Milan Koljanin, "The Holocaust in Yugoslavia and Serbia," in Koljanin et al, *Final Destination Auschwitz*, 99–101, here 100.

31. Koljanin, "Holocaust in Yugoslavia and Serbia," 101.

32. Koljanin, "Holocaust in Yugoslavia and Serbia," 101.

Jewish refugees from central Europe (mostly Austria and Czechoslovakia) who in 1939 sailed from Vienna down the Danube attempting to reach Palestine but had to interrupt their voyage in Serbia when the Danube froze over during the winter. This large group of refugees is known as the "Kladovo transport" (after the Serbian town where they stopped). When Serbia came under occupation in 1941, these refugees were first interned in the Šabac concentration camp, the men separated and all shot in the wave of reprisal shootings on October 12–13, 1941; the women were then transported to concentration camps in Belgrade and gassed.[33]

In March 1944, as part of the SS operation Sonderaktion 1005, a group of Jews and Roma brought in from elsewhere were ordered to dig up and burn the bodies buried in mass graves at Jajinci, on the outskirts of Belgrade.[34] After they completed their gruesome job, they were killed. The Germans then loaded the ashes onto seven trucks and dumped the contents at the mouth of the Topčiderka river in Belgrade's Čukarica neighborhood. The local population sifted through the ashes in search of valuables—most often gold teeth or rings—which they then sold on the Belgrade market. This went on for a month and became known as the "Čukarica golden fever."[35]

Of the seventeen thousand Jews who lived in German-occupied Serbia, 82 percent were killed very early into the war, including almost all of Belgrade's eleven thousand Jews. To give a sense of the global Holocaust timeline, the Wannsee conference where the Final Solution was put in motion took place in January 1942 and the first transports of Jews to Auschwitz began in March 1942, to Treblinka in July 1942.[36] By then, there were almost no Jews left alive in Serbia.

---

33. Sanja Petrović Todosijević, "Jewish Refugees in Serbia (the Kladovo Transport)," in Koljanin et al, *Final Destination Auschwitz*, 90–91. On the Kladovo transport, also see the documentary film by Vesna Lukic, *Two Emperors and a Queen* (2018).

34. Sonderaktion 1005 was a process of massive exhumations and burning of Jewish remains across occupied East Central Europe aimed at hiding the evidence of the Holocaust.

35. Milovan Pisarri and Nikola Radić Lucati, *Oktobar 1941: 31 dan Holokausta, genocida i terora nacističke i kolaboracionističke vlasti u Srbiji* [October 1941: Thirty-one days of the Holocaust, genocide, and terror of Nazi and collaborationist authorities in Serbia] (Belgrade: Istorijski arhiv Beograda, 2016), 54; and Milovan Pisarri, "Zaboravljena mesta stradanja" [Forgotten sites of suffering], paper presented at the "The First Stage of the Holocaust in Serbia and Croatia" conference, Belgrade, July 1, 2017.

36. Auschwitz-Birkenau camp was established in 1940. In the first few years of the camp, until mid-1942, transports to Auschwitz included Poles, Soviet prisoners of war, other political prisoners from the Spanish civil war, and partisan resistance fighters. Only in mid-1942 did Auschwitz become primarily an extermination camp for the Jews.

Communist Pan-national Remembrance: Memory without Ethnicity

Fewer than five thousand Jews in Serbia survived the war, most by joining the partisans, some by hiding in the countryside under protection of Serbian peasants, some by fleeing to territories controlled by Italy.[37] In the immediate postwar years, the most pressing activity for the slowly reconstituting Jewish community was humanitarian aid, property restitution (a task particularly daunting and rarely successful because Jewish property was first Aryanized during the German occupation, and then confiscated by the communist regime, or simply taken over as abandoned by various war refugees or returning partisans), family reunification, and basic economic assistance organized through the activities of the Autonomous Relief Committee.[38] Since the economic situation of the surviving Jews was so desperate in the years immediately after the Holocaust and many vibrant prewar Jewish communities were no more, the Federation of Jewish Communities of Yugoslavia resorted to selling dozens of synagogues across the country—some partially destroyed in the war and too expensive to renovate, but also some well preserved—and using the money for further aid and reconstruction efforts. Some of these sold synagogues were then destroyed, some were preserved to be used as cultural objects, and some were repurposed for a variety of services, including restaurants.[39] This further eviscerated any traces of prewar Jewish religious and cultural presence in the country.

The Serbian Jewish community was further reduced when, between 1948 and 1952, about 3,200 Jews left Serbia for Israel in a series of *aliyahs*, leaving fewer than 2,600 remaining in Serbia.[40] In a clear departure from Soviet doctrine, the Yugoslav state allowed Jewish emigration under condition they renounced their property rights and their Yugoslav citizenship.

---

37. Milan D. Ristović, *U potrazi za utočištem: jugoslovenski Jevreji u bekstvu od Holokausta 1941–1945* [In search of shelter: Yugoslav Jews fleeing the Holocaust 1941–1945] (Belgrade: Službeni list SRJ, 1998).

38. Emil Kerenji, "Rebuilding the Community: The Federation of Jewish Communities and American Jewish Humanitarian Aid in Yugoslavia, 1944–1952," *Southeast European and Black Sea Studies* 17, no. 2 (2017): 245–62.

39. Author interview with Barbara Panić, curator of the Jewish Historical Museum, May 30, 2017, Belgrade.

40. Byford, "Between Marginalization and Instrumentalization," 523.

Holocaust Remembrance as Brotherhood and Unity

When it came to remembering the Holocaust, the Yugoslav communist experience largely followed that of the rest of communist Europe, with some important exceptions. As was the case elsewhere in Europe, in the immediate aftermath of WWII, the Holocaust in Yugoslavia was remembered primarily as an event *within* the parameters of the war and not as a separate event with its own dynamics. Communist Yugoslavia, however, was ideologically committed to thinking of the Holocaust as primarily an antifascist struggle and as an atrocity that was universal to all Yugoslav nations, which served to further bolster two main pillars of communist Yugoslav identity—socialism and pan-nationalism.

This is why most public memories of the Holocaust were in fact public memories of the war, and especially public memories of Yugoslav partisan heroism, sacrifice, and, eventually, triumph. This mnemonic strategy left little to no space for memorialization, or even conceptualization of "victims." This is again not uniquely Yugoslav, but rather a much larger European phenomenon, especially prior to the 1960s, when Holocaust survivors did not fit the narrative of resistance or heroic defeat of fascism. In the Yugoslav context, this glorification of the heroes of the revolution served to affirm new socialist values by universalizing victims and universalizing memory.

This lack of interest in or even recognition of victims is also evident in monuments built in this period to commemorate WWII. An overwhelming majority of monuments were built to "heroes," "fighters," or "liberators," and to the extent that any victims were memorialized, they posthumously became reconstructed as heroes themselves. The category of a civilian victim who was not a heroic resister, but was simply killed or died in camps, was not part of this political memory space and was not memorialized.[41] This is why the only concentration camp on the territory of Serbia memorialized in any way during the 1950s was the Crveni krst camp in Niš, one of the largest German detention camps for Jews, partisans, and a smaller number of Yugoslav army officers and Chetniks, that operated from 1941–44. In 1950, the camp became the site of an early memorial in the shape of a small pyramid, but this memorialization is the consequence of the fact that, conveniently, the Niš camp witnessed a rare rebellion and successful escape and as such could fit into the main narrative template of resistance and not victimization.[42]

---

41. Heike Karge, "Sajmište, Jasenovac, and the Social Frames of Remembering and Forgetting," *Filozofija i društvo* 23, no. 4 (2012): 106–18.

42. Jovan Bajford, *Staro sajmište: Mesto sećanja, zaborava i sporenja* [Staro Sajmište: A site remembered, forgotten, contested] (Belgrade: Beogradski centar za ljudska prava, 2011), 96.

While the focus on universal victims of fascism, resistance, and heroism is one shared across the communist space, what was also of paramount importance for Yugoslav postwar legitimacy was the shoring up of the ideology of Yugoslav multicultural "brotherhood and unity," according to which all nations suffered equally in the war and all were committed to the socialist future together. This focus on brotherhood and unity was evident from the very first days of postwar reconstruction and immediately colored WWII remembrance. Since there was no separate mnemonic space for Holocaust remembrance, any Jewish suffering was included as suffering of "Yugoslav peoples." Tito made this point repeatedly, including in an early speech in March 1945: "Our peoples, *all jointly*, Slovenes, Serbs, Croats, Montenegrins, Macedonians—have suffered together and together given enormous sacrifices in this great struggle of the freedom loving nations."[43] At the same time, Tito made sure that any responsibility for the atrocities, other than the obvious one by the German occupier, would be equally spread out across Yugoslav nations, making sure that no constitutive nation was disproportionally singled out: "Did you see how the German conqueror in that terrible year of 1941, with the help of his servant Pavelić [of Croatia], and later also with the help of the traitors of the Serbian people, Nedić and Mihailović, and the traitor of the Slovene people, Rupnik, did everything to deepen the chasm not only between the Croatian and Serbian peoples, but also between all the peoples of Yugoslavia?"[44]

Another critical aspect of postwar reconstruction involved destroying memories of the war and filling the void with new, positive experiences.[45] The Youth Labor Actions (YLA), or the Youth Brigades, as they were colloquially known, were a regular feature of the early postwar period. This program was voluntary—but highly encouraged—and it would send Yugoslav youth on work programs lasting a few weeks to build infrastructure projects such as railroads and highways.[46] From 1948 to 1950, the main headquarters of the YLA program for the construction of the New Belgrade neighborhood was housed in the surviving buildings of the Semlin camp complex. One of the newly distributed YLA leaflets read, "We will forget the days of

43. Josip Broz Tito, *Izgradnja nove Jugoslavije I* [Building new Yugoslavia I] (Belgrade: Kultura, 1948), 22, emphasis added.

44. Tito, May 21, 1945, quoted in Tea Sindbæk, *Usable History?: Representations of Yugoslavia's Difficult Past from 1945–2002* (Aarhus: Aarhus Universitetsforlag, 2012), 13.

45. Carol S. Lilly, *Power and Persuasion: Ideology and Rhetoric in Communist Yugoslavia, 1944–1953* (Boulder: Westview Press, 2001).

46. Dragan Popović, "Youth Labor Action (Omladinska radna akcija, ORA) as Ideological Holiday-Making," in *Yugoslavia's Sunny Side: A History of Tourism in Socialism (1950s–1980s)*, ed. Hannes Grandits and Karin Taylor (Budapest: Central European University Press, 2010), 279–303.

war, the horrors of Semlin, and build on what is now swampy, sandy, and empty space."[47] The focus here was on the bright socialist future, reconstruction, and rebuilding, and remembrance of horrors past was seen as an impediment to this socialist progress.

Jewish Remembrance as Affirmation of the Yugoslav Project

While Jewish identity in communist Yugoslavia has sometimes been described as a form of "submergence," in which loyalty to Yugoslav socialist and multiethnic ideology suppressed any distinct Jewish identity, in actuality Jewish identity after the Holocaust was much more layered, as Emil Kerenji notes: the postwar Jewish community reconstruction "was a part of a wider Yugoslav narrative, [which] defined Jewishness as an identity firmly rooted in the new Yugoslav political project."[48]

This multilayered identity is nicely captured in the words of Albert Vajs, the president of the Federation of Jewish Communities in 1950: "From the very moment in which we reestablished our Federation of Jewish Communities, our leadership was guided by two basic principles . . . we were part of the larger Yugoslav community of our country, and we are bound by thousands of threads to that community . . . and we are members of the larger Jewish community of the world."[49] It is because of this dual space that Yugoslav Jews could carve out—to be both "Yugoslav" but also confidently "Jewish," and presumably not have the two be in conflict—that, in the words of Ivan Ceresnjes, the onetime head of the Sarajevo Jewish community, Tito's Yugoslavia "afforded Jews opportunities that were the envy of Jewish communities throughout [postwar] Eastern Europe."[50]

In the immediate postwar years, members of the decimated Yugoslav Jewish community, the "remains of the remains," organized to erect a few memorials marking the deaths of their loved ones.[51] Out of a total of fourteen memorials built to commemorate Yugoslav Jews, the most prominent were five monuments built in 1952 at five major sites in Yugoslavia (Belgrade and Novi Sad in Serbia, Zagreb and Đakovo in Croatia, and Sarajevo in Bosnia-Herzegovina). The monuments' unveiling was accompanied by

47. Aleksandar Ignjatović and Olga Manojlović Pintar, "Staro sajmište i sećanja na II sv. rat" [Old Fairgrounds and memories of World War II], *Helsinška povelja* 117–18 (March–April 2008): 33–35, here 34.

48. Kerenji, "Jewish Citizens," vii–viii.

49. Quoted in Kerenji, "Jewish Citizens," 175.

50. Quoted in Byford, "Between Marginalization and Instrumentalization," 524.

51. Author interview with Ruben Fuks, former president of the Federation of Jewish Communities in Serbia, May 29, 2017, Belgrade.

high-level cultural events, including official representation by the state of Israel and many Jewish organizations in the region. The Yugoslav state did not itself organize the building of monuments and accompanying cultural events, but it fully supported them.[52]

Significantly, these monuments explicitly separated the Jewish experience during the war from that of other Yugoslav civilians. This memory intervention was, importantly, introduced by the Jewish community itself, not by the larger Yugoslav state:

> We believe that these monuments are not only important for the 6,500 surviving Jews who live in Yugoslavia at the present-day, but also for all the peoples of Yugoslavia, with whom the Jews in this country have lived together for centuries and shared both good and ill, and among whose victims of two million people our victims should be included. . . . But our victims were not killed simply as citizens of Yugoslavia, but also as members of the Jewish people whom Fascism wanted completely to exterminate and from whose over six million victims, our victims cannot be separated.[53]

In 1953, the Jewish Federation of Yugoslavia organized the planting of sixty thousand trees in Israel, to commemorate every "Jewish victim of fascism." The funds for this expensive project were provided by the Yugoslav government, state owned companies, and trade unions, and the event was widely covered by the Yugoslav media.[54] Since 1952, another forty monuments to the victims of the Holocaust have been erected in Serbia alone, the most prominent of which was the first monument, designed by the internationally famed Yugoslav architect Bogdan Bogdanović and unveiled in 1952 at the Jewish Sephardic Cemetery in Belgrade.[55] This unique monument incorporated elements of the demolished Jewish houses in the Belgrade neighborhood of Dorćol, subtly indicating the Jewish identity of the victims.[56]

---

52. This is in important contrast to other socialist countries of the time. As I discuss more in chapter 4, in the Soviet Union all individual memorials to Jewish victims of the Holocaust were forcefully removed by the state. See Mordechai Altshuler, "Jewish Holocaust Commemoration Activity in the USSR under Stalin," *Yad Vashem Studies* 30 (2002): 271–96.

53. Quoted in Olga Manojlović Pintar, "Places of Memory—and Oblivion," in Koljanin et al, *Final Destination Auschwitz* (Belgrade: Historical Museum of Serbia, 2015), 113–14, here 113.

54. Kerenji, "Jewish Citizens," 21–22.

55. As part of this burst in activity by the Jewish Federation, the Jewish Historical Museum was founded in 1959 in Belgrade.

56. Vladimir Kulić, "The Scope of Socialist Modernism: Architecture and State Representation in Postwar Yugoslavia," in *Sanctioning Modernism: Architecture and the Making of Postwar Identities*, ed. Vladimir Kulić, Timothy Parker, and Monica Penick (Austin: University of Texas Press, 2014), 37–62.

FIGURE 2. Monument to the Jewish victims of fascism, designed by Bogdan Bogdanović, unveiled in 1952. Jewish Sephardic Cemetery, Belgrade, Serbia (photograph by Vladimir Kulić).

Even more explicitly, the monuments in this series all include translated inscriptions in Hebrew, clearly identifying the object of representation as Jewish victims of WWII, a direct identifier highly unusual so early after the war and especially unusual in communist Eastern Europe. Hebrew inscriptions also provided a private space for Jewish-only mourning and remembrance, detached from the dogmatic insistence on multicultural brotherhood and unity.[57] Over the years, families have affixed their own memorial plaques commemorating individual victims of the Holocaust, private initiatives not sanctioned by the state. This commemorative practice, then, fits within the framework of "mediated remembrance," which points to far more space for local remembrance practices carved out during communism, and argues against the static view of memory being frozen during communist Yugoslavia.[58]

These monuments, artistically innovative and critically acclaimed, were some of the earliest public Holocaust monuments anywhere in Europe, the

57. Kerenji, "Jewish Citizens."

58. Heike Karge, "Mediated Remembrance: Local Practices of Remembering the Second World War in Tito's Yugoslavia," *European Review of History* 16, no. 1 (2009): 49–62.

only older one being the memorial to the Warsaw Ghetto Uprising.[59] However, they were mostly hidden from public view within the confines of the Jewish cemetery.[60] A visitor would only notice the monument if they were making a special visit to the Jewish cemetery, which means it was a monument to the Jews for the Jews. It was not a monument to the Jews for all Yugoslav citizens to see.

Heroes, Fighters, and Victims of Fascism

While there was some space in the immediate postwar years for uniquely Jewish remembrance, over time the focus on partisan resistance gave way to the focus on the immense civilian suffering of Yugoslavs during the War.[61] To that end, socialist Yugoslavia invested in building many memorial parks, commemorative centers, and elaborate monuments on major execution sites or the sites of civilian massacres. During this entire period, however, the unique *Jewish* aspect of the Holocaust was, although not denied, never emphasized. It was enveloped in the larger memory of civilian devastation and Nazi cruelty. The public memory of the Holocaust, then, was universalized to all civilians.

In this period, Jewish victims were mentioned as victims of fascist terror, usually in the same breath as communist partisans and other antifascists. The leveling of all victims as "victims of fascism" accomplished two major things for the Yugoslav communist ideological project: it removed ethnicity as the principal motivating factor in WWII genocides—both the Holocaust of Yugoslavia's Jews and the genocidal killing among various Yugoslav ethnic groups—and it grouped all anticommunist forces as "fascist," regardless of whether they were ideologically fascist (like the Croatian Ustasha of the Serbian Ljotić militia) or primarily anticommunist (such as Serbian Chetniks), or, most problematic of all, whether they were simply prewar anticommunist bourgeoisie. This categorization of victims and perpetrators then provided a

59. Another early Holocaust memorial, the Tomb of the Unknown Jewish Martyr in Paris, is often referred to as the first of its kind, but it was built in France over three years (1953–56). Stijn Vervaet, "Staging the Holocaust in the Land of Brotherhood and Unity: Holocaust Drama in Socialist Yugoslavia in the 1950s and 1960s," *Slavonic & East European Review* 92, no. 2 (2014): 228–54, here 232.

60. Similarly, in 1959, the Jewish Community of Vienna erected a memorial to the victims of the Kladovo transport. This memorial is also placed within the confines of the Jewish cemetery in Belgrade, hidden from general public view.

61. Total population losses in Yugoslavia were above one million. Jozo Tomasevich, *War and Revolution in Yugoslavia, 1941–1945: Occupation and Collaboration* (Stanford: Stanford University Press, 2001).

rigid mnemonic framework for permissible Holocaust remembrance during the communist period.

Attempts to isolate the Jewish experience from the larger Yugoslav experience in WWII was often swiftly rejected by Yugoslav authorities, as in 1980, when the Jewish Federation's proposal for the Yugoslav post service to issue a stamp "in memory of the tragedy of the Jews in Yugoslavia" was immediately rejected with this stinging rebuke: "Several of our nations were subjected to the policy of physical extermination," therefore "singling out one constitutive nation or national minority as a victim of genocide would represent a violation of the legacy of our Revolution— the unity, or rather the equality of all the people of Yugoslavia."[62]

This universalization of victimhood is visible in the memorial treatment of Holocaust sites. One of the three main Nazi concentration camps in Belgrade—the Banjica camp with the adjacent execution site Jajinci—became a prominent memorial site of fascist terror in general. The commemorative plaque at the Jajinci memorial designates its victims as "patriots," but fails to mention that it was the execution site for Jews transported to these killing fields from two other concentration camps in Belgrade—Topovske šupe and Semlin. The Jajinci monument again represents these events as acts of heroism—an artistic plaque depicts adult men and women in a defiant posture facing the shooting squad, conveniently ignoring the fact that Semlin victims buried there died in circumstances much different, and much less fitting to the resistance master narrative.[63] The only reason the Jajinci memorial was even built was because Jajinci was also the site of partisan martyrdom. Other camps and killing sites of mostly Jews (Topovske šupe, Jabuka) did not receive almost any attention at all.

The importance of heroism and resistance as the main narrative of the Yugoslav antifascist struggle also colored public and political reception of (rare) art projects that dealt with the Holocaust in this period. For example, in 1956, the Auschwitz survivor Đorđe Lebović coauthored a play titled *Celestial Squad*, which was performed in Belgrade to critical acclaim.[64] However, mainstream reviews harshly criticized the play's main plotline—about Auschwitz prisoners, the *Sonderkommando*, being forced to dispose of other prisoners' remains in camp's crematoria—as bending the truth and glorifying

62. Quoted in Byford, "Between Marginalization and Instrumentalization," 526–27.

63. Bajford, *Staro sajmište*.

64. Lebović was deported to Auschwitz from his hometown of Sombor in northern Serbia in 1944, at the age of fifteen.

violence.[65] The anguish of survival at Auschwitz was largely incomprehensible within the confines of the heroism narrative of the time.

Victims of Semlin as the Last Yugoslavs

As Yugoslav ideology shifted and metamorphosed over time, so did the sources of Yugoslav state ontological insecurity, anxiety, and stress—all of which are visible through larger WWII, and especially Holocaust, memorialization. The changing memorialization of Semlin points clearly at this subtle shift. The very first memorial plaque at Semlin was mounted as late as October 20, 1974, the thirtieth anniversary of the liberation of Belgrade. It was a small white marble stone, with the following inscription: "On the location of old Sajmište, German Gestapo in 1941 established the camp Semlin in which, aided by domestic collaborators, more than 40,000 people from various parts of our country were cruelly tortured and killed." Next to the inscription was a small flower with the communist red star at the center. The plaque was placed unremarkably on the side of one of the buildings, mostly hidden from public view.[66]

The second monument, a concrete stone, was erected in 1984. It had the identical textual inscription as the 1974 plaque (since removed), but it was located more centrally within the Sajmište complex. Its unveiling was a ceremonial affair headed by then Belgrade mayor Bogdan Bogdanović, the same architect who designed the first Holocaust memorial at Belgrade's Sephardic Jewish cemetery in 1952. The erection of the 1984 monument, however, is ideologically significant because it came at a time of profound Yugoslav socialist anxiety in the aftermath of Tito's death in 1980, and great fear among the communist leadership that socialist ideals, especially among the youth, were weakening. This is why the Yugoslav government at this time made repeated calls to local organizations to "construct and maintain material evidence of revolutionary consciousness such as monuments, memorials, sculptures, buildings, important sites."[67]

These messages were quite explicit in the annual commemorations the government organized in the late 1980s at the Semlin site. A particularly memorable speech was given in 1989 by then Belgrade mayor Aleksandar Bakočević who, after repeating the main themes of inspirational heroism and resistance of Semlin victims (again not identified as Jews, but

65. Byford, "Between Marginalization and Instrumentalization," 528.

66. Bajford, *Staro sajmište*, 107.

67. Quoted in Bajford, *Staro sajmište*, 113.

instead as victims of fascism "from all over our country"), urged today's youth to "maintain the integrity of equal brotherly nations represented in Yugoslavia."[68] Two years before Yugoslavia's bloody dissolution, the victims of Semlin seemed to have represented a rapidly disintegrating ideal of a multinational socialist Yugoslavia. For a state facing anxiety about leadership transition, the weakening legitimacy of the socialist order, and, most significantly, burgeoning nationalist voices threatening to destabilize the multinational union, Holocaust remembrance of "all Yugoslavs"—and Jews as suitable examples of "all Yugoslav" people—represented a link to a simpler past when ethnicity did not matter, victims and perpetrators were clearly identified, and Yugoslavia was an internationally respected, successful socialist role model. Holocaust remembrance, in other words, was a celebration of the Yugoslav project.

Appropriation of Memory after Communism

The violent death of Yugoslavia in a series of wars from 1991 to 1999 introduced a completely rearranged public memory of WWII and the Holocaust in new successor states.[69] In fact, the wars themselves were discursively waged as continuations of WWII, but not as a repeat of the antifascist struggle against the Nazis, but instead as a repeat of the smaller-scale ethnic wars that, under the umbrella of the larger war, pitted ethnic groups against each other. The persecution by the Ustasha, the fascist Croat militia, against ethnic Serbs was one big memory pillar that got reused in the 1990s on the Serbian side, and the atrocities committed by the Serbian Chetniks and other right wing militias against Croatian and Bosnian civilians was activated on the Croatian side.[70] What is relevant for my larger argument, however, is the documented appropriation of not only WWII but specifically the Holocaust

68. Quoted in Bajford, *Staro sajmište*, 124.

69. The wars also further reduced the Serbian Jewish community, as many Jews emigrated to Israel in another wave of aliyah in the 1990s, mostly because of the very difficult economic situation in the country, as well as the ongoing war. The 2011 census listed as few as 578 self-identified Jews (by religion) in Serbia, but the Serbian Jewish Community counts around three thousand members, as it includes those who are Jewish by marriage as well as others with more extended family links. Panić, interview. 2011 census summary available at "2011 Census of Population, Households and Dwellings in the Republic of Serbia," accessed March 2, 2019, http://pod2.stat.gov.rs/ObjavljenePublikacije/Popis2011/Knjiga4_Veroispovest.pdf.

70. The literature on this appropriation of WWII in the 1990s is vast. See Tamara Banjeglav, Nataša Govedarica, and Darko Karačić, eds., *Re:vizija prošlosti: Politike sjećanja u Bosni i Hercegovini, Hrvatskoj i Srbiji od 1990. godine* [Re:vision of the past: Politics of memory in Bosnia-Herzegovina, Croatia and Serbia since 1990] (Sarajevo: ACIPS, 2012); Srdjan Cvijic, "Swinging the Pendulum: World War II History, Politics, National Identity and Difficulties of Reconciliation in Croatia

and Holocaust imagery (of concentration camps, emaciated bodies, torture camps) by both the Yugoslav war parties in the 1990s, as well by as the international media covering atrocities in the Balkans.[71]

As the rest of this chapter demonstrates, since the dissolution of Yugoslavia, Holocaust remembrance has served multiple ontological security needs for the Serbian state: it has provided framing for nationalist mobilization in the run up to, during, and in the aftermath of the wars of the 1990s; it has offered continuing narrative purchase for Serbia's insecure relationship with its principal significant other—Croatia; and, most significantly, it has allowed for the complete delegitimation of Serbia's communist—including its deep antifascist—past in order to provide a legitimacy shield for its nationalist postcommunist present.

Serbs as Jews

The Holocaust was an important memory marker in the development of Serbian nationalism in the run up to the Yugoslav wars in the late 1980s and early 1990s. Of course, it was not the Holocaust itself—its global history or its Serbian chapter—that was of use to the Serbian nationalist project. Instead, it was a very specific narrative comparing Serbs to the Jews—persecuted, victimized, terrorized—that served nationalist mobilization purposes. These Jews always remained nameless, placeless, and completely decontextualized, and were only relevant to the extent that they could garner up images of horror, suffering, and pain. This narrative was made most explicit when the novelist (later turned politician) Vuk Drašković famously wrote in his 1985 *Letter to the Writers of Israel*, "Serbs are the thirteenth, lost and the most ill-fated tribe of Israel."[72] Drašković went on to write, "Both Serbs and Jews have been exterminated at the same concentration camps, slaughtered at the same bridges, burned alive in the same ovens, thrown together into the same pits."[73]

---

and Serbia," *Nationalities Papers* 36, no. 4 (2008): 713–40; Jelena Subotić, "Genocide Narratives as Narratives-in-Dialogue," *Journal of Regional Security* 10, no. 2 (2015): 177–98.

71. David Bruce MacDonald, *Balkan Holocausts?: Serbian and Croatian Victim-Centred Propaganda and the War in Yugoslavia* (Manchester: Manchester University Press, 2002). The calls for an international intervention in response to the Serbian campaign of ethnic cleansing in Kosovo in 1999, for example, were made explicitly using the language and imagery of the Holocaust. See Daniel Levy and Natan Sznaider, "Memory Unbound: The Holocaust and the Formation of Cosmopolitan Memory," *European Journal of Social Theory* 5, no. 1 (2002): 87–106, here 99–100.

72. Vuk Drašković, "Piscima Izraela" [To the writers of Israel], *Naša reč* 373 (1985): 8–9.

73. Drašković, "Piscima Izraela," 8.

Serbs as Jews, or Serbs as people who suffered *even more* than the Jews, was a narrative framework that primed Serbian nationalist mobilization in the 1990s. This mobilization itself was rooted in the fear of a "renewed genocide" against the Serbs by Kosovo Albanians in the late 1980s and then by Croats in the 1990s. A leading Serbian nationalist intellectual at the time, Dobrica Ćosić (who later went on to briefly serve as president of rump Yugoslavia), explicitly warned of Serbs succumbing to the Jews' fate: "We Serbs feel today as the Jews did in Hitler's day. . . . Today, Serbophobia in Europe is a concept and an attitude with the same ideological motivation and fury as anti-Semitism was during the Nazi era."[74] Another Serbian writer claimed, "The departure point for the genocide of the Jews was anti-Semitism, and of the Serbs, Serbophobia."[75]

This spiritual kinship between Serbs and Jews was also built on the narrative of Serbian compassion for other peoples, such as the Jews. The understanding that Serbia has no history of anti-Semitism and that everyday Serbs were quick to help their Jewish neighbors during WWII is so heavily embedded in contemporary Serbian national consciousness that it has become a social fact, an example of "collective innocence" for the Holocaust.[76] For example, the authors of one contemporary Serbian history textbook publicly argued against spending "too much attention to the suffering of Jews in relation to the suffering of other Balkan nations" during German occupation, as "it is well documented" that "Jews died mainly in Central Europe, not in the Balkans."[77]

A further important element of this Jewish trope was the emphasis on Serbian sacred territory—Kosovo—which was seen as emotionally indivisible for the Serbs in the same manner that Jerusalem was indivisible for the Jews.[78] This complex identification with the abstract "Jews"—their suffering and their territory—then provided a fitting background to the larger Serbian narrative of victimization, sacrifice, and historical injustice at the hands of

74. Quoted in David B. MacDonald, "Globalizing the Holocaust: A Jewish "Useable Past" in Serbian Nationalism," *PORTAL Journal of Multidisciplinary International Studies* 2, no. 2 (2005): 1–31, here 16.

75. MacDonald, "Globalizing the Holocaust," 16.

76. John-Paul Himka and Joanna B. Michlic, eds., *Bringing the Dark Past to Light: The Reception of the Holocaust in Postcommunist Europe* (Lincoln: University of Nebraska Press, 2013), 17.

77. Kosta Nikolić and Suzana Rajić, "Balkanska povest s oksfordskim akcentom" [Balkan history with an Oxford accent], *Prosvetni pregled*, December 15, 2005.

78. Filip Ejdus and Jelena Subotić, "Kosovo as Serbia's Sacred Space: Governmentality, Pastoral Power and Sacralization of Territories," in *Politicization of Religion, The Power of Symbolism: The Case of Former Yugoslavia and its Successor States*, ed. Gorana Ognjenovic and Jasna Jozelic (Basingstoke: Palgrave, 2014), 159–84.

their ethnic others (as well as at the hands of great powers), a strategic narrative that has outlasted the 1990s war and continues into Serbia's present.[79] The linkage between Jerusalem and Kosovo, and the Holocaust and genocide against the Serbs, was also activated in relationship to Serbia's claims of Kosovo Albanian "demographic genocide," the fear of rising Albanian birthrates that would annihilate Serbian presence in their ancestral home.[80] All of these perceived threats and warnings that "Serbs were the new Jews" inevitably led to considerations of a Serbian armed response, which to a great extent explains the popular success of Serbia's nationalist mobilization for the wars of Yugoslav succession. Throughout the 1990s, Serbian history—including the appropriated narratives, images, and frames of the Holocaust—became directly weaponized and used as "a war training manual."[81]

The Museum of Genocide as a Site of Nationalist Mobilization

This appropriation of the Holocaust for contemporary war purposes was quite explicit. In 1992, at the height of the Croatian war, the Serbian government established the Museum of Genocide, a "museum of victims of crimes against the Serbian people committed in the NDH [Nezavisna država Hrvatska, or Independent State of Croatia]," to inform the public of the "unprecedented suffering of the Serbian people in the state of the *Croatian Nazis*—the NDH."[82] The founding documents of the museum define its mission as remembrance of the "genocide perpetrated against the Serbs," while it also "*may* engage" in activities pertaining to the genocide against the Jews, Roma, and others.[83] The justification for this exclusive focus on the Serbs was, in the words of the founding museum director Milan Bulajić, because "Jews have over ninety museums and institutions about the Holocaust" (presumably around the world), while this one would be "the only institution dedicated to *Serbian* suffering."[84] The museum, however, was not really a museum, having neither a permanent exhibition nor material objects to

79. Jelena Subotić, "Narrative, Ontological Security, and Foreign Policy Change," *Foreign Policy Analysis* 12, no. 4 (2016): 610–27.

80. Marina Blagojević, "The Migrations of Serbs from Kosovo during the 1970s and 1980s: Trauma and/or Catharsis," in *The Road to War in Serbia: Trauma and Catharsis*, ed. Nebojša Popov (Budapest: Central European University, 2000), 212–46.

81. Dubravka Stojanović, *Ulje na vodi: Ogledi iz istorije sadašnjosti Srbije* [Oil on water: Essays on the history of Serbia's present] (Belgrade: Peščanik, 2010), 18.

82. Jovan Byford, "When I Say 'The Holocaust,' I Mean 'Jasenovac,'" *East European Jewish Affairs* 37, no. 1 (2007): 51–74, here 56, emphasis added.

83. Byford, "When I Say 'The Holocaust,'" 57, emphasis added.

84. Byford, "When I Say 'The Holocaust,'" 57, emphasis added.

display. Instead, it functioned more as a research and, increasingly, propaganda center in the run-up to, during, and after the Yugoslav wars.

The use of the Holocaust to tell the story of Serb suffering was a direct, and not a secondary, goal of this state project. The museum included members of the Jewish community on its executive board and it also nurtured relationships with major international Holocaust centers, such as Yad Vashem in Jerusalem, the US Holocaust Memorial Museum in Washington, DC, the Simon Wiesenthal Center in Vienna. However, the purpose of this nominal focus on the Holocaust was, again, not on the Holocaust itself but rather on what the Holocaust framework (and, more disturbingly, what the international connections established with "powerful" Holocaust institutions) could accomplish for the principal narrative goal of the state—popular mobilization for Serbian nationalist endeavors.

This objective was quite unambiguous and never hidden from public view. In one of his reports, the founding museum director bluntly stated that the purpose of his institution was to "demonstrate the suffering of the Serbian people via the Jews,"[85] an approach to Holocaust remembrance Serbian Jewish leaders called "necrophiliac."[86] This Museum of Genocide was, then, not about the genocide of the Nazi Holocaust at all, but instead about the victimhood of Serbs (not Jews) by the Croats (not Germans).

The since renamed Museum of Genocide Victims continues to play an important public memory role in contemporary Serbia, decades after it served its purpose in the nationalist mobilization of the 1990s. The museum has continued its activity in promoting exhibition and publication content on the genocide of the Serbs in the NDH but has also actively engaged in other memory projects important for Serbia's continuing identity and ontological security needs. Equally important for Serbia's maintenance of its foundational self-image as a victim nation (an image that the focus on the NDH genocide of Serbs supports) is maintaining its claim to innocence and a forceful denial of war crimes it itself has perpetuated during the Yugoslav wars.

The importance of maintaining myths of innocence is very well documented and is hardly unique to Serbia.[87] What is interesting for my purposes here is how the Museum of Genocide Victims, an institution which is at least in part tasked with Holocaust remembrance and which proudly displays its affiliation with major international Holocaust institutions, has used its perch to promote Serbia's own genocide denialism. In July 2017, the

85. Cited in Byford, "Between Marginalization and Instrumentalization," 532.

86. Fuks, interview.

87. Stanley Cohen, *States of Denial: Knowing about Atrocities and Suffering* (Cambridge: Polity, 2001).

museum presented its new project, *Rethinking Srebrenica*, a collection of revisionist and semi-revisionist articles that claim to "demonstrate that all media propaganda, all Hague verdicts, all attempts at silencing and censorship have failed," and that what happened in 1995 in Srebrenica "was only the culmination of what happened in 1914, and not an isolated incident."[88] This recontextualization of the Srebrenica genocide is remarkable in its bluntness—its argument against "Hague verdicts" is a direct negation of the determination by the International Criminal Tribunal for the former Yugoslavia (ICTY) that the massacre in Srebrenica in July 1995 was, indeed, an act of genocide, committed by the Bosnian Serb army and Serbian paramilitaries against Bosniac (Muslim) civilians. Further, it places Srebrenica not within the context of the wars of Yugoslav succession (1991–95) and Serbian territorial expansionism, but in the context of the long Serbian history of suffering in the twentieth century that began in 1914 with the onset of World War I, and then continued throughout World War II, the communist era, and the most recent wars.

The invocation of the Holocaust to deflect remembrance of the Srebrenica genocide has also become a frequent narrative crutch for various Serb political leaders. Milorad Dodik, the president of Bosnia's Serb entity, Republika Srpska, asked in 2009, "When so many are studying the tragedy in Srebrenica, where some thousand Muslims perished . . . should we then continue to shy away from telling the truth about our own national tragedy and the tragedy of Jews and Roma in the Ustasha camps in Pavelić's Croatia?"[89]

The Museum of Genocide Victims has also engaged in remembrance practices of Serbian suffering that decidedly do not fit the category of genocide, its purported mission. In August 2017, it cohosted an event commemorating "the death of Srpska Krajina," a Serbian rebel stronghold in Croatia, armed and supported by Serbia proper from 1991–95, that was dissolved in the sweeping Croatian military operation Storm, which took control of this territory but in the process expelled, under threat and intimidation, almost the entire Serbian civilian population of the region. In the museum's interpretation, this event is remembered as "an aggression of the Croatian army against Republic of Srpska Krajina which ended in the great tragedy of the

88. "Predstavljanje zbornika radova 'Preispitivanje Srebrenice'" [Presentation of the volume "Revisiting Srebrenica"], accessed March 2, 2019, http://www.muzejgenocida.rs/85-novosti/329-медија-центар,-београд,-10-јул-2017-представљање-зборника-радова-„преиспитивање-сребренице.html.

89. "Počinje snimanje grandioznog filma o Jasenovcu" [The making of a grand film on Jasenovac begins], *Vesti*, March 9, 2009. Dodik's sleight of hand here is also to minimize the number of victims at Srebrenica. It is between seven and eight thousand, not "a thousand" as he claims.

Serbian people and the destruction of that four year old *state*."[90] Equally important for the Serbian nationalist project here is both the implicit designation of operation Storm as genocide (hence the interest of the museum) and the museum's reference to Krajina as a state, thus creating a narrative of military aggression by Croatia (already established in the museum's narrative as a genocidal state) against an internationally legitimate political entity.

A similar discursive move was the museum's remembrance of the NATO air war against Serbia in 1999, which was instigated by reports of campaigns of ethnic cleansing of Kosovo Albanian civilians at the hands of Serbian police and military. The Museum of Genocide Victims, of course, did not accept this framing of the 1999 NATO war, but instead commemorated it with a 2014 exhibition that was breathtaking both in its historical revisionism (even fabrication) and in its explicit, almost obsessive anti-Americanism. Reminiscent of the heights of Serbian nationalist mobilization under Milošević and using language by now mostly abandoned by mainstream Serbian cultural institutions, the museum in 2014 explained the breakup of the former Yugoslavia by noting, "Communist Yugoslavia was destroyed by the will of the Vatican, Germany, other European states, and especially the United States." Comparing the aerial bombardment in 1999 to the series of air raids of Belgrade during WWII, the exhibit authors argue that the "Anglo-American" (Allied) bombing in 1944 was worse than the German bombing in 1941, but the 1999 bombing used a force "so far not seen in the world." Making as explicit as possible the link between WWII and the 1999 NATO air war, the authors claim, "German Wehrmacht soldiers joined the 1999 operation as aggressors, the first time since WWII." The exhibition catalog then ends with a call to Never Forget.[91] The use of both the Holocaust remembrance slogan and the very strongly implied argument that the NATO war itself was a genocide against Serbia is yet another example of the way in which Holocaust remembrance serves contemporary state identity building and ontological security needs: to preserve the view of the state as a victim; to justify the (negative) relationship between Serbia and its international others (Europe, United States); and to shift the blame for Yugoslavia's dissolution from Serbian nationalist territorial expansionism to the Vatican, Americans,

90. "Otvaranje izložbe 'Oluja–nestanak Srpske krajine, avgust 1995'" [Exhibition opening "Storm–the destruction of Srpska Krajina, August 1995"], accessed March 1, 2019, http://www.muzejgenocida.rs/85-novosti/382-кикинда,-дом-културе,-5-август-2017-отварање-изложбе-„олуја—нестанак-српске-крајине,-август-1995".html.

91. "Agresija na SR Jugoslaviju 24. mart—10. jun 1999" [Aggression against FR Yugoslavia March 24–June 10, 1999], accessed February 5, 2019, http://www.muzejgenocida.rs/images/izlozbe/1999_opt.pdf.

or some other international actor whose ill intent toward Serbia has become a broadly shared, and unchallenged, social fact.

Cooptation of Holocaust Memorials

The complete appropriation and nationalization of Holocaust remembrance was also manifest in new memorials. In 1990, the Serbian-Jewish Friendship Society (unaffiliated and often in conflict with the Federation of Jewish Communities in Serbia) successfully lobbied for the erection of a monument to Jewish victims of the Holocaust called "Menorah in Flames," a very dramatic sculpture by the distinguished artist Nandor Glid, whose parents were killed at Auschwitz and who had already created many artworks about the Holocaust, including the major art piece at the entrance to the Dachau concentration camp memorial site. This sculpture was placed on the Danube riverbank in the neighborhood of Dorćol, Belgrade's prewar Jewish quarter. How, exactly, this location was chosen is unclear, as the sculpture, while beautiful and very evocative, sits awkwardly in front of a semi-decrepit gray socialist-era apartment complex, without any local contextualization and seemingly without proper maintenance, as small pieces of its bronze have since chipped off.

Menorah in Flames served a dual purpose for the Serbian government at the time. It provided a convenient location for a Holocaust memorial, silencing stubborn calls from the Jewish community for proper memorialization of Semlin. In fact, it is possible that the unveiling of the Menorah further set back efforts to create a Semlin memorial, as the issue of memorialization of Jewish victims had been taken off the agenda. Simultaneously, it also introduced another opportunity for the maintenance of the Serbian narrative about its own righteousness, as witnessed in the media reports on the unveiling of the monument with headlines such as "Testament to our Openness" or "Suffered Together."[92] Once again, Holocaust memorialization was not about the Jews, but about the Serbs.

Even more directly, in 1993, the city of Belgrade granted permission for the building of an Orthodox church next to Memorial Park Jajinci, with the following justification: "After Jasenovac, Jajinci is the greatest Serbian mass grave—bigger than Kragujevac, than Kraljevo . . . than Kosovo."[93] For a variety of reasons—some political, some financial—the construction work on

92. "Znamenje naše otvorenosti" [A testament to our openness], *Novosti plus*, October 22, 1990, "Stradali zajedno," *Politika ekspres*, October 22, 1990.

93. Ignjatović and Manojlović Pintar, "Staro sajmište," 35.

the church began only in 2005, and by then the justification for this project had further evolved: "This was the place where the occupiers shot, buried, burnt alive, and brought in a gas van *mostly Serbian youth* imprisoned in Banjica map. . . . Today there is no *cross*, no name, no guide, nor any word on such a huge killing site!"[94] Obviously missing from this memorial project is any recognition at all that the victims killed or buried at Jajinci were Jewish and communist, and that an Orthodox Christian church is not an appropriate way to commemorate either group.[95]

And just as ultranationalist Polish Catholics tried to put a Polish Catholic stamp on the memory of Auschwitz by literally planting hundreds of crosses immediately outside the memorial site, what the new Serbian state did with this memory intervention was to fully nationalize victims of the Holocaust and victims of WWII and posthumously make them all Serbs and Christian.[96] This is not just a trivial manipulation of history. It serves a very direct role for states seeking ontological security—it uses political memory for the construction of the new national body politic. In postcommunist Serbia, the new polity is constructed on the foundations of ethnic and religious homogeneity.

Holocaust Remembrance as Foreign Policy

In addition to nationalist mobilization, Serbia's contested, contentious, and unresolved relationship with its most significant international other—Croatia—is the second pillar of its problematic postcommunist Holocaust remembrance. Serbia's relationship with Croatia (and Croatia's with Serbia, as the next chapter of the book demonstrates) has always been fraught, best resembling sibling rivalry elevated to the level of the state. Serbs and Croats share the same language (although nationalists in each state insist on treating the two dialects as linguistically distinct), they share a history in Yugoslavia, both when it was a kingdom and during the socialist experiment, and their nationalisms and expansionist projects toward Bosnia have formed the axis of the wars of Yugoslav succession.[97]

---

94. Ignjatović and Manojlović Pintar, "Staro sajmište," 35, emphasis added.

95. Still unfinished, as of 2017, the church is half built and is supposed to be part of a much larger church complex that would include a cultural center, sports arena, movie theater, offices, kitchen, and two apartments. Daliborka Mučibabić, "Hram u Jajincima i nedovršen—živi" [The church in Jajinci unfinished, yet living], *Politika*, May 4, 2013.

96. On the Auschwitz controversy, see Geneviève Zubrzycki, *The Crosses of Auschwitz: Nationalism and Religion in Post-communist Poland* (Chicago: University of Chicago Press, 2009).

97. Sabrina P. Ramet, *Balkan Babel: The Disintegration of Yugoslavia from the Death of Tito to the Fall of Milosevic* (Boulder: Westview Press, 2002).

Serbia-Croatia relations have become further complicated as their paths toward the European Union have diverged—while Croatia was an early enthusiastic EU candidate, and was rewarded for it by entry in 2014, Serbia has been a reluctant Europeanizer, watching Croatia's EU success with a mixture of envy, resentment, and sense of betrayal, as its own path to Brussels has seemingly stalled.[98]

It is in this context of Serbia's deep insecurity regarding its relations with Croatia that the rich repertoire of Serbian Holocaust remembrance as fundamentally anti-Croatian begins to make sense. This project was, and continues to be, an all-out state effort that includes multiple memory actors. In addition to the Museum of Genocide Victims discussed above, another critical actor in this effort is the Serbian Orthodox Church, which has spearheaded a certain revival of the interest in the Holocaust among the Serbian general public. As we shall see, however, the Church is not really interested in discussing the actual Holocaust, but rather in using the Holocaust—its symbols, imagery, and narrative—to pursue its own claims of Serbian, Christian martyrdom at the hands of Catholic Croats and godless communists.

The Serbian Orthodox Church's interest in leading Holocaust-themed remembrance projects is particularly notable because the Church has a deep history of anti-Semitism, most clearly personified in Bishop Nikolaj Velimirović, whom the Church canonized in 2003 despite abundant public evidence of his extreme anti-Semitic teachings during the interwar period.[99] Further, some of the contemporary publications of the Church, including the Church's samizdat *Bogoslovija*, continue to publish anti-Semitic articles, while the Church-affiliated youth movements *Dveri* and *1389* have also openly expressed anti-Semitism in their public rallies.[100]

Against this background, in 2003, the Serbian Orthodox Church established its Jasenovac Committee of the Synod of Bishops, whose stated purpose was to "draw the attention of the Ministries of Education of Serbia and Republika Srpska to the importance of the Stockholm Declaration on education regarding the Holocaust, the signing of which offers many opportunities for the accurate and proper presentation of the tragedy of the Second World War and its transmission to generations to come."[101] While

98. Jelena Subotić, "Europe is a State of Mind: Identity and Europeanization in the Balkans," *International Studies Quarterly* 55, no. 2 (2011): 309–30.

99. Jovan Byford, "Distinguishing 'Anti-Judaism' from 'Antisemitism': Recent Championing of Serbian Bishop Nikolaj Velimirović," *Religion, State & Society* 34, no. 1 (2006): 7–31.

100. Fuks, interview.

101. Communique of Jasenovac Committee of the Holy Assembly of Bishops of the Serbian Orthodox Church, 2005, http://www.jasenovac-info.com/2005/?lang=en&s=sednica-050714.

citing European Holocaust remembrance architecture, this Church institution, however, immediately moved the focus away from the Holocaust, and just like the Museum of Genocide Victims, turned it squarely onto the Serbian victims of the Ustasha genocide. This is evident in its commitment to "the preservation of remembrance of this new Serbian Kosovo, of the Great-martyred Jasenovac," where the reference to Kosovo indicates that it is now Jasenovac, the site of Serbian suffering, that should be the identity core of the Serbian nation.[102]

To the extent that this religious institution couched its narrative within the larger framework of the Holocaust, it argued for a direct equivalency of Jewish and Serbian suffering, stating explicitly, "Nazis killed Serbs and Jews equally," "The bones of Serbian and Jewish victims are mixed together in mass graves," and "Serbs and Jews are [today] living together again, as the remnants of a slaughtered people."[103]

These Church activities did not pass unnoticed by international observers. In 2005, giving a huge boost to these kinds of Holocaust remembrance practices, the Organization for Security and Cooperation in Europe (OSCE) officially cited the Jasenovac Committee as an "example of good practice in the field of commemorating the Holocaust."[104] Whether the OSCE genuinely believed that this Holocaust practice was good, whether they did not understand its problematic nature, or whether they did not care too much to double-check beyond noting the presence of Holocaust education, which they promote, the fact remains that a major European institution praised Holocaust remembrance that can most charitably be described as Holocaust appropriation.[105]

The "Croatization" of Holocaust remembrance (replacing Holocaust remembrance with remembrance of Jasenovac) has also created a public narrative that the Croats were worse than the Germans, a narrative that has taken such deep roots that it has become hegemonic. The trope that "Jasenovac was worse than Auschwitz" is widely used and promoted by major state and religious institutions. At a 2013 presentation of a new book by the Serbian art historian Dinko Davidov, *Total Genocide*, on the NDH genocide against

---

102. Communique of Jasenovac Committee.

103. Serbian Patriarch, press release, September 26, 2003, http://www.spc.rs/old/Vesti-2003/09/26-9-03_l2.html.

104. Organization for Security and Cooperation in Europe (OSCE), *Education on the Holocaust and Anti-Semitism* (Warsaw: OSCE Office for Democratic Institutions and Human Rights, 2005), 52.

105. Lea David, "Holocaust Discourse as a Screen Memory: The Serbian Case," in *(Mis)Uses of History: History as a Political Tool in the Western Balkans 1986–2012*, ed. Srdjan M. Jovanović and Veran Stančetić (Belgrade: CSDU Press, 2013).

the Serbs, another well-known Serbian historian Vasilije Krestić—who had gained some notoriety in the 1990s by arguing that the Croats were "a genocidal people"—claimed that it was the communists who, after the war, purposefully placed the blame for the genocide against the Serbian people at the feet of the Germans, instead of with Croatia's Ustasha, where it belonged.[106] Krestić went on to argue, "Nowhere in Europe during WWII were so many cultural monuments destroyed as in Croatia," describing the destruction of "more than 450 Serbian Orthodox shrines" as "culturicide." That hundreds of synagogues were destroyed during Kristallnacht alone in November 1938 is simply not part of the Serbian WWII memory repertoire.[107]

An important focal point of the Jasenovac narrative in Serbian historiography is that it was a camp not only as horrific as any Nazi concentration camp, but actually much, much worse. Much of the Serbian historiography on Jasenovac consists of in-depth description of gruesome conditions and horrific killing methods in the Ustasha camp. Some of the accounts in both Serbian academic scholarship and also the popular press are over-the-top gruesome and often not substantiated with any evidence, so gratuitous in their description of horrors as to be impossible to read and improbable to take seriously as historical fact.

This idea that Jasenovac (and, following from that, the Ustasha and Croatia) is much worse than the Holocaust is also evident in high-profile publications such as, for example, a major volume on Jasenovac, *The Yugoslav Auschwitz and the Vatican*, by Vladimir Dedijer, a premier Serbian historian from the communist era. This book not only declares that the horrors of Jasenovac were just as gruesome, if not worse, than Auschwitz, but also links the NDH to the Vatican, a narrative frame that was used to great success in Serbian nationalist propaganda during the Croatian war and that lives on to this day, as we saw in the description of the contemporary activities of the Museum of Genocide Victims.[108]

The "Holocaust is Jasenovac" homily has been put to direct use for Serbian foreign policy needs on multiple occasions. On January 27, 2017, International Holocaust Remembrance Day, the Serbian Ministry of Foreign Affairs organized a high-profile exhibition and conference on Jasenovac in

---

106. For an example of his incendiary arguments, see Vasilije Krestić, *Through Genocide to a Greater Croatia* (Belgrade: BIGZ, 1998).

107. "Knjiga sa teškim naslovom" [A book with a heavy title], *Radio Televizija Srbije*, November 27, 2013, http://www.rts.rs/page/rts/sr/Dijaspora/story/1518/vesti/1455307/knjiga-sa-teskim-naslovom.html.

108. Vladimir Dedijer, *The Yugoslav Auschwitz and the Vatican: The Croatian Massacre of the Serbs during World War II* (Buffalo: Prometheus Books, 1992).

New York. Initially planned to be held at the United Nations headquarters, this conference ended up in a rented gallery space in Hoboken, New Jersey, as the organizers presumably failed to ensure the necessary UN permits.[109] Regardless of this setback, the Serbian delegation still promoted the exhibition at the UN during the events commemorating International Holocaust Remembrance Day by distributing leaflets about the new location. The Serbian government spared no resources for this major event that included witness testimonies, newly commissioned artwork, and an academic symposium that, the organizers announced, was "intended to *mobilize the global public* to contribute to the preservation of the universal values such as peace, freedom and the protection of human rights"—a clear jab at Croatia's increasing revisionism regarding its WWII fascist atrocities, especially those at Jasenovac.[110]

But the goal was much broader than this and involved using International Holocaust Remembrance Day to remember crimes against the Serbs, and in so doing improve Serbia's insecure international relationships, especially with Europe. One of the main intellectual sponsors of the conference, historian Vasilije Krestić, already discussed above, said that the exhibition was "in line with the foreign policy interests of the Republic of Serbia—the only country charged for genocide twice before the International Criminal Court in the Hague" and "addressed the challenges in the international arena, while contributing to the protection of Serbia's foreign policy interests."[111]

Similarly, one of the conference participants, Serbian Orthodox Bishop Irinej (of the Metropolitanate of Australia and New Zealand) said, "I always ask myself when will us Serbs have the chance to, in major world centers such as New York and Washington, present the facts about the suffering of our people so that everyone knows what happened to us."[112] This focus on Serbian suffering is evident in the title of the exhibition—*Jasenovac—Right to Not Forget*—which itself insinuated that Serbian victims were being marginalized

109. Mirjana Sretenović, "Izložba 'Jasenovac—pravo na nezaborav' otvorena u Americi" [The exhibition "Jasenovac—Right to not forget" opens in New York], *Politika*, January 29, 2017.

110. Milivoje Pantovic, "Serbia to Highlight Croatia Concentration Camp at UN," *Balkan Insight*, August 11, 2016, http://www.balkaninsight.com/en/article/serbia-to-highlight-croatia-concentration-camp-at-un-08-10-2016, emphasis added.

111. Krestić was referring to Bosnia's and Croatia's unsuccessful lawsuits against Serbia for genocide in the wars of 1991–95 in front of the International Court of Justice. Serbian Ministry of Foreign Affairs, press release, January 26, 2017, http://www.mfa.gov.rs/en/press-service/statements/16132-27-january-2017-international-holocaust-day-and-exhibition-jasenovac-the-right-to-rememberance.

112. Sretenović, "Izložba."

by the centrality of Holocaust memory and that the exhibition was a way of making Serbian victimhood a part of global Holocaust remembrance.[113]

In 2018, the exhibition opened again, this time at the UN Headquarters in New York, as part of the International Holocaust Remembrance Day series of commemorations. It was again mired in controversy, as the government of Croatia issued an official protest to the UN for hosting an exhibition that falsified history.[114] In response, the UN issued a statement clarifying that the content of the exhibition was the mandate of the organizer and that the UN did not necessarily condone it.[115]

The influence of Serbian-Croatian unresolved relations in Holocaust remembrance is also evident in the often contradictory memorializations at the Semlin site. Against all historical evidence, a narrative has gradually emerged in Serbia that shifts the blame for Semlin from Nazi Germany to Croatia. Part of this rhetorical coup is the insistence that the Semlin camp was on the territory of the NDH, which, while technically accurate, is hardly relevant, since the German administration asked permission from the NDH to place the camp at Semlin and, after obtaining it, ran the camp independently from any NDH input or personnel.[116]

In 1995, at the height of Serbian nationalist frenzy under Slobodan Milošević, a new monument was erected at Semlin. For the first time, it introduced the ethnic background of Semlin victims as Serbs, Jews, and Roma, a precise ordering of suffering that has since become canonized. In a departure from communist remembrance practices, however, the monument was unveiled on April 22, the day of the mass escape of Serbian inmates from Jasenovac– a date of no significance to the story of Semlin, but of central significance to the inversion of Serbian memory of genocide, where the Holocaust is replaced with the memory of Serbian suffering at the hands of Croatia's fascist militia.[117] It is also notable that the monument—a sculpture by the artist Miodrag Popović—was not commissioned for Semlin, but

113. I thank an anonymous reviewer for this astute insight.

114. Croatia specifically objected to the inflated number of victims and the linking of a revered WWII Croatian cardinal, Alojzije Stepinac, to Jasenovac atrocities. Filip Rudic, "Serbia, Croatia Spar Over Concentration Camp Exhibition," *Balkan Insight*, January 26, 2018, http://www.balkaninsight.com/en/article/serbia-croatia-spar-over-jasenovac-exhibition-01-26-2018.

115. I. D, "Nedopustive su bilo kakve manipulacije žrtvama" [Any manipulation regarding victims is unacceptable], *Dnevnik.hr*, January 29, 2018, https://dnevnik.hr/vijesti/hrvatska/marija-pejcinovic-buric-o-srpskoj-izlozbi-u-un-u-nedopustive-su-bilo-kakve-manipulacije-zrtvama---504850.html.

116. Bajford, *Staro sajmište*.

117. Jovan Byford, "Semlin Judelanger in Serbian Political Memory," accessed February 6, 2019, https://www.open.ac.uk/socialsciences/semlin/en/.

instead was a runner-up in the competition for the Jajinci memorial site.[118] So seemingly unimportant was the visual representation of the Holocaust in Serbia that monuments were simply replaceable from one atrocity site to another.

In another notable shift, the standard memorialization language of previous monuments was replaced in the 1995 monument with an inscription that now included Serbian victims of Croatian and Hungarian fascists, including Serbian victims of Jasenovac, a mnemonic strategy that marginalized the history of Semlin and removed its centrality to the Holocaust.[119] In fact, throughout this period, annual commemorations of the Day of Remembrance for the Victims of Genocide (April 22) began with a ceremony at the Semlin site, further replacing the commemoration of the Holocaust of Serbia's Jews with the commemoration of the Croatian genocide of Serbs.[120] It is this very specific "memorial geography" of Serbia's Holocaust remembrance—the dislocation of all Holocaust memory onto both the physical and the mnemonic territory of Croatia—that serves Serbia's contemporary identity as well as its foreign policy needs.[121]

This political use of Holocaust remembrance is also evident in contemporary memorialization—and the lack thereof—at the Semlin camp site. In 2017, the Serbian government proposed a law that would establish a memorial complex on the Semlin site, which its authors envisaged would become the Serbian Yad Vashem.[122] Unlike Yad Vashem, however, the proposed memorial center would commemorate general themes of "genocide, terror of the occupation and war crimes" over the course of Serbia's twentieth century, guided by the "proud Serbian tradition of freedom."[123] The preamble of the draft law spends considerable time describing Serbia as a "small nation but one of large historical character," fighting only "wars of liberation and defense," and "honorably belonging to nations with the greatest victims in

118. Bajford, *Staro sajmište*.

119. Bajford, *Staro sajmište, 174*.

120. The fact that the Day of Remembrance for the Victims of Genocide is memorialized on the day of Serbian prisoners' escape from a Croatian fascist camp itself indicates that genocide in the Serbian public discourse means Croatian genocide against the Serbs and does not include the Holocaust.

121. Byford, "When I Say," 53.

122. According to the draft law, this will be one institution to commemorate all victims of WWII, with three museums under one roof—the Museum of Genocide (of Serbian people in Croatia), the Museum of the Holocaust, and the Museum of Porajmos (Holocaust of Roma / Sinti). Draft Law on the Establishment of Memorial to Victims, February 2017, on file with author. After the Jewish community complained about the lack of autonomy for the Holocaust museum, the draft law was amended in February 2018 to provide for institutional autonomy. The nationalist preamble remained. The second draft of the law is also on file with author.

123. Draft Law on the Establishment of Memorial to Victims.

recent history, and especially in the two world wars, symbolized by the Albanian Golgotha and Jasenovac."[124]

Completely missing from the text of the proposed memorial is any mention of the Serbian government's collaboration in the Holocaust or the role Serbian paramilitaries played in rounding up the Jews for execution. It also again marginalizes the exclusively Jewish suffering at Semlin and the fundamentally different experience of Jews under Nazi occupation from that of other groups, instead de facto equating their victimhood with that of the Serbs.[125] The Serbian Yad Vashem, therefore, like many other memorial projects already discussed, was designed to be a memorial to the unimpeachable character of the Serbian nation.[126]

The draft law—in the writing of which the Serbian Jewish community was not invited to participate—also claims that the Serbian people were the victims of genocide committed by the "Independent State of Croatia, as well as Germany and its allies and helpers, and especially *Albanian collaborators* in Kosovo and Metohija during WWII."[127] Within this context, then, the proposed memorial center at the Semlin site would focus mostly on Serb victimization at the hands of Croats and Albanians that have at most tangential relationship, and often no relationship at all, to the Holocaust and the Jewish suffering at Semlin, but are of significant importance to Serbia's continuing contested relationship with Croatia, Kosovo, and the larger European Union.

Despite an almost complete absence of Holocaust memory, the Semlin site, however, continues to be used as the physical location of the "Serbs as Jews" narrative. On May 10, 2017, at a small ceremony observing the Day of Remembrance of the Victims of the Holocaust at Semlin, Aleksandar Vulin, Serbia's labor minister, said, "Each wound of the Jewish people is the wound of the Serbian people, their joy is our joy, the struggle of the Jewish people for freedom and independence is the struggle of the Serbian people for freedom and independence," because "the Serbian and the Jewish people are the people of freedom and dignity."[128]

---

124. Draft Law on the Establishment of Memorial to Victims.

125. Author interview with Haris Dajč, former vice president of the Belgrade Jewish Community, February 22, 2018, Belgrade.

126. The former president of the Serbian Jewish Community, Ruben Fuks, developed a plan for the Holocaust memorial, which would include an educational facility and a memorial devoted to Jewish life in Serbia before the war (the "memorial to absence"), the Holocaust, the postwar period, and Serbian Righteous Gentiles (Serbs who risked their lives to save Jews). Fuks, interview.

127. Draft Law on the Establishment of Memorial to Victims.

128. "Vulin: Srpski i jevrejski narod—narodi slobode i ponosa" [Vulin: Serbian and Jewish people—The people of liberty and pride], *Novosti*, May 10, 2017.

Instead of clearing out the barracks at Semlin in preparation for the construction of the memorial complex, though, in January 2018, the Serbian ruling party, misleadingly named the Serbian Progressive Party (SNP), moved into one of the abandoned buildings and hung the party banner from the windows.[129] The draft law and the memorial complex project had stalled. The Semlin site had new owners.

Holocaust Remembrance for the European Gaze

In addition to its use as ammunition in Serbian-Croatian continuing bilateral provocations, Holocaust remembrance has also been used by Serbian political leaders to demonstrate the country's international commitments—and, especially its European outlook. This has been evident in the stark difference between the way in which the Holocaust is memorialized (or rather, unmemorialized) in the Serbian everyday and the government's use of discrete moments—such as the unveiling of monuments—to send direct messages to Brussels about Serbia's readiness to join Europe. And yet as this heightened rhetorical focus on the Holocaust—or what the Holocaust represents for Serbia's European aspirations—has seemingly blossomed, the actual state interest in Holocaust remembrance has remained almost nonexistent. On January 27, 2005, at the commemorative event marking the sixtieth anniversary of the liberation of Auschwitz, Serbia was the only European country not to send a single state delegate.[130]

As part of its slow progression toward European Union membership, Serbia has joined a number of international organizations that promote Holocaust memory and education. In 2006, Serbia became an observer at the Task Force for International Cooperation on Education about the Holocaust (ITF), thus obligating itself to promote Holocaust education. In 2009, Serbia became an affiliate, and in 2011, a full member of the now renamed IHRA (International Holocaust Remembrance Alliance). With full membership, Serbia accepted the responsibility to fully integrate Holocaust education and research into its official curricula, to observe International Holocaust Remembrance Day on January 27, to open archives related to Holocaust

---

129. Filip Rudic, "Serbia Ruling Party Opens Office at Concentration Camp," *Balkan Insight*, January 24, 2018, http://www.balkaninsight.com/en/article/serbia-s-progressives-open-office-at-wwii-camp-s-location-01-24-2018.

130. "Ne zaboraviti Aušvic" [Don't forget Auschwitz], *B92*, January 27, 2005, http://www.b92.net/info/vesti/index.php?yyyy=2005&mm=01&dd=27&nav_id=160879.

research, and to guarantee "academic, educational, and public examination of the country's historical past as related to the Holocaust period."[131]

As discussed earlier, by entrusting the Church—which has become increasingly politically assertive and socially present after the collapse of communism—to carry out Holocaust education and training, the state simultaneously used the Holocaust for domestic political needs and attained international legitimacy by conducting education under the patronage of the IHRA. In addition to education activities carried out by the Church-run Jasenovac Committee, Serbia also embarked on a flurry of other activities to demonstrate its commitment to fulfilling IHRA requirements.

One of the first high-profile projects was the exhibition *Holocaust in Serbia 1941–1944* at the Museum of Yugoslav History in 2012.[132] While certainly the first major state effort to provide a comprehensive account of the Holocaust in Serbia, it was a hastily and clumsily prepared exhibition, with some embarrassingly unprofessional displays. For example, in describing Jewish prewar life in Serbia, one caption read: "[Jews] participated in industrial, commercial and banking affairs *where they, very often, had majority and predominant influence*," an old and tired anti-Semitic trope that somehow made it to the exhibition walls.[133] Other questionable arguments included the caption, "On account of the international political situation, Yugoslavia started to pass restricting measures because the Jewish emigrants from Europe in the beginning of 1933 began to pass or inhabit the territory of the Kingdom. It culminated with the Kladovo transport." This interpretation of anti-Jewish measures as being a defense of Serbia against migrants is not only historically inaccurate, but it also justifies anti-Semitism as regular immigration control. The inclusion of the Kladovo transport is also bizarre because, as discussed earlier, Central European Jewish refuges found themselves in Serbia in 1939 because they were fleeing Nazism. They did not "emigrate" into Serbia, taxing its resources. They were all killed in 1941–42. That these errors could

131. IHRA, Membership and Application Procedure, accessed March 2, 2019, https://www.holocaustremembrance.com/node/533.

132. An earlier exhibition in 1997, "A Tale of the Neighbours That Are No More," was an excellent presentation of the Jews of Belgrade before, during, and after the Holocaust, and was received to great critical acclaim. However, this was a very small event put up by the Jewish Historical Museum and the independent Radio B92 in an alternative cultural space, not a museum, and it was not a state endorsed affair.

133. Emphasis added. The choice of display text is even more bizarre when compared to the exhibition catalog. For example, in the catalog, the quoted sentence in Serbian ends at "Jews were present in industry, trade, banking, and manufacturing." The English translation in the same catalog, however, extends the sentence to include "where they often had a major and crucial influence." It was this anti-Semitic ending that was then included in the exhibit. Museum of Yugoslav History, *Holocaust in Serbia 1941–1944* (Belgrade, 2012), 7, 20.

have easily been avoided—by consulting the meticulous work of Serbia's own Holocaust historians—demonstrates a lack of interest and the shallowness of Serbia's commitment to IHRA at the time.

However superficial the commitment, IHRA membership was also hugely important for Serbian officials, who used it on multiple occasions to showcase Serbia's increasing European outlook. "Membership in this organization represents international recognition of many decades of activities of the Republic of Serbia, which has regularly commemorated all important dates in the history of suffering of Jews, Serbs, Roma, and others on the entire territory of our state in WWII and has carried out many activities in the fields of Holocaust education, remembrance and research," the Serbian Ministry of Foreign Affairs proudly boasted.[134]

In 2016, Serbia also passed the Law on Removing the Consequences of Confiscating the Property from Holocaust Victims with No Living Descendants,[135] basically a Restitution Act, and is a signatory to the 2009 Terezin Declaration on Holocaust Era Assets.[136] These Serbian efforts did not pass unnoticed internationally, and the Serbian media gave much attention to the visit of Robert Singer, the executive director of the World Jewish Congress, who emphasized the "historical and cultural links of our two peoples [Serbs and Jews]," and congratulated Serbia for "everything it has accomplished in terms of Jewish property restitution, for which it should be especially praised internationally."[137] Grateful for the praise from the European

---

134. Ministry of Foreign Affairs of the Republic of Serbia, "Međunarodna alijansa za sećanje na Holokaust" [International Holocaust Remembrance Alliance], accessed February 6, 2019, http://www.mfa.gov.rs/sr/index.php/spoljna-politika/multilaterala/itf?lang=lat.

135. The text of the law is available at Republic of Serbia, Restitution Agency, Law on Removing the Consequences of Confiscating the Property from Holocaust Victims with No Living Descendants, accessed March 2, 2019, http://restitucija.gov.rs/doc/zakoni/Zakona%20o%20otklanjanju%20posledica%20oduzimanja%20imovine%20zrtvama%20holokausta.pdf. By May 2017, the Serbian Jewish community received restitution property in the amount of fourteen million euros. "Jevrejima u Srbiji vraćena imovina od 14 miliona evra" [Property valued at 14 million Euro returned to the Jews in Serbia], *Alo*, May 17, 2017. The law also obligates Serbia to compensate the Federation of Jewish Communities in Serbia with annual donation of 950,000 euros for twenty-five years. Jelena Popadić, "Četrdeset nekretnina vraćeno jevrejskim opštinama" [Forty properties returned to the Jewish community], *Politika*, February 28, 2017. The Jewish community planned to use the funds for education, programs to fight prejudice, Holocaust victims remembrance, and support to survivors. Katarina Subasic, "Serbia Returns Property Taken in Holocaust to Tiny Jewish Community," *Times of Israel*, March 30, 2016.

136. The Terezin declaration is non-binding, but it calls for signatory states to set up restitution policies, strengthen Holocaust education and research, and memorialize sites of Holocaust atrocities. Prague Holocaust Era Assets Conference: Terezin Declaration, June 30, 2009, US Department of State website, https://www.state.gov/p/eur/rls/or/126162.htm.

137. Ministry of Foreign Affairs of the Republic of Serbia, "Zajednički napori na sprečavanju relativizacije Holokausta i revizije istorije" [Joint efforts to prevent relativization of the Holocaust

Parliament, the director of the Serbian Restitution Agency proudly proclaimed, "Our country again chose the right side."[138]

The example of the tragically disrespected remains of the Topovske šupe camp, whose history as a Jewish and Roma execution site was outlined above, is further illustrative of this dual dynamic. After years of complete neglect, in 1994, the Serbian government finally decided to memorialize the camp, but instead of being placed at the location of Topovske šupe, the memorial plaque was erroneously placed at Tramvajske šupe, a tram depot in central Belgrade, and a site of no connection to the Nazi camp. So apparently irrelevant was both the history of Topovske šupe and the topography of the Holocaust in Serbia that it took full twelve years for this error to be corrected and the plaque to be moved to the proper location. On January 27, 2006, the first year that International Holocaust Remembrance Day was observed in Serbia, a small memorial plaque in the shape of a Torah with a short text in Serbian, Hebrew, and English was unveiled.

That the unveiling of a commemorative plaque at Topovske šupe was predominantly an internationally oriented and not a domestically driven event was evident in the relatively small crowd in attendance, but even more so in the speech by Milorad Perović, the president of the Belgrade city assembly, who said, "This event is especially significant today when Serbia is making huge efforts to join the European Union."[139]

This connection between memorializing the Holocaust and Serbia's EU aspirations was made by political leaders time and time again. On International Holocaust Remembrance Day in 2012, then Serbian president Boris Tadić said, "Serbia is eager to join the EU, thus, there is no place here for those who committed crimes against humanity."[140] In 2014, then president Tomislav Nikolić was even more determined to use International Holocaust Remembrance Day for very contemporary political purposes, completely decoupled from the Holocaust: "As the Jewish people were objects of stigmatization, so today some are trying to slander the entire Serbian people. Some historians, helped by Serbian media, are laying the blame for World War I,

---

and historical revisionism], May 23, 2017, http://www.mfa.gov.rs/sr/index.php/pres-servis/saopstenja/18113-2017-05-23-13-28-02?lang=lat.

138. V. Crnjanski Spasojević, "Odnos Srbije prema Jevrejima uzor Evropi" [Serbia's relations with Jews an example for Europe], *Novosti*, April 29, 2017.

139. "U petak otvaranje spomen-parka 'Topovske šupe'" [Memorial park "Topovske šupe" opens on Friday], *Belgrade portal*, January 25, 2006, http://www.beograd.rs/cir/beoinfo/1221343-u-petak-otvaranje-spomen-parka-topovske-supe/.

140. Rade Ranković, "Dan sećanja na žrtve Holokausta" [Holocaust Victims Remembrance Day], January 27, 2012, *Glas Amerike*, https://www.glasamerike.net/a/serbia-holocoust-01-27-138217154/734967.html.

with no evidence, on Serbia. This is why we need more serious research and studies of Serbian history in the First and Second World Wars."[141]

And as Serbian politicians have continued each year to give high profile speeches on International Holocaust Remembrance Day and tie Serbian EU aspirations to global Holocaust memory, in everyday practice on the ground, the Holocaust has continued to be neglected, its victims forgotten. In 2013, just seven years after the memorial plaque at Topovske šupe was unveiled, a major retail tycoon purchased the land on which the former camp was located and announced the construction of a massive mixed-use complex that would include "the largest shopping mall in the region."[142] Awkwardly, the architectural firm behind the project was Israeli. After objections were raised by the Serbian Jewish community, the partner companies—both Israeli and Serbian—revised their plans and committed to maintaining the memorial character of the site. How, exactly, the site of a Holocaust death camp could be "integrated" into the new mixed-use development remains unclear and a source of great anxiety for the local Jewish community.[143] Worried that direct accusations of Serbia's anti-Semitism would be met with a backlash, a representative of the Jewish community at one of the protests against the shopping mall construction called Serbia's negligence about Holocaust memory "not anti-Semitic, but profoundly anti-civic."[144]

As of 2019, all that remains of the former camp is a segment of the crumbling wall, the memorial plaque invisible beneath overgrown foliage and the Hebrew letters peeled off, making the inscription unreadable. The plaque has been stolen multiple times, sold as scrap metal, replaced, and stolen again.[145] There is garbage strewn all over the small area where the memorial—although it can hardly be called such—is located, including discarded tires

---

141. Rade Ranković, "Nikolić: Nećemo dopustiti reviziju istorije" [Nikolić: We shall not allow historical revisionism], *Glas Amerike*, January 27, 2014, https://www.glasamerike.net/a/serbia-holocaust/1838713.html. Nikolić was referring to the publication of Christopher M. Clark, *The Sleepwalkers: How Europe Went to War in 1914* (London: Allen Lane, 2012). This book was hugely controversial in Serbia due to Clark's argument that it was Serbia's broader expansionist policies that motivated the terrorist group Young Bosnia and its member Gavrilo Princip to assassinate Archduke Franz Ferdinand on July 28, 1914, leading to World War I.

142. Federico Sicurella, "Topovske Šupe: Memory of the Holocaust at Stake," *Osservatorio Balcani e Caucaso*, June 19, 2013, https://www.balcanicaucaso.org/eng/Areas/Serbia/Topovske-Supe-memory-of-the-Holocaust-at-stake-137662.

143. Fuks, interview. For a personal plea for remembrance by a noted Serbian Jewish writer and Holocaust survivor whose father was killed at Topovske šupe and mother at Semlin, see Ivan Ivanji, "Topovske šupe: Naše smrti i vaš život" [Topovske šupe: Our deaths and your life], *Vreme*, 1184, September 13, 2013.

144. Sicurella, "Topovske Šupe."

145. Fuks, interview; Panić, interview.

from a tire shop nearby. There are no signs pointing to the camp location anywhere in the vicinity for potentially interested visitors. There is no designated parking (or parking of any kind), or even a sign pointing to a site of historical interest. This is all despite the fact that the Topovske šupe site is in the center of Belgrade, next to one of the busiest traffic junctions. Yet it lingers as a site of nonmemory over which victims' families continue to speak out in anguish.

Rehabilitation of Fascist Collaboration

The assault on the commemorative legacy of partisan resistance in Serbia started immediately after Milošević was ousted from power in 2000. Just a few days after the October 5 revolt, Belgrade's newly elected democratic mayor Milan Protić, a historian himself, announced that October 20, the day of Belgrade's liberation from Nazi occupation in 1944, would no longer be observed because "this was a day of occupation, not liberation."[146] Soon after, the Day of Victory over Fascism and the Day of Uprising (the start of partisan resistance) were also removed from the national calendar.[147]

As in many other postcommunist countries, in Serbia the courts played a primary role in establishing a new, revisionist remembrance of WWII and, within it, of the Holocaust. In December 2004, the Serbian government passed the Law on Amendments and Supplements to the Law on Veterans' Rights, a document with a seemingly innocuous name that in fact provided the legal basis for recognizing the political and economic equivalence of two Serbian WWII groups—the partisans and the Chetniks—each of whose descendants could now claim veteran status and benefits, regardless of whether they fought with or against the Axis forces in WWII.[148]

That the purpose of the law was a much broader political break with communist legacy and a complete realignment of the Serbian state identity vis-à-vis its history is evident in the justification provided by Kosta Nikolić, a historian at the Institute for Contemporary History of Serbia and a notable proponent of the Law: "If we are truly dedicated to transition, we must

---

146. Stojanović, *Ulje na vodi*, 135.

147. As a sign of how conflicted and unsettled this remembrance is, in 2014, the two former national holidays were returned to the state calendar, but not as official national holidays of remembrance.

148. Milan Radanović, "Zakonodavna politika Vlade Republike Srbije (2004–2011) u službi revizije prošlosti" [Legislative policies of the Serbian government (2004–2011) in service of historical revisionism], in *Antifašizam pred izazovima sadašnjice*, ed. Milivoj Bešlin and Petar Atanacković (Novi Sad: AKO, 2012), 81–114.

create a society discontinued from an unnatural movement that committed violence against history, and emerged right after WWII. . . . There is no argument in the world about what communism was: a totalitarian ideology in its objectives and methods very close to Nazism in Germany and fascism in Italy."[149] This law, therefore, marked the beginning of a full scale historical revisionism of WWII in Serbia, which began with equating the partisan and Chetnik movements as both antifascist patriotic movements (one from the left, and one from the right) and led to the establishment of the Chetnik movement as the most important resistance movement in WWII.

Serbia did not make these political decisions in an international vacuum.[150] In April 2006, the Serbian government passed the Rehabilitation Law, modeled after the 2006 Council of Europe Resolution, which condemned crimes of totalitarian communist regimes.[151] The Serbian law allows for "the rehabilitation of all individuals who were killed or denied rights in an extrajudicial manner for political or ideological reasons from April 6, 1941 (the beginning of the German occupation of Serbia) until the day the current law comes into effect."[152] The law thus sanctioned a sweeping rehabilitation of anyone declared an enemy of the state by the communist regime, without making a distinction between whether these individuals were truly innocent civilians (certainly the case in many instances) or whether they were in fact members of the Chetniks or other profascist militia, or collaborators with the Nazi regime (which, as historical data show, constituted the majority of those declared enemies of the state).[153] All that was necessary to file a claim for rehabilitation was evidence of prosecution by the communist regime—for what crime, the law did not ask.

---

149. Ilija Stamenović, "Kosta Nikolić, istoričar: 'Ni potomak Svetog Save ne bi ga majci dobio penziju'" [Even St. Sava's descedant would not qualify for pension], *Srpska reč* 358 (November 10, 2004), 10.

150. Ana Milosevic and Heleen Touquet, "Unintended Consequences: The EU Memory Framework and the Politics of Memory in Serbia and Croatia," *Southeast European and Black Sea Studies* 18, no. 3 (2018): 381–99.

151. Council of Europe Resolution 1481/2006 (January 25, 2006), "Need for International Condemnation of Crimes of Totalitarian Communist Regimes," Council of Europe website, http://assembly.coe.int/nw/xml/XRef/Xref-XML2HTML-en.asp?fileid=17403&lang=en. This resolution builds on Council of Europe Resolution 1096/1996 (June 27, 1996), "Measures to Dismantle the Heritage of Former Communist Totalitarian Systems," Council of Europe website, http://assembly.coe.int/nw/xml/XRef/Xref-XML2HTML-EN.asp?fileid=16507&lang=en.

152. Zakon o rehabilitaciji [Rehabilitation law], *Službeni glasnik Republike Srbije*, 33/2006, on file with author.

153. Milan Radanović, *Kazna i zločin: Snage kolaboracije u Srbiji* [Crime and punishment: Forces of collaboration in Serbia] (Belgrade: Rosa Luxemburg Stiftung, 2015).

Noting the expansive scope of the Council of Europe's anticommunist resolutions, proponents of the law, while happy it was passed, argued for an even broader law that would not deal with individual cases but would instead criminalize the entire communist regime, in order to, "*in line with Council of Europe recommendations*, collectively rehabilitate the entire category of victims . . . and condemn the communist regime."[154] Again using the language of international human rights, the law's proponents, many of them revisionist WWII historians themselves, argued that the Rehabilitation Law was, simply, "a tool of transitional justice." As another pro-rehabilitation historian said, "For the victims of the communist terror to be rehabilitated, it is necessary to first reject the communist past, *like the Germans rejected their Nazi past*."[155] That most victims of "communist terror" being rehabilitated actually collaborated with the Germans *during* their Nazi past is a connection almost too obvious to mention, yet it was completely absent from the rehabilitation discussion in Serbia.

The passing of the Law was couched in the language of national reconciliation. One Serbian government minister said that the law "affirmed the historical reconciliation among the Serbs around the world, as well as among the citizens of Serbia."[156] Similarly, the judge who passed the first rehabilitation verdict also took upon himself a bit of political analysis, praising the law as providing "a healthy foundation for Serbian national reconciliation without which there is no effective democratic statebuilding."[157] Another noted revisionist historian welcomed the passing of the law for "symbolically ending WWII."[158]

That the purpose of the law was political rehabilitation of Serbian collaborationist and Chetnik forces was evident in the early filing of a claim for the rehabilitation of Draža Mihailović, the leader of the Chetnik movement. Soon thereafter, another claim was filed for the rehabilitation of Milan Nedić, the head of the collaborationist government. In 2009, two former collaborationist gendarmes were rehabilitated in a district court in Šabac, in a decision that listed their 1941 conviction in a partisan court as being ideologically and politically motivated, thereby setting the legal precedent

---

154. Srđan Cvetković, "I loš zakon bolji je ni od kakvog" [Even bad law is better than no law], *Politika*, October 13, 2009, emphasis added.

155. Aleksandar A. Miljković, "Osuda komunisti" [Condemnation of a communist], *Hereticus* 2, no. 2 (2004): 37–46, here 43, emphasis added.

156. Milan Parivodić, "Istorijski značaj Zakona o rehabilitaciji" [Historical significance of the rehabiliation law], *Hereticus* 6, no. 2 (2008): 91.

157. Miroljub Mijušković, "Zločini pobednika" [The crimes of victors], *Politika*, August 6, 2007.

158. Marijana Milosavljević, "Ofanziva SPO-a: Čičini unuci" [SPO offensive: The duke's grandsons], *NIN*, 2817, December 23, 2004.

that the partisan movement itself was repressive and its convictions for collaboration illegitimate.[159] Thousands of further claims for rehabilitation followed, including those for senior officials in the Nedić government, the main apparatus of Serbian collaboration with the Nazi occupation.

Interestingly, the Law on Restitution and the Law on Rehabilitation came to a head, as the families of the newly rehabilitated collaborationists began to request restitution for property confiscated by the communist government after the war.[160] While the EU explicitly demanded that the Serbian government pass a rehabilitation law, it raised not a single objection to an implementation that de facto rewarded descendants of collaborators and quislings.[161]

The 2006 Rehabilitation Law's broad mandate proved too ambitious, and the subsequent 2011 amended law somewhat narrowed the scope of rehabilitation, no longer allowing claims for rehabilitation of "members of occupation or quisling forces and people convicted of or declared to have been war criminals by the Yugoslav authorities."[162] However, the amended law's Article 2 allows for cases of claims for rehabilitation to be brought even of known quislings and war criminals, as long as their innocence is proven during rehabilitation proceedings. This article, then, continued to be used as a vehicle to claim rehabilitation for some of the most well-known WWII war crimes perpetrators and collaborators, as the claimants relitigated what constituted a war crime during WWII seventy year later. On May 14, 2015, Mihailović, sentenced to death as an enemy of the Yugoslav state in 1946, was officially rehabilitated by the Serbian Higher Court, his earlier sentence nullified, and all his rights as a citizen posthumously restored.[163]

The Chetnik rehabilitation project has also been evident in education. Contemporary Serbian history textbooks describe Chetniks as "national patriots" and the Chetnik movement as an "anti-fascist movement from the right."[164] Chetniks are today favorably portrayed as "traditional" and as

---

159. Jelena Đureinović, "Istorija, sećanje i pravo: još jedan osvrt na problem sudske rehabilitacije u Srbiji" [History, memory and the law: Another look at the problem of judicial rehabiliation in Serbia], *Godišnjak za društvenu istoriju* 3 (2016): 89–111.

160. Jelena Popadić, "Rehabilitacija zavadila Ministarstvo finansija i Agenciju za restituciju" [Rehabilitation pits the Ministry of Finance against the Agency for Restitution], *Politika*, June 24, 2017.

161. European Parliament Resolution on the 2013 progress report on Serbia (2013/2880(RSP), January 7, 2014, European Parliament website, http://www.europarl.europa.eu/sides/getDoc.do?type=MOTION&reference=B7-2014-0006&language=EN.

162. Djureinovic, "Serbian Courts."

163. Vuk Z. Cvijić, "Rehabilitovan Draža Mihailović" [Draža Mihailović rehabilitated], *Blic*, May 14, 2015.

164. Helsinki Committee for Human Rights in Serbia, *Human Rights Reflect Institutional Impotence* (Belgrade: HCHRS, 2011), 27.

"protecting the interests of the Serbian people."[165] While maintaining the narrative that the partisans were bad and the Chetniks good, the textbooks vacillate between arguing that partisans were ineffective and that they were bloodthirsty war criminals and the only group that had committed war crimes.[166]

While rehabilitation of the Chetniks and delegitimization of partisans have become commonplace narratives, perhaps most alarming was the claim for rehabilitation of Nedić. On January 27, 2017 (incredibly, International Holocaust Remembrance Day), the court hearing the Nedić claim rejected the amicus brief from the Federation of Jewish Communities in Serbia to participate in the trial as interested observers.[167] The media portrayed the Jewish perspective as one of personal interest, but not of mainstream historical consensus. "Jewish community *claims* that Nedić actively participated in the Holocaust. They *object* to his confiscation of property and arrests," one article reported; the article's headline read, "Jewish Community against Nedić."[168] This move again separated the Jewish community from the rest of the Serbian body politic and placed on them the responsibility for fighting Holocaust revisionism, as if the Holocaust and Serbian complicity were only a Jewish problem.

The revisionism of Nedić's direct participation in the Holocaust of Serbia's Jews has become mainstream in elite intellectual circles. Bojan Dimitrijević, a historian at the Institute for Contemporary Serbian History, was the main expert witness at the Nedić rehabilitation trial, where he testified that Nedić's administration only registered the Jews and provided them with fake Serbian documents, while the Germans did all the rounding up and the actual killing. What Nedić was most interested in, argued Dimitrijević, was "fighting communism as that was the biggest evil confronting Serbia at the time." Dimitrijević joined the Nedić trial because he was "motivated to clear the Serbian name from the attempt to implicate Serbia in the Holocaust, which is

165. Jovana Mihajlović Trbovc and Tamara Pavasović Trošt, "Who Were the Anti-Fascists? Multiple Interpretations of WWII in Post-Yugoslav Textbooks," in *The Use and Abuse of Memory: Interpreting World War Two in Contemporary European Politics*, ed. Christian Karner and Bram Mertens (New Brunswick: Transaction Publishers, 2013), 173–92, here 177.

166. This argument is presented in the textbook by Kosta Nikolić, Nikola Žutić, Momčilo Pavlović, and Zorica Špadijer, *Istorija za IV razred gimnazije* [History for high school, fourth grade] (Belgrade: Zavod za udžbenike i nastavna sredstva, 2003), 142–43.

167. V. Crnjanski Spasojević, "Jevrejska zajednica će se žaliti Strazburu?" [The Jewish community will appeal to Strasbourg?], *Novosti*, February 4, 2017.

168. V. C. S. "Jevrejska opština protiv Nedića" [The Jewish community against Nedić], *Novosti*, October 20, 2016, emphasis added.

scandalous."[169] These are not fringe views. Dimitrijević is a public intellectual often called to comment on Serbian history as well as current affairs in the media. Contemporary Serbian textbooks also describe Nedić's collaboration favorably, explaining it as an attempt to "save the biological essence of the Serbian nation," using the exact same language Nedić himself used during the occupation.[170] The contemporary justification for Nedić's rehabilitation with the argument "Nedić saved the Serbs" just indicates which members of the political community count, and which are not considered necessary for saving. In July 2018, the Nedić rehabilitation claim, however, was ultimately denied by the Serbian High Court.[171]

In addition to the delegitimization of communism, another way to interpret this wave of rehabilitations is as a new historical framework for understanding Serbian behavior in more recent Yugoslav wars. Chetnik rehabilitation transforms unpleasant memories through historical distortion and fully exonerates the Serbian WWII political, military, and religious leadership that built and sustained the Serbian nationalist program that ultimately led to the wars of the 1990s. Rehabilitation of Chetniks, then, can be understood as rehabilitation of Serbia's role—and of the war crimes committed—in these wars.[172]

Delegitimation of Partisan Resistance

The new historical narrative that Chetniks and other WWII collaborators were also part of the antifascist movement and were themselves victims of fascism has since become hegemonic. Multiple state museum permanent exhibitions on WWII—most egregiously those in Niš, Kraljevo, Kragujevac, and Šabac—have now relativized and even inverted any memory of

169. "Istoričar: Nedićeva vlada nije progonila Jevreje" [Historian: Nedić's government did not persecute the Jews], *Tanjug*, May 23, 2016. Dimitrijević did face some political backlash for his historical revisionism. He was expelled from the Democratic Party in 2015 for his steadfast defense of Nedić.

170. Dubravka Stojanović, "Vinovnici i žrtve u srpskim udžbenicima istorije" [Perpetrators and victims in Serbian history textbooks], *Peščanik*, September 19, 2013, http://pescanik.net/2013/09/vinovnici-i-zrtve-u-srpskim-udzbenicima-istorije/.

171. This ruling, however, is subject to appeal. Belgrade High Court. "Odbijen zahtev za rehabilitaciju Milana Nedića" [Appeal for Nedić's rehabilitation denied], July 26, 2018, https://www.bg.vi.sud.rs/vest/1439/odbijen-zahtev-za-rehabilitaciju-milana-nedica.php.

172. Rehabilitation of Chetniks is so pervasive that it even interferes in the narratives put forward by Holocaust survivors themselves. A memoir of survival by Aleksandar Ajzinberg was published in 2006 with this editorial note on the book jacket: "This lively and convincing testimony simultaneously uncovers half a century of prejudices about Chetniks and partisans, which for decades passed for official historical truth." Aleksandar Ajzinberg, *Pisma Matveju* (Belgrade: Prosveta, 2006).

Yugoslav partisans as either resistors or victims of Nazism. They have now been replaced in discourse and in physical displays with Chetniks, the Serbian royal gendarmerie, and other anticommunist movements as the true victims of Nazi crimes.[173]

In Niš, the new exhibition opened in 2013 treats the Crveni krst concentration camp as a camp for mostly Chetniks, not partisans. When partisans are mentioned they are no longer discussed as members of the armed resistance that liberated Niš, but only as "members of the communist party." This discursive move is important because it portrays partisans as primarily communists and therefore political enemies not worthy of remembrance. It is because this mnemonic intervention has already been carried out that the contemporary Niš exhibit can also completely downplay the heroic escape on February 12, 1942, of more than a hundred communist prisoners from the camp—one of the largest mass escapes from any Nazi camp—and instead attribute the organization and execution of the escape to one Chetnik "duke" interned at the camp, whom the museum posthumously named "commander of the Yugoslav Royal Homeland Army."[174]

In Šabac, the National Museum's narration of WWII focuses on the October 1944 partisan execution of wartime collaborators in the city. It also portrays the Chetnik movement as antifascist, completely ignores the large German concentration camp outside the city (where 2,600 victims were killed), and does not mention at all the fate of the Kladovo transport Jews, whose WWII experience is central to the history of wartime Šabac.[175]

In Kragujevac, the Memorial Museum of 21 October has also completely revamped its permanent exhibit, which now fully equates the partisan and Chetnik movements, describing them in one of the exhibition displays as the "two liberating movements: the 'national' and the communist," while Draža Mihailović and Josip Broz Tito are depicted as leading two resistance movements, both fiercely fighting the Germans—a new historical interpretation that completely ignores the fact that Chetniks fought on the side of the Axis from 1941 until the end of the war.

Similarly, the Museum of Military History in Belgrade has been slowly replacing its permanent exhibition since the mid-2000s. The curators were given instructions by museum leadership to reorganize the exhibit without

---

173. Author interview with Olga Manojlović Pintar and Sanja Petrović Todosijević, Institute for Recent Serbian History, July 11, 2016, Belgrade.

174. Vladimir Veljković, "Lager Niš", *Peščanik*, February 12, 2016, http://pescanik.net/lager-nis/print/.

175. Udruženje ReEX, ed. *Politički ekstremizmi u muzejima Srbije* [Political extremism in Serbia's museums] (Belgrade: ReEX, 2018), 50.

ideology, which they interpreted to mean without the communist ideology that focused on the heroism of the partisan movement. The new, "non-ideological exhibition," however, has just replaced the communist narrative with the postcommunist one, which gives preeminence to the Chetnik movement in the history of Serbia's WWII resistance, presenting it as "composed of Yugoslav officers who refused to surrender, turning instead to guerilla warfare 'against the occupation troops,'" while the partisans only began their resistance once they had "support from [the] Comintern."[176]

The exhibition display also includes a large map of wartime Europe, which identifies with pin needles major concentration and extermination camps in Europe, including those in Serbia. However, the map includes no accompanying text and never mentions the Holocaust to contextualize the map of the camps. This major Serbian museum, then, narrates the story of WWII without the Holocaust, and the story of Serbia without the Jews. That the museum sits within the old fortress of Kalemegdan, right on top of the field where Belgrade Jews had to register in April 1941, makes this omission that much more jarring.

As part of this larger project of reconfiguring the role of communism in Serbia's past, in 2009, the Serbian government formed a State Commission for Secret Mass Graves, a body tasked with discovering all locations with remains of "those shot after the liberation in 1944," which meant: shot by communist Yugoslavia. This commission became very active and emerged as another memory actor in the changing landscape of postcommunist remembrance. Its work was followed by numerous sensationalist reports in the press, creating a picture of a vast web of secret mass graves left all over Serbia by the communists, with some reports claiming that there were as many as a hundred fifty thousand secret mass graves of communist terror.[177] The more mundane fact, however, was that, as was common practice in the immediate aftermath of WWII, those convicted of war crimes were unceremoniously buried in unmarked graves.[178] More to the point, a vast majority of the victims the commission identified were in fact Chetniks killed in battle with the partisans, as well as POWs who died in camps, and at least fourteen victims

176. Museum exhibition display. This argument that the partisans were not an indigenous resistance movement but were plants of the Soviet Communist Party has also become part of the broader postcommunist historical narrative.

177. For a thorough historical debunking of these claims, case by case, see Milan Radanović, "Kontroverze oko kvantifikovanja i strukturisanja stradalih u Srbiji nakon oslobođenja 1944–1945" [Controversies regarding quantifying and configuring the casualties in Serbia after liberation 1944–1945], in *Politička upotreba prošlosti: O istorijskom revizionizmu na postjugoslovenskom prostoru*, ed. Momir Samardžić, Milovoj Bešlin, and Srđan Milošević (Novi Sad: AKO, 2013), 157–220, here 159.

178. Bešlin, "Četnički pokret."

of the Holocaust who died at Auschwitz, Mauthausen, Bergen-Belsen, and Jasenovac.[179] By putting together a report that conflates enemies killed in action, POWs, and people actually murdered in the Holocaust under the label of "innocent victims of communist terror," the government commission contributed to yet another building block in the narrative delegitimation of the communist past that inverted the remembrance of victims and perpetrators in WWII.

The results of the commission's work were then presented to the public in a major 2014 exhibition at the Historical Museum of Serbia, *In the Name of the People—Political Repression in Serbia 1944–1953*. To give a sense of scale of how comprehensive the inclusion of former collaborationists was in this project, the list of "innocent victims of communist terror" included Milan Aćimović, the president of the Council of Commissioners in Serbia's first quisling government in 1941; Svetislav Stevanović, a racial thinker; and Krsta Cicvarić, a noted anti-Semitic journalist, famous for writing, "I am an anti-Semite because the Jews are a pest. They spoil everything: economy, morale, race. . . . The sacrifices of this war would not have been adequately justified if the Jews again became the masters of European economic life."[180]

The direct and crude replacement of victims of the Holocaust with victims of communism also affected the memorialization of Semlin. At the 2014 Historical Museum exhibition, next to the photograph of Buchenwald camp that was captioned as "living conditions in the communist camp at Goli otok," there was another photograph. This was a prewar image of the main tower of the Belgrade Fairgrounds, the building that housed the administration of the Judenlager Semlin during the occupation. The photograph caption read: "The parachute tower becomes a machine gun nest, period 1952–1953 . . . enemies of all colors were held at Sajmište."[181] This completely fabricated statement then gives the visitor an impression that Semlin camp was a communist prison for enemies of the state, with discipline maintained through machine gunfire, giving no hint that Semlin was the place where half of all Serbia's Jews were killed in a few spring months of 1942.

179. Radanović, "Kontroverze oko kvantifikovanja"; Milan Radanović, "Kako su dželati postali žrtve" [How the executioners became the victims], *E-novine*, April 18, 2014, http://www.e-novine.com/srbija/srbija-tema/102144-Kako-delati-postali-rtve.html.

180. Quoted in Milan Radanović, "Kuća terora u Muzeju revolucije" [House of terror at the Museum of the Revolution], *Peščanik*, June 2, 2014, http://pescanik.net/kuca-terora-u-muzeju-revolucije.

181. Radanović, "Kuća terora u Muzeju revolucije."

Unofficial Holocaust Remembrance and Official Backlash

While all this historical revisionism has been disturbing, there have also been encouraging projects of new Holocaust remembrance. In 2010, Radio B92 (since closed) organized a series of conferences on Semlin, which included site visits to various camps and killing sites in Serbia and the creation of a comprehensive website with a trove of documents—primary and secondary—on the Holocaust in Serbia.[182] Out of this project, a serious new Center for Holocaust Research and Education (CHRE) emerged in 2014. CHRE has organized teacher training, seminars, site visits, and the mapping of Holocaust sites in Serbia, and it has maintained a vibrant publication program and a content-rich website.[183] The Historical Museum of Serbia has maintained an active database of Holocaust victims in Serbia and Serbian historians have regularly published new findings on various aspects of the Holocaust. A major exhibition at the Historical Museum of Serbia, called *Final Destination Auschwitz* (2015), tells the story of transports to Auschwitz from Serbia and was a product of this research.

Scholarly conferences and academic projects with participation by some state institutions (Historical Archive of Belgrade and the National Library of Serbia have been most active) have produced useful pedagogical and research resources, such as a new website that included many resources for teachers preparing lesson plans on the Holocaust.[184] *Invisible Monuments*, a play about the Holocaust in Serbia, was performed at the major international theater festival in Belgrade in 2015 by a group of high school students who worked on this as a school project, apparently inspired by reading memoirs of Serbian Holocaust survivors.[185]

At the same time, each attempt to discuss the Holocaust in Serbia that mentions Serbian complicity or the responsibility of the Nedić administration is met by fierce resistance from establishment historians, and is widely criticized in the press.[186] For example, *October 1941*, a 2016 exhibition at the Historical Archive of Belgrade coorganized by the CHRE that discussed only

182. "A Visit to Staro Sajmište," accessed February 6, 2019, http://www.starosajmiste.info/en/#.

183. The project has already identified two previously unknown execution sites of Serbian Jews—at Rakovica and Bubanj potok, both on the outskirts of Belgrade. "Killing Sites: The First Stage of the Holocaust in Serbia and Croatia," accessed February 6, 2019, www.killingsites.org. CHRE has approached local authorities to propose collaborative memorialization, but has received almost no interest from municipalities. Author interview with Milovan Pisarri, Center for Holocaust Research and Education, March 8, 2018 (Skype).

184. The website is available at www.ester.rs.

185. For a moving letter of gratitude to the students from a Holocaust survivor, see Ivan Ivanji, "Moj krik iz dečjih usta" [My scream from the children's mouths], *Vreme*, 1274, June 4, 2015.

186. Author interview with Milovan Pisarri, May 31, 2017, Belgrade.

a very narrow segment of the Holocaust—the October 1941 shooting spree of Jewish men and the detentions at Semlin—met with massive opposition in the press. A leading public historian, Čedomir Antić, accused the exhibition organizers of "post-Nazification of Serbia" by implying that "the Serbian people had a role in the Holocaust, when the Holocaust was only carried out by the German occupiers." But Antić also added, "Belgrade had no anti-Semitic outbursts such as those in Sarajevo in 1941, for, *unlike its neighbors,* the vast majority of Serbs chose anti-Nazism."[187] Significant in this angry rebuttal to the Holocaust exhibit (the author called the exhibition "racist" against the Serbs) are the small jabs at Serbia's neighbors—Bosnia, but especially Croatia—with the implication that Serbia's behavior during WWII (and, presumably, since) has always been more honorable. To maintain this narrative of Serbia always being on the right side of history, evidence of WWII complicity or apathy must be delegitimized.

Holocaust remembrance in Serbia was never really about the Holocaust. During socialist Yugoslavia, Holocaust remembrance was placed within a larger narrative of Yugoslav antifascism and resistance—its multiculturalism and commitment to a pan-national socialist identity. To the extent that the Jewish victims of the Holocaust were ever memorialized, this remembrance was either a product of Jewish organizations and initiatives or, in state efforts, a nonethnic remembrance that subsumed Jewish suffering under the larger framework of antifascist struggle and triumph.

After the end of communism, however, Holocaust remembrance became a critical element in the total delegitimation of communism. This erasure of the communist past was built around an attack on Yugoslav multiculturalism, an attack which then provided legitimacy to the role of nationalism as the ordering principle in the postcommunist state and the increasing importance of maintaining an ethnically homogeneous body politic. A significant part of this project involved breaking the commitment to pan-national brotherhood and unity and thus making Yugoslavia retrospectively seem unnatural and artificial.

In other words, communism was delegitimized not because it was undemocratic but because it was antinationalistic. Holocaust remembrance in this context, then, necessitated decoupling Hitler and Nazism from domestic collaboration—rejecting the former while justifying the latter. This type of inverted Holocaust remembrance strengthens Serbian identity along nationalist lines and it strengthens Serbia's move away from communism—two

187. Čedomir Antić, "Postnacifikacija Srbije" [Post-Nazification of Serbia], *Politika*, June 24, 2016.

principal goals if Serbia is to maintain its ontological security—the security of its own identity and its biography—as a state.

In contemporary Serbia, Holocaust remembrance has served the needs of a retrospective totalitarianization of the Yugoslav communist past. That this process has gone unchallenged and, in fact, has received the full support of the European Union during Serbia's rocky road to Brussels speaks to the lack of differentiation of varieties of communism and communist experiences across the postcommunist European landscape.

This Serbian search for its better, more usable past excludes Jews from the Serbian body politic. In this imagined Serbia, there is no room for memory of the Jews who once lived as neighbors down the street.

CHAPTER 3

Croatia's Islands of Memory

As the 1930s approached, politics in Croatia were becoming tense, the Croatian political elite increasingly dissatisfied with their marginal status in the Serb-dominated Kingdom of Yugoslavia. Unlike in Serbia, where the commitment to the multinational kingdom was stronger—based largely on the fact that it was the Serbian dynasty that ruled—in Croatia the enthusiasm by both the elites and the mass public for a joint union was always tempered. In many ways, Yugoslavia felt forced on the Croatians; they resented Serbian hegemony and did not feel like the arrangement quite fit their national aspirations.[1]

It is in this period of growing national resentment that the Croatian Revolutionary Movement—the Ustasha—was formed in 1929 as a political movement organized around fascist, racist, extreme nationalist, and increasingly terrorist ideas.[2] Ustasha ideology was also expansionist—it called for the establishment of a Greater Croatia that would incorporate much of Slovenia and Bosnia-Herzegovina and end at the gates of Belgrade.[3]

1. Ivo Goldstein, "Croatia in the Kingdom of Serbs, Croats and Slovenes and the Independent State of Croatia (1918–1945)," *Croatian Studies Review* 5, no. 1 (2008): 64–74.

2. Jozo Tomasevich, *War and Revolution in Yugoslavia, 1941–1945: Occupation and Collaboration* (Stanford: Stanford University Press, 2001).

3. John K. Cox, "Ante Pavelić and the Ustasha State in Croatia," in *Balkan Strongmen: Dictators and Authoritarian Rulers of South Eastern Europe*, ed. Bernd J. Fischer (West Lafayette: Purdue University

The Ustasha at first did not have much political success in Croatia and their leaders were expelled from the Croatian Party of Rights in 1929. The most prominent Ustasha then left Croatia, most to Italy, some to Germany. They regrouped in exile in Europe and North and South America and began organizing terrorist actions against Yugoslav interests.[4] Their most successful terrorist act was the assassination of King Aleksandar of Yugoslavia on October 9, 1934, in Marseille, France. The Ustasha influence slowly grew in Croatian right-wing intellectual circles, where, by the start of WWII, they had gained a significant national presence in religion, politics, media, and academia, exemplified by the Catholic organizations Križari and Domagoj and the youth organization Hrvatski junak (Croatian hero).[5] More extensive organizing and increasing anti-Semitism followed the return of some of the exiled Ustasha to Croatia in 1937 and 1938.[6]

Throughout the 1930s, the Ustasha forged close ties with fascist Italy and Nazi Germany and copied much of their developing fascist ideological scaffolding, such as the "cult of the nation, the state, and the leader."[7] Already in 1933, the Ustasha published the movement's *Seventeen Principles*, the document which proclaimed the Croatian nation to be "unique" and declared those not Croat by "race" and "blood" to be excluded from all political life. Anti-Semitism (and racialized anti-Serbism) was central, not epiphenomenal, to Ustasha ideology.

Also central to their nationalist project was the creation of an independent Croatia and the destruction of the Yugoslav union, and Jews—seen as inherently pro-Yugoslav—were seen as an obstacle to this goal. In his 1936 manifesto *The Croatian Question*, Ustasha leader Ante Pavelić wrote,

> Jews greeted the foundation of the so-called Yugoslav state with great joy, because a Croatian nation-state would by no means suit them as well as did Yugoslavia—a state made up of various peoples. . . . On every occasion, Jews in Croatia showed in their own and noisy way their loyalty to Yugoslavism and to state unity.[8]

Press, 2007), 199–238; Sabrina P. Ramet, *The Three Yugoslavias: State-Building and Legitimation, 1918–2005* (Washington, DC: Woodrow Wilson Center Press, 2006); Mark Biondich, "'We Were Defending the State': Nationalism, Myth, and Memory in Twientieth-Century Croatia," in *Ideologies and National Identities: The Case of Twentieth-Century Southeastern Europe*, ed. John R. Lampe and Mark Mazower (Budapest: Central European University Press, 2004), 54–81.

4. Tomasevich, *War and Revolution*.

5. Ivo Goldstein and Slavko Goldstein, *The Holocaust in Croatia* (Pittsburgh: University of Pittsburgh Press, 2016), 95.

6. I. Goldstein and S. Goldstein, *Holocaust in Croatia*, 96.

7. I. Goldstein, "Croatia in the Kingdom of Serbs," 68.

8. Quoted in I. Goldstein and S. Goldstein, *Holocaust in Croatia*, 93–94.

The Ustasha vision for Croatia was also totalitarian, as they declared in 1941:

> In the Ustasha state . . . one must think like an Ustasha, speak like an Ustasha and most importantly—work like an Ustasha. In one word, life in its totality in the Independent state of Croatia [NDH] must be Ustasha.[9]

But its principal motivating ideology was that of racial purity and the elimination of non-Croats, primarily Serbs, Jews, and the Roma. Violence was a crucial element of this strategy and was announced as early as 1932, in an editorial in the inaugural issue of *Ustasha* magazine, signed by Pavelić: "The KNIFE, REVOLVER, MACHINE GUN AND TIME BOMB, these are the idols, these are the bells that will announce the dawning of the RESURRECTION OF THE INDEPENDENT STATE OF CROATIA."[10]

Unraveling of Jewish Life

As the national tensions within the kingdom heightened in the interwar period, so did the rise in anti-Semitism, which arrived to Croatia in a more systematic way in the late 1920s with the 1929 publication in Split—the first time the book appeared anywhere in Yugoslavia—of the *Protocols of the Elders of Zion*, and began to spread more broadly in the 1930s.[11] Mainstream publications, such as *Luč, Nova revija*, and the Catholic Church affiliated *Hrvatska prosvjeta* started to run standard anti-Semitic fare, accusing the Jews of oversized influence on the intellectual, political, and economic life of the country.[12]

In 1932, swastikas began to appear on the building of the Jewish Community office in Zagreb, as well as on some Jewish-owned businesses. Leaflets calling for the boycott of Jewish businesses, of "those obedient servants of every foreign government, [who] have been warned not to challenge us in this way again, because they will share the fate of their 'fellow-nationals' in

---

9. Quoted in I. Goldstein, "Croatia in the Kingdom of Serbs," 68.

10. Quoted in I. Goldstein and S. Goldstein, *Holocaust in Croatia*, 92 (emphasis in original).

11. In this period there were a total of four separate issues of the *Protocols* published in Serbo-Croatian. The first was the 1929 Split edition, followed by the 1934 and 1939 publications in Belgrade and the 1936 edition published in Berlin but in Croatian translation. Laslo Sekelj, "Antisemitizam u Jugoslaviji (1918.–1945.)" [Anti-Semitism in Yugoslavia (1918–1945)], *Revija za sociologiju* 11, no. 3–4 (1981): 179–89, here 185. Unfortunately, historical data about circulation numbers of these editions are not available. Author correspondence with Ivo Goldstein, professor of history, University of Zagreb, June 27, 2018.

12. I. Goldstein and S. Goldstein, *Holocaust in Croatia*, 14–16.

Germany" appeared on the streets of Zagreb.[13] Other anti-Semitic papers proliferated. In 1936, Jewish organizations in Zagreb were placed under police surveillance, and the Jewish community grew increasingly worried about the rumored introduction of anti-Jewish laws in Croatia. Starting en masse in 1938, many Jews began to convert to Catholicism, change their last names, or both, for fear of persecution.

The two anti-Jewish measures passed by the Yugoslav government in October 1940—and discussed in the previous chapter—hit Croatian Jews hard. Particularly distressing was the *numerus clausus* regarding enrollment at universities, as Croatian, Jews were overrepresented in higher education, especially in Zagreb—they made up 16 percent of the student population in the fields of medicine and law. Following the ban on handling food items, many Jewish-owned grocery shops, bakeries, and food import businesses closed and were taken over by the government or handed out to other, Gentile merchants.

By the spring of 1941, the Jewish community was increasingly realizing that life as they knew it would end. The Zagreb-based magazine *Židov*, the main voice of Yugoslav Jewry, stopped publication in March 1941, and the last public activity Croatian Jews openly participated in was the football match between the Jewish club Makabi and Ličanin from Zagreb. The Makabis won 1:0 in the last minute of the match.[14]

A week later, on April 6, 1941, the Axis powers occupied Yugoslavia.

Establishment of the Independent State of Croatia

Germany immediately carved up the country into occupied zones. On April 10, Vladko Maček, the leader of the Croatian Peasant Party, the majority party in the Croatian parliament, refused to head the new government under conditions of occupation. Instead, Slavko Kvaternik, the senior Ustasha not in exile, took control of the police in Zagreb and declared the establishment of the Independent State of Croatia (NDH). The Ustasha "poglavnik" (Führer) Ante Pavelić promptly returned to Croatia from Italy and declared the formation of the new government on April 16.

The Ustasha numbers swelled—from a small group of extremists before the war, they steadily grew to a force of more than two hundred sixty thousand troops, including seventy thousand "Domobran" (Home Guard) militia

13. Quoted in I. Goldstein and S. Goldstein, *Holocaust in Croatia*, 19.

14. I. Goldstein and S. Goldstein, *Holocaust in Croatia*, 85.

and twenty-two thousand "Blackshirts."[15] The participation in the Ustasha apparatus of force, therefore, was extensive. This is important because most of the violence that was to come in Croatia during the war was perpetrated by the Ustasha, not by the Germans, and with massive participation of local state officials.

As soon as the NDH was established, the new government instituted a series of anti-Semitic laws. In a departure from German laws, the Ustasha expanded the racial categories to include not only Jews and Roma, but also Serbs, thus making them immediately vulnerable to persecution. On April 30, the Legal Decree on Racial Origins (which defined Jews and Roma—but not Serbs—as non-Aryan) and the Legal Decree on the Protection of Aryan Blood and the Honor of the Croatian People (which prohibited marriage between Aryans and non-Aryans) were passed, defining the status of Jews, Roma, and Serbs in the new Croatia.[16] In a somewhat unusual arrangement, the Ustasha allowed some six hundred Jews—about 170 doctors and others who in some way were seen as contributing to the Croatian cause, as well as their families—to be designated "honorary Aryans" and excluded from racial laws.[17] This designation protected these Jews from deportations, but only for a while.

Arrests of Jews began immediately upon the establishment of the NDH in April 1941. Destruction and plunder of Jewish property followed, mostly by local Croatian Ustasha and sympathetic ethnic Germans, the *Volksdeutsche*. It was the Volksdeutsche youth who on April 14 set fire to the old Osijek synagogue and took over Jewish shops in town.[18] On May 22, 1941—months before the measure was introduced in the Third Reich in September—the Ustasha passed a decree ordering all Jews to wear Jewish insignia.[19] Soon thereafter, all Jews were dismissed from employment.

One of those Jews was the fourteen-year-old Lea Deutsch—a popular Croatian child actress known as the Croatian Shirley Temple, who started performing at the Croatian National Theater at the age of five and achieved international fame. After May 1941, she was banned from performing at the theater and was soon dismissed from her school. One of her theater contemporaries remembered, "She used to sit motionless on a bench across from the

15. Cox, "Ante Pavelić," 222.

16. Milovan Pisarri, "Holokaust u Jugoslaviji" [Holocaust in Yugoslavia], *YU Historija*, 2017, http://www.yuhistorija.com/serbian/drugi_sr_txt01c5.html.

17. Nevenko Bartulin, *Honorary Aryans: National-Racial Identity and Protected Jews in the Independent State of Croatia* (New York: Palgrave Macmillan, 2013).

18. I. Goldstein and S. Goldstein, *Holocaust in Croatia*, 104–5.

19. I. Goldstein and S. Goldstein, *Holocaust in Croatia*, 121.

theater in a little herringbone pattern coat with a yellow Star of David on her sleeves, staring for hours at the building where once she was a star, and now she couldn't even enter."[20]

The Holocaust and the Genocide

The Ustasha's anti-Semitism was matched only by their racialization of the Serbs. The Ustasha newspaper *Hrvatska gruda* wrote in 1941, "The Serbs are a people who always bring evil and misfortune—the entire life of the Serb people is filled with corruption and usury. . . . The Serbs left us a horrible, disgusting and unwanted heritage, which we must resolutely end."[21] And to this end they swiftly turned. In their attempt to decimate the large Serbian minority—Serbs, at two million, were one third of the population of prewar Croatia—the Ustasha deported between one hundred fifty thousand and two hundred thousand Serbs from the country and forcefully converted two hundred thousand of those who stayed to Catholicism.[22] Three hundred thousand Serbs—17 percent of the prewar Serbian population in Croatia—were killed.

The genocidal policies and extermination practices against the Serbs, the Jews, and the Roma were sometimes similar, sometimes different; the victims were sometimes killed together and sometimes they followed different tragic paths.[23] What is important, however, is that the ideology of violence that was at the core of the NDH regime was genocidal toward all three groups. The clear intent was to transform Croatia into a homogeneous ethnic nation-state.[24] The genocide against the Serbs followed its own historical trajectory and was complicated by the ensuing ethnic civil war between various Croatian and Serb militias—a separate war under the larger dynamics of WWII. The Holocaust of Croatia's Jews and Roma followed more directly

---

20. Nina Ožegović, "Film o tragičnom usudu dječje zvijezde" [Film about the tragic fate of a child star], *Nacional* 565, September 11, 2006.

21. Quoted in Ivo Goldstein, "The Independent State of Croatia in 1941: On the Road to Catastrophe," *Totalitarian Movements and Political Religions* 7, no. 4 (2006): 417–27, here 418.

22. Cox, "Ante Pavelić," 224. Full demographic breakdown of the NDH was three and a half million Croats, two million Serbs, eight hundred thousand Muslims, one hundred fifty thousand ethnic Germans, between twenty-five thousand and forty thousand Roma, and between thirty-five thousand and forty thousand Jews. Pisarri, "Holokaust u Jugoslaviji."

23. For an attempt to analytically distinguish between the Holocaust of Croatian Jews and the genocide of Croatian Serbs and Roma during the NDH, see Tomislav Dulić, "Mass Killing in the Independent State of Croatia, 1941–1945: A Case for Comparative Research," *Journal of Genocide Research* 8, no. 3 (2006): 255–81.

24. Alexander Korb, "Understanding Ustaša Violence," *Journal of Genocide Research* 12, no. 1–2 (2010): 1–18.

Nazi principles and methodologies and was carried out by Ustasha forces, with some German support. In fact, while the Germans obviously approved of Ustasha extermination of the Jews and Roma, they on multiple occasions reprimanded the NDH for its massive violence against the Serbs, a policy they did not see as integral to the Reich's aims and one that often backfired, as it recruited more Serbs to partisan resistance.[25]

Croatian Catholicism was an integral part of Ustasha ideology, which is why the policy of forced conversion to Catholicism and the targeted killing of Serbian Orthodox priests were both widespread during the genocide. As part of this policy, local Catholic priests frequently participated in both the forced conversion and the larger implementation of Ustasha principles.[26] Anti-Semitism within the Catholic Church was also notable. For example, the Catholic Bishop of Sarajevo wrote, "The movement of liberation of the world from the Jews is a movement for the renewal of human dignity. Omniscient and omnipotent God stands behind this movement."[27]

Camps and Deportations

Soon after the start of the war in April 1941, the Ustasha established an expansive system of twenty-six concentration and death camps. The very first concentration camp was Danica in the town of Koprivnica, to which in May 1941 the Ustasha deported 165 young Jewish men from Zagreb (aged seventeen to twenty-five), members of the Jewish sports club Makabi. All but three were killed.[28]

Other camps were established in quick succession, including Jasenovac, Stara Gradiška, Kerestinec, Jadovno, Đakovo, Loborgrad, and Slana on the island of Pag.[29] Among the unimaginable horrors of this camp system was a uniquely monstrous camp at Sisak, which housed more than six thousand Serbian, Jewish, and Romani children, including infants, forcibly removed from their parents; 1,600 of these children were left to die from starvation,

25. Korb, "Understanding Ustaša Violence."

26. Pisarri, "Holokaust u Jugoslaviji."

27. Quoted in Michael Phayer, *The Catholic Church and the Holocaust, 1930–1965* (Bloomington: Indiana University Press, 2000), 35.

28. Narcisa Lengel-Krizman and Mihael Sobolevski, "Hapšenje 165 židovskih omladinaca u Zagrebu u svibnju 1941. godine" [The arrest of 165 Jewish youth in Zagreb in May 1941], *Novi omanut* 5759, December 1998.

29. As a ten-year-old, my father, Gojko Subotić, was interned with his mother, first in Stara Gradiška, then in a smaller camp at Caprag during the summer of 1941. The camp was closed in September 1941 when all Serbian prisoners were loaded onto trains and deported to Serbia.

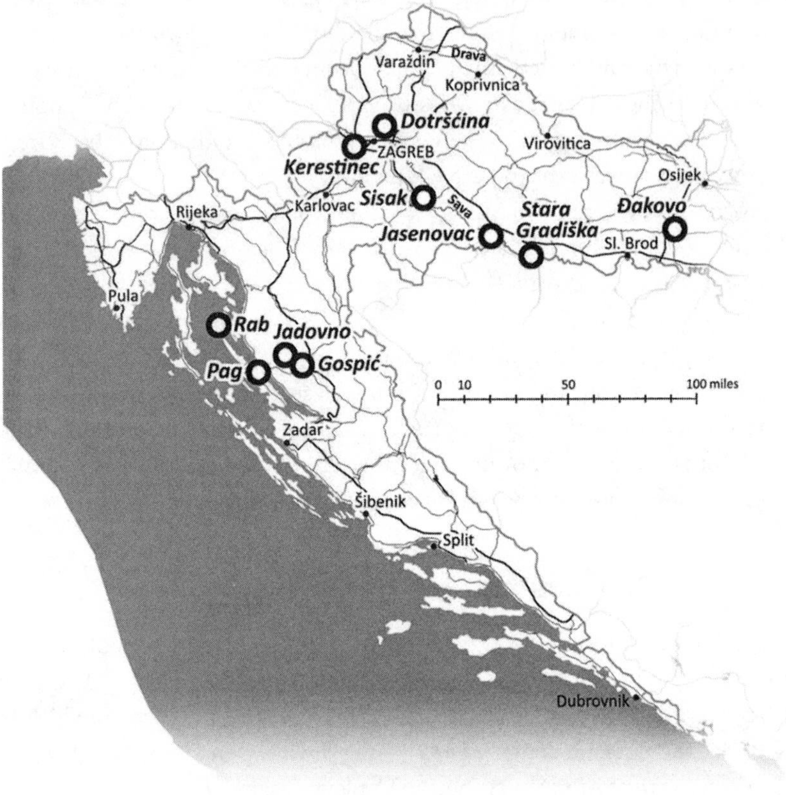

Map 2. Camps and execution sites in Croatia (map by Aleksandar Stanojlović)

disease, exposure, and neglect.[30] This was the only concentration camp for unaccompanied children anywhere in Europe, in the entire span of WWII.[31]

By far the largest of these camps was Jasenovac, less than two hours east of Zagreb. Jasenovac itself was a complex of five camps, established in August 1941, on the bank of the river Sava, the same river that flows south to reach Belgrade's Semlin camp. After decades of controversies about the

30. Only very recent research has uncovered that Diana Budisavljević, a Croatian humanitarian, managed to save 7,500 children from various Ustasha camps, including Sisak. Nataša Mataušić, "Diana Budisavljević: The Silent Truth," in *Revolutionary Totalitarianism, Pragmatic Socialism, Transition: Tito's Yugoslavia, Stories Untold*, ed. Gorana Ognjenovic and Jasna Jozelic (Basingstoke: Palgrave Macmillan, 2016), 49–97.

31. Nataša Mataušić, *Žene u logorima Nezavisne Države Hrvatske* [Women in the Independent State of Croatia's camps] (Zagreb: Savez antifašističkih boraca i antifašista Republike Hrvatske, 2013).

exact number of victims of Jasenovac, the scholarly consensus today sits at around eighty-five thousand killed, fifty thousand of whom were Serbs, thirteen thousand Jews, sixteen thousand Roma (almost the entire Croatian Roma population), and the remainder communists and enemies or perceived enemies of the Ustasha regime.[32]

Jasenovac was truly a dreadful place, its gruesome and low-tech technology of extermination (starvation, burning alive, decapitations) so pervasive and well documented that consequent Serbian attempts to make it appear even more gruesome (described in detail in the previous chapter) were simply unnecessary. Jasenovac was hell.

As the new camps were established, they began to be populated by Jewish refugees who had fled Germany and other occupied territories and found themselves in Croatia at the start of the war. Throughout the summer of 1941, groups of Jews from all over Croatia and Bosnia-Herzegovina were deported to camps. Women with children were often removed from men and sent to separate camps. Sexual violence was rampant.[33]

In July, many arrested Jews were sent to Gospić, and from there to death camps in Jadovno and Slana, on the island of Pag. Jadovno was in fact the very first death camp in all of WWII Europe.[34] In its three months of operation (May–August 1941), before it was closed and replaced with a much larger Jasenovac complex, twenty-four thousand people—mostly Serbs, but also approximately 2,500 Jews—were killed by being thrown, often alive, into the deep ravines of Velebit Mountain.[35] Killing continued across

32. The exact number of those killed in Jasenovac has been an issue of intense debate in both Serbian and Croatian historiography. Other than the tendentiously small number (ten thousand) offered by Croatian nationalists or the unreasonably high number (six hundred thousand) insisted on by Serbian nationalists, most scholarly consensus puts the number of dead between eighty-three thousand and a hundred thirty-five thousand. The numbers I listed above are the confirmed identified victims by the Jasenovac Memorial Site, which is a database in progress ("List of Individual Victims of Jasenovac Concentration Camp," Jasenovac Memorial Site, last updated March 2013, http://www.jusp-jasenovac.hr/Default.aspx?sid=6711). Since this number includes only identified victims, the actual death toll is likely higher. The US Holocaust Memorial Museum estimates the total number of victims at Jasenovac at 77,000–97,000, of whom 8,000–20,000 were Jews, 45,000–52,000 Serbs, and 8,000–15,000 Roma ("Holocaust Era in Croatia: Jasenovac 1941–1945," US Holocaust Memorial Museum website, accessed February 10, 2019, https://www.ushmm.org/exhibition/jasenovac). Among the many problems with finding an accurate victim count is that whole families and communities were deported, leaving no survivors. Another major problem is that the Ustasha burned official records from the camp in 1943 and again upon the evacuation and partisan takeover of Jasenovac in 1945.

33. Mataušić, *Žene u logorima*.

34. The first Nazi extermination camp at Chełmno in occupied Poland did not begin operations until December 1941.

35. It is incredibly difficult to determine the exact number of those killed at individual camps in the NDH camp network as many prisoners were moved or killed elsewhere. Jadovno poses a

Croatia. Throughout the war, more than eighteen thousand communists, Serbs, Jews, and other "enemies" were arrested, killed, and dumped in mass graves in Zagreb's meandering Dotršćina nature preserve, on the outskirts of town.

On October 10, 1941, the Legal Decree on the Nationalization of the Property of Jews and Jewish Companies was declared, confiscating all Jewish property. That same month, the demolition of the Zagreb Synagogue began—it was fully destroyed by April 1942. In December 1941, three thousand women and children, most of whom were Jewish, were taken to Đakovo concentration camp—650 died there, the rest were transported to Jasenovac and killed.[36]

By 1942, only around seven thousand Jews remained in Croatia. In February 1942, Andrija Artuković, the Ustasha minister of interior affairs, addressed the Croatian parliament and declared, to much cheering from assemblymen,

> The Independent State of Croatia through its decisive action has solved the so-called Jewish question. . . . This necessary cleansing procedure finds its justification not only from a moral, religious and social point of view, but also from the national-political point of view: it is international Jewry associated with international communism and Freemasonry, that sought and still seeks to destroy the Croatian people."[37]

This declaration of *Judenfrei* Croatia, however, was premature, to the great annoyance of Germany, which dispatched from Berlin Hauptsturmführer Franz Abromeit to inspect the situation. The Ustasha were under pressure to finish the job, and so they organized the mass detention of the remaining five thousand or so Jews from Zagreb, Osijek, Sarajevo, and elsewhere under NDH control. In April 1942, the Jews of Osijek were ordered to build their own ghetto, to which they were moved in June and July. From this ghetto, two hundred Jews were deported to Jasenovac on August 18, and 2,800 directly to Auschwitz on August 15, 1942.[38] Jews detained in Zagreb—in a school—were first taken to the main Zagreb train station and from there to Auschwitz. For a few brief hours, their friends and "Aryan" relatives were allowed next to

particularly vexing problem because it is in an extremely unreachable and dangerous location where exhumations are almost impossible to carry out because of the highly treacherous mountainous terrain. The estimates for Jadovno victims range between twenty thousand and forty thousand.

36. I. Goldstein and S. Goldstein, *Holocaust in Croatia*, 278.

37. "'U NDH je riješeno židovsko pitanje', rekao je Artuković, iz saborskih klupa čuli su se povici odobravanja: 'Tako je!'" ['The NDH solved the Jewish question,' Artuković announced, to approving cheers by assemblymen], *Jutarnji list*, August 21, 2012.

38. Zlata Živaković-Kerže, "Od židovskog naselja u Tenji do sabirnog logora" [From a Jewish settlement in Tenja to a concentration camp], *Scrinia Slavonica* 6 (2006): 497–514, here 509.

the boxcar to say their final, anguished goodbyes. None of those on the two Zagreb transports—August 13 and 24, 1942—survived.[39]

This left two thousand Jews in Croatia, who had so far been spared due to political connections, mixed marriages, or sheer luck. On May 5, 1943, Reichsführer Heinrich Himmler himself visited Zagreb for talks with Pavelić, likely imprinting the urgency of the Final Solution. Pavelić made a deal according to which NDH would compensate Germany with 30 Reichsmarks for every Jew the Nazis took out of Croatia.[40] Two days after Himmler's visit, the last roundup of Zagreb Jews began, this time organized by the Gestapo. After a week, 1,700 Jews from Zagreb and three hundred from neighboring towns were deported to Auschwitz.[41] The child actress Lea Deutsch, whose family and friends had desperately tried to hide her (including converting her to Catholicism), was on this transport. She never made it to Auschwitz. She died on the train at the age of sixteen.[42]

Until Italian capitulation on September 8, 1943, those Croatian Jews who lived in Dalmatia and Istria—regions under Italian control—had a degree of protection. Italy also detained some three thousand Jews in a camp on the island of Rab. Most of these Jewish prisoners (around 2,500) were rescued in a daring action by the Yugoslav partisans in August 1943, and many of them then joined the partisan ranks, where for a while they even had their own "Jewish battalion." Of the five hundred who did not go with the partisans, around three hundred survived by hiding in various Italian controlled regions, and the remaining two hundred who stayed in the camp because they were too weak and infirm were sent to Auschwitz-Birkenau when the Germans retook the camp. Almost all of them were killed.[43]

After Italian capitulation, Germany annexed Croatia's provinces of Pula and Rijeka in the northern region of Istria. On January 25, 1944, the German occupation administration demolished the Rijeka Synagogue. In April 1944, the Jews of the Međimurje region under Hungarian control were rounded up in the wave of deportations of Hungarian Jews and sent to Auschwitz. By then, the only Jews who survived in Croatia were either in territories still under Italian control or in hiding, or they had joined the partisans. Between

39. I. Goldstein and S. Goldstein, *Holocaust in Croatia*, 368.

40. Cox, "Ante Pavelić", 226.

41. I. Goldstein and S. Goldstein, *Holocaust in Croatia*, 395–96.

42. I. Goldstein and S. Goldstein, *Holocaust in Croatia*, 397. A powerful novel based on the life of Lea Deutsch is by Miljenko Jergović, *Ruta Tannenbaum* (Evanston: Northwestern University Press, 2011).

43. Emil Kerenji, "'Your Salvation is the Struggle Against Fascism': Yugoslav Communists and the Rescue of Jews, 1941–1945," *Contemporary European History* 25, no. 1 (2016): 57–74, here 66.

1941 and 1945, a total of around twenty thousand Jews were killed in Croatia or deported to Nazi concentration camps in Auschwitz, Bergen-Belsen, and elsewhere, and killed there. Another twelve thousand Jews were killed in or deported from parts of Bosnia-Herzegovina that were under NDH control.[44] Close to 80 percent of Croatia's Jewry was exterminated.

One of the very first Jews to be arrested in Croatia on April 13, 1941, just a few days after the establishment of NDH, was Ivo Goldstein, who ran a bookstore in the town of Karlovac, a popular gathering spot of left-leaning intellectuals. From Karlovac he was taken to Danica camp, where his family could briefly visit him, and from there to the death pits at Jadovno, where he was killed. In 2005, sixty-four years after his father's murder, Slavko Goldstein received a call from the National University Library in Zagreb. While arranging the personal papers of an Ustasha official, a local archivist stumbled upon a faded, unfinished letter Ivo Goldstein wrote from prison to his then thirteen-year-old son, which in part read:

> Dear Slavko!
>
> I heard from mother that you were crying last Saturday because I am in prison. The news saddened me more than it pleased me. I know that you were not crying from shame that your father is behind bars! You should know that there are times when it is a greater honor to be in prison than outside it. Perhaps you were crying because your father is suffering an injustice. It is better to bear an injustice than to commit one. . . . You are now thirteen years old, and I've always wanted you to become a hero. When you were younger, I showed you how one can be brave in a physical sense . . . , but later I tried to show you another kind of heroism. As happy as your athletic and academic successes make me, I would like you to be both in that other sense, and primarily in that other sense, a hero.[45]

---

44. This is the estimate of the US Holocaust Memorial Museum ("Holocaust Era in Croatia: Jasenovac 1941–1945"). Other scholars have provided slightly different estimates. Complicating the victims count in Croatia is the problem of mass Jewish conversions to Catholicism on the eve of and during the Holocaust, which also often included changing and Croatianizing last names. This made it extremely difficult after the war to reconstruct who the Jews were prior to conversions and what their ultimate fate was. This problem, coupled with the systematic Ustasha destruction of records, means that it is unlikely that there will ever be a definitive count of Croatian victims of the Holocaust.

45. Slavko Goldstein, *1941: The Year That Keeps Returning* (New York: New York Review of Books, 2013), 59–61. Slavko Goldstein survived the Holocaust by joining the partisans—together with his mother and a ten-year-old younger brother—and after the war became a well-known Croatian journalist, a historian of the Holocaust, and, for a number of years, head of the Zagreb Jewish Community. He died in 2017. His son Ivo is a leading Croatian historian and founding president of the Bet

"They Are No More Because They Wanted to Be": Communist Remembrance in Croatia

Only three thousand Croatian Jews survived the war. After liberation in 1945, the few survivors gathered in the Zagreb Jewish Community and began sending hundreds of letters all over Yugoslavia and abroad in search of any news about their friends and families. Almost always, the letters returned with confirmation of death, deportation, or disappearance. The community worked mostly on property restitution, financial support to camp returnees, and family placement for Jewish children orphaned in the war.[46]

As was the case in Serbia discussed in the previous chapter, any remembrance of the Holocaust in Croatia by the Yugoslav state was subsumed by the much larger, totalizing narrative of WWII and Yugoslav heroism in defeat of fascism. These trends largely followed the same pattern in both Yugoslav republics, but significant for Croatia was the insistence by the Yugoslav government of tying the criminal NDH regime with the larger criminality of Nazi ideology, therefore immediately delegitimizing any attempts at NDH or Ustasha revival.

The 1961 Eichmann trial in Jerusalem provided this opportunity quite directly. The Yugoslav media followed the trial very closely and reported in detail on trial findings. Not surprisingly, the most attention was paid to crimes committed in Yugoslavia or against Yugoslav citizens in Nazi camps abroad. Specifically, the Yugoslav press reported on the ties between Eichmann, the genocidal project of the Final Solution, and top NDH leadership such as Andrija Artuković, the NDH minister of interior affairs in charge of mass deportations and exterminations, who had fled to the United States at the end of the war and whom Yugoslavia had desperately tried to capture and prosecute.[47] In addition to seeking extradition, the Yugoslav government in this period often resorted to summary justice—many Ustasha officials were hunted down and killed in exile, the most notorious being Vjekoslav Maks Luburić, the former commander of Jasenovac, who was assassinated in 1969 in Spain.

To the extent that there was any Holocaust-specific remembrance to speak of in the early postwar years, it mostly was reduced to projects organized by

---

Israel Jewish Community in Zagreb. The comprehensive volume *The Holocaust in Croatia*, written together by father and son, remains the most authoritative source on this topic to date.

46. I. Goldstein and S. Goldstein, *Holocaust in Croatia*.

47. Artuković was finally extradited to Yugoslavia in 1986. He was tried and found guilty of crimes against humanity in the NDH, and was sentenced to death. However, the sentence was commuted due to his advanced age and deteriorating health and he died in custody in 1988.

the Jewish community itself, such as the series of five Holocaust memorials erected across Yugoslavia in 1952 (discussed in the previous chapter).

In line with the commemorative code of the time, the inscription at the 1952 memorial unveiled in Zagreb read, "To Jewish fighters fallen in the struggle for liberation of the peoples of Yugoslavia and to Jews victims of Fascism."[48] The monument featured a large statue of Moses holding the Ten Commandments tablets. The Zagreb memorial also contained the Hebrew inscription, which differed in a subtle way from the inscription in Serbo-Croatian, as it mentioned fighters and victims in Croatia (not in Yugoslavia, as the Serbo-Croatian version read).

As Kerenji notes, this nuance is likely the result of the reluctance of Yugoslav authorities to showcase the larger crimes against "victims of fascism in Croatia" as that would include the Holocaust but also the larger genocide against the Serbs—a result of Croatian (not German) policies against the Serbs that communist Yugoslavia did much to silence.[49] A few days after the unveiling of the Zagreb monument, the memorial was vandalized. The words *Thou shalt not* were erased from one of the tablet commandments, so the only word remaining was *kill*.[50]

Representing Yugoslavia at Auschwitz

A vivid example of the many paradoxes of Holocaust remembrance during communist Yugoslavia, and especially the way in which Holocaust remembrance was used to represent the contemporary Yugoslav state internationally, is the Yugoslav national exhibition at the Auschwitz Memorial Museum in Oświęcim, Poland. Auschwitz-Birkenau is an important site for Yugoslav Holocaust remembrance as twenty thousand victims from Yugoslavia and more than seven thousand from Croatia, were interned in the death camp. The Yugoslav national exhibition at Auschwitz was opened on September 29, 1963, on the initiative of the Yugoslav Veterans Association of the National Liberation War. In preparing to mount the exhibit, members of the Yugoslav Veterans Association insisted that it be of "international, not national character."[51] Yugoslavia's decision to participate in an international memorial

48. Emil Kerenji, "Jewish Citizens of Socialist Yugoslavia: Politics of Jewish Identity in a Socialist State, 1944–1974" (PhD diss., University of Michigan, 2008), 211.

49. Kerenji, "Jewish Citizens of Socialist Yugoslavia," 212.

50. Kerenji, "Jewish Citizens of Socialist Yugoslavia," 220.

51. Minutes from the meeting of the Central Committee of the Association of Veterans with General Secretary of the International Committee Auschwitz, February 23, 1960, Archives of Yugoslavia, 297/4/36.

was therefore driven by the desire to be part of the larger European antifascist resistance narrative and secure its place as an important actor in the new global order after WWII.[52]

The Yugoslav exhibition included mostly photographs and documents of the Yugoslav struggle against fascism and some original artwork, including sculptures by Vida Jocić, herself an Auschwitz survivor. All other artifacts represented political prisoners and partisans at Auschwitz, many portraying the resistance of Yugoslav fighters interned in the camp, as well as many photographs depicting the torture and suffering of Yugoslav inmates.[53]

This ideological character of the Auschwitz memorial display is also evident from media coverage announcing the opening of the pavilion in 1963:

> The opening of the Yugoslav exhibit will honor the memory of *all Yugoslavs* who suffered in this notorious camp, whose resistance despite horrific torture and suffering was very highly respected by all inmates from various countries.[54]

Like other news reports—and like the Yugoslav exhibit itself—this description presents an image of Auschwitz without the Jews.

The first comprehensive book on Yugoslavs at Auschwitz, published as late as 1989, still memorialized Auschwitz victims primarily through their antifascist struggle:

> Yugoslav inmates were not passive in any camp, and the same was the case in Auschwitz. Under conditions of the worst possible terror they kept their unity, morale, and the ideational purity of the national liberation struggle in their country, of which they were an inseparable part. In the joint resistance front in camp Auschwitz, Yugoslavs left the most beautiful memories of true friendship, sustained character, and courageous spirit.[55]

---

52. On this point also see Heike Karge, "Sajmište, Jasenovac, and the Social Frames of Remembering and Forgetting," *Filozofija i društvo* 23, no. 4 (2012): 106–18. As part of this effort, Yugoslavia even offered the Auschwitz Memorial Committee free Yugoslav granite stone to be used in the building of the new memorial at the campsite. Letter from Odette Elina, International Committee Auschwitz, to Đorđe Lebović, member of the Auschwitz Committee of the Association of Veterans of Yugoslavia. May 29, 1962, Archives of Yugoslavia, 237/56/813–24.

53. List and images of contents of the 1963 exhibition on file with author, courtesy of staff of the Institute for Recent History of Serbia. Also, author interview with Kaja Širok, director of the Slovenian Museum of Contemporary History, June 24, 2016, Ljubljana.

54. *Politika*, September 29, 1963, emphasis added.

55. Tomislav Žugić and Miodrag Milić, *Jugosloveni u Koncentracionom logoru Aušvic 1941–1945* [Yugoslav citizens in the concentration camp Auschwitz 1941–1945] (Beograd: Institut za savremenu istoriju, 1989), 103.

In another section of this monograph, the authors describe Yugoslav inmates' political activity in Auschwitz:

> Yugoslav prisoners did not ignore the discussion of various theoretical issues of Marxism-Leninism. They discussed developing a communist morale and proletarian humanity, and this also included criticism and self-criticism.[56]
>
> In the international committee Yugoslavs were very respected because of their fight, political determination and revolutionary traditions they carried away from freedom and continue to nurture in the darkest of days.[57]

The discussion of the communists' resistance is so detailed that there is even a description of a scene in which a newly transported group of Yugoslav women partisans supposedly refused to let SS camp guards shave their heads on arrival in Auschwitz in defiance of camp practice and explicit orders:

> The news about the resistance of Yugoslav women partisans travelled fast throughout the camp. Their courage was admired by prisoners of all countries.[58]

The absurdity, even grotesqueness of describing the life of Auschwitz prisoners as one spent discussing Marxism-Leninism and defying orders aside, what is striking in these depictions is that they are, in fact, descriptions not of Auschwitz prisoners, but of the Yugoslav state itself. The tropes of resistance, status, defiance, and international reputation are the exact same tropes on which socialist Yugoslavia built its own sense of identity and the image it wanted to project to the world. Holocaust remembrance, then, served Yugoslavia's international goals. The historical narrative of the actual Holocaust was largely irrelevant to this project.

The Proliferation of Communist Memorials

In the immediate aftermath of the war, on July 6, 1945, the Yugoslav government issued a decree that all graveyards and memorials to the occupiers and their collaborators (Ustasha, Chetniks, etc.) be destroyed.[59] This meant that the only type of memorialization permitted was that of communist heroism,

---

56. Žugić and Milić, *Jugosloveni u Koncentracionom logoru Aušvic 1941–1945*, 108.
57. Žugić and Milić, *Jugosloveni u Koncentracionom logoru Aušvic 1941–1945*, 110.
58. Žugić and Milić, *Jugosloveni u Koncentracionom logoru Aušvic 1941–1945*, 131.
59. Mila Dragojević and Vjeran Pavlaković, "Local Memories of Wartime Violence: Commemorating World War Two in Gospić," *Suvremene Teme* 8, no. 1 (2016): 66–87, here 74.

antifascist partisan struggle, and civilian victims. Thousands of memorials of various sizes, prominence, and artistic expression—from huge sculptures to murals, cemeteries, and memorial parks—were built all over the country, often organized by local war veterans associations. In Croatia alone, 2,700 local monuments were erected by 1960, two thirds of which commemorated local fighters or events in a particular region.[60] By 1990, there were six thousand monuments of various sizes and sophistication memorializing WWII, but almost never specifically the Holocaust.[61]

While they varied in appearance and ambition, these monuments all shared the same basic narrative features: first, the celebration of the partisans for both their heroism and their rejection of ethnic nationalism; and second, a general ambiguity and vagueness of what, exactly, had happened on the memorialized site, against which victims and by which forces. For example, a small memorial in Levanjska Varoš that commemorates thirty-seven killed partisans read, "These are not grave pits, but cradles of new forces!"—a vacuous slogan in place of historical context.[62]

Despite the proliferation of monuments, many sites remained unmemorialized for many decades. The Jadovno death camp, an important marker of the Holocaust in Croatia, only received a small memorial in 1975. Local commemorations at the site included mostly student visits and military drills, with a local politician occasionally making a vague and abstract speech, such as the one in 1973 by the vice president of the Executive Council of the Croatian Parliament,

> You are here to honor and remember the tens of thousands of men, women, and children who were thrown into pits and abysses across the Velebit mountain range for one single reason: because they hated fascism and they rose up against the enemy and the quisling forces. In Jadovno everyone who rose up against fascism and refused to acknowledge the occupation was killed, these were all patriots and were of all nations and nationalities (. . .)[63]

60. Heike Karge, "Mediated Remembrance: Local Practices of Remembering the Second World War in Tito's Yugoslavia," *European Review of History* 16, no. 1 (2009): 49–62, here 51.

61. Juraj Hrženjak, ed. *Rušenje antifašističkih spomenika u Hrvatskoj: 1990–2000* [The destruction of antifascist monuments in Croatia: 1990–2000] (Zagreb: Savez antifašističkih boraca Hrvatske, 2002), ix. Around twelve thousand communist monuments were built on the territory of the entire Yugoslavia. Tamara Banjeglav, "Sjećanje na rat ili rat sjećanja?" [Memory of war or war of memory?], in *Re:vizija prošlosti: Politike sjećanja u Bosni i Hercegovini, Hrvatskoj i Srbiji od 1990. godine*, ed. Tamara Banjeglav, Nataša Govedarica, and Darko Karačić (Sarajevo: ACIPS, 2012), 91–162, here 99.

62. Hrženjak, *Rušenje antifašističkih spomenika*, 129.

63. Quoted in Dragojević and Pavlaković, "Local Memories," 79.

A young student listening to this speech would not know that most of the victims at Jadovno were Serbs and Jews, killed because of genocidal policies of extermination by the Croatian Ustasha.[64] After increasing appeals by the families of Jadovno victims for more detailed memorialization, a bigger monument was erected in 1988, which was to include a dedication to Serbian priests and other camp victims. The complete monument was never finished.

Other camps were mostly neglected, with some receiving small signs of memorial attention. In 1960 a memorial plaque was placed on the side of the remains of the Reis salt factory, which housed the children's camp in Sisak. A children's cemetery was built in 1974, with a small monument indicating that two thousand children were buried there.[65] In 1975 a small memorial plaque was placed on the location of the former Slana camp on the island of Pag.[66] A small monument was also built near the site of the Tenja Jewish ghetto outside Osijek memorializing the "camp" in 1968—but it was a monument "to the fallen Yugoslav partisans and victims of fascism from Tenja."

Another plaque was placed next to the Kerestinec prison outside of Zagreb in 1961. Again in line with communist remembrance of the time, even though Kerestinec was the prison camp in which the majority of the nine hundred victims were Jews (and the camp had separate sections for Jews, Serbs, and communists), the memorial plaque commemorates the victims as "antifascist fighters," and mentions the heroic but ultimately futile escape by famous Croatian communists imprisoned there.

Some of the memorialization projects were more ambitious. In 1953, a big early memorialization complex was the Kampor memorial cemetery of victims of the Italian concentration camp on the island of Rab. The memorial was built by the esteemed Slovenian architect Edvard Ravnikar and contains several groupings of gravestones, a large open stone hall, and an obelisk column. It sits at a particularly attractive scenic location and its artistic rendition was a source of great pride for the Yugoslav state.[67]

---

64. For a related argument on the history of silence about WWII atrocities in a Bosnian community, see Max Bergholz, *Violence as a Generative Force: Identity, Nationalism, and Memory in a Balkan Community* (Ithaca, NY: Cornell University Press, 2016).

65. "Komemoracija za decu žrtve ustaškog logora u Sisku" [Commemorating children victims of the Ustasha camp in Sisak], *Radio Televizija Srbije*, February 9, 2012, http://www.rtv.rs/sr_lat/region/komemoracija-za-decu-zrtve-ustaskog-logora-u-sisku_346049.html.

66. Saša Šimpraga, "Tri mjeseca strave" [Three months of horror], *Zarez*, January 21, 2015, http://www.zarez.hr/clanci/tri-mjeseca-strave.

67. Vladimir Kulić, "Edvard Ravnikar's Eclecticism of Taste and the Politics of Appropriation," in *Terms of Appropriation: Modern Architecture and Global Exchange*, ed. Ana Miljački and Amanda Reeser Lawrence (Abingdon: Routledge, 2017), 75–93.

As was the case with similar memorialization projects on the territory of Serbia at the time, Kampor was selected because it carried a narrative of heroism—both the daring partisan rescue and (even more important) the subsequent formation of a partisan battalion by the liberated inmates. Kampor was also a convenient commemorative choice because it was an Italian- (not Croatian-) run camp and so the atrocities could cleanly be deflected onto the foreign enemy, not disturbing the multinational postwar Yugoslav peace. In that sense, Kampor was a perfect mnemonic fit for socialist Yugoslavia.[68]

Another large project was a series of memorial sculptures erected at various locations across Zagreb's expansive Dotršćina park. As it was the graveyard of eighteen thousand people—some executed there, some killed elsewhere in and around Zagreb and buried in unmarked mass graves—in the immediate postwar years families began to place individual burial stones with the communist red star, marking the victims as communists. However, in 1960, all of these individual memorials were removed by the government, which implemented a centralized strategy of memorialization at the site. Starting in 1963 a total of five monuments were unveiled at the site. The most prominent was a memorial designed by the famed Yugoslav sculptor Vojin Bakić, which was dedicated in 1968. Over the years new memorials were added, including a large monument in 1981 bearing the verse "They are no more because they wanted to be," from the poem "Spring" by the Croatian poet Ivan Goran Kovačić, who was killed by Serbian Chetniks in 1943.[69]

Constructing and Weaponizing Jasenovac

The Jasenovac site, even though—or precisely because—it was by far the largest camp in the NDH, was completely destroyed and razed at the end of the war, first by the retreating Ustasha and then by the advancing partisans. What remained from the rubble local villagers took away as cheap building material.[70] Jasenovac, therefore, remained officially unmemorialized for the first few decades after the war, even though a local group, the Initiative Board for Erecting a Monument to the Victims of Fascism at Jasenovac, started to appeal to the authorities as early as 1952.[71] While no expense was spared for

---

68. Karge, "Sajmište, Jasenovac."

69. Saša Šimpraga, "Najveći zločin u povijesti Zagreba" [The biggest crime in the history of Zagreb], Virtuelni Muzej Dotršćina, Tekstovi, accessed March 13, 2019, http://www.dotrscina.hr.

70. Nataša Mataušić, *Jasenovac 1941.-1945: logor smrti i radni logor* [Jasenovac 1941–1945: Death camp and labor camp] (Jasenovac: Javna ustanova Spomen-područje Jasenovac, 2003).

71. Karge, "Mediated Remembrance," 56.

the memorial at Kampor, Yugoslav leadership was reluctant to dedicate as many resources to Jasenovac, as this comment by a high party official on the War Veterans Committee indicates:

> Memorials are expensive and we should only turn to solutions that speak of something sublime, something great in another sense—for example a memorial of the Revolution. Jasenovac should be made attractive and modest. Our country doesn't have a lot of money and it would not be a good idea to waste money on expensive memorials.[72]

But this was not just about the money. Jasenovac clearly caused a mnemonic problem for the communist state. While the extent of the atrocities was so vast that the population, especially the surviving Serbian and Jewish population, knew about the death camp, the precise nature of Jasenovac's administration and the identity and number of its victims remained fluid and contested (and it still remains so even today). Immediately after the war, the Croatian State Commission tasked with determining war crimes on its territory declared Jasenovac the site of between five hundred thousand and eight hundred thousand victims—a number clearly unrealistic since the total number of Yugoslav casualties in the war was around 1.7 million.[73] But the bigger problem for the Yugoslav government was that the intraethnic character of the massacres and the clearly Croatian (Ustasha) administration of the camp with almost no supervision by Nazi Germany seriously complicated the narrative of brotherhood, unity, and multinational cooperation. Jasenovac was itself a testimonial to ethnic conflict, racism, and genocide perpetrated by one Yugoslav nation against the others, and as such was a memory knot difficult to unravel. It is not insignificant that throughout his long reign, Tito never once visited Jasenovac.[74]

The plans to build a memorial at Jasenovac were put in motion in 1963, after increasing pressure from survivor groups who had by then begun annual commemorations at the site.[75] At the same time, there was tremendous anxiety within the Croatian War Veterans Union about how to properly depict the atrocities without singling out Croatian culpability, while also not completely deflecting all responsibility onto the Germans, a historical mischaracterization that survivors would be able to immediately challenge.

72. Quoted in Karge, "Sajmište, Jasenovac," 116.

73. Karge, "Mediated Remembrance," 54.

74. "FAQs," Jasenovac Memorial Site, accessed February 10, 2019, http://www.jusp-jasenovac.hr/Default.aspx?sid=7619.

75. Karge, "Mediated Remembrance," 57.

The task of memorializing Jasenovac was given to architect Bogdan Bogdanović, who had already designed early memorial monuments to victims of the Holocaust in Serbia. The huge monument, in the shape of a flower, was erected in 1966, and has since become iconic, a premier example of Yugoslav communist architectural representation of WWII. The Jasenovac

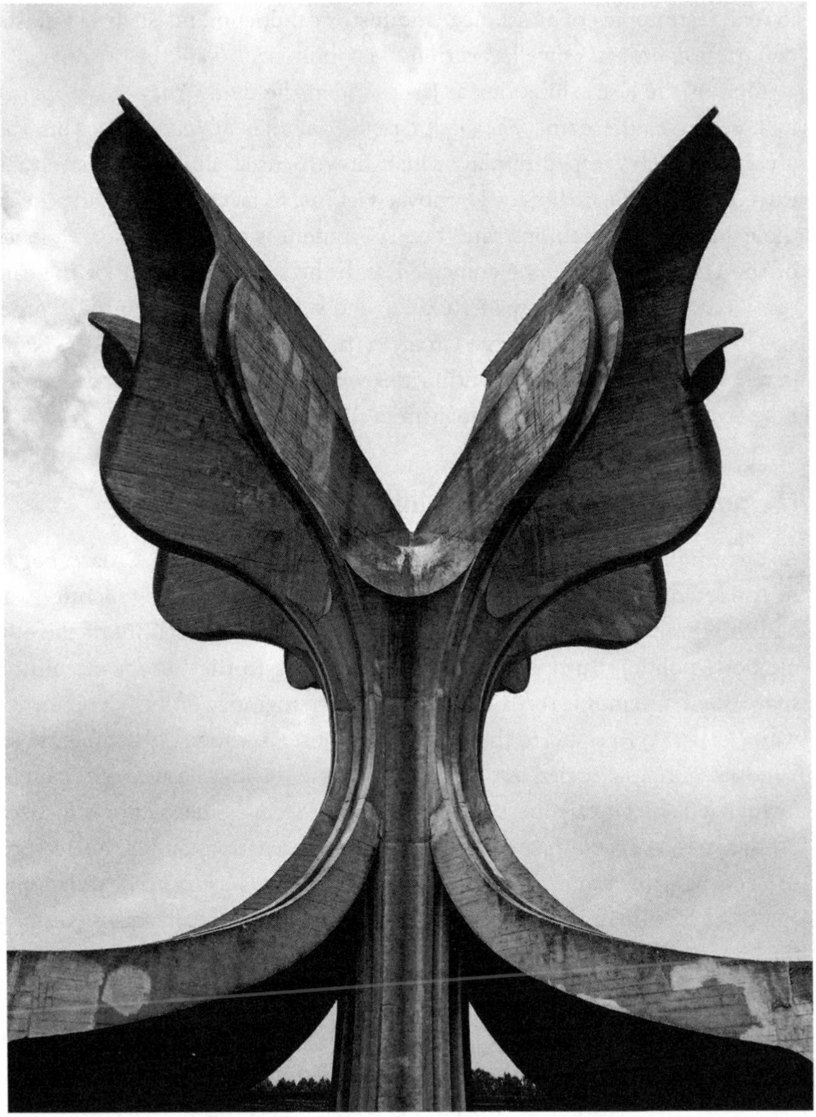

FIGURE 3. The flower monument at Jasenovac, designed by Bogdan Bogdanović, unveiled in 1966 (photograph by Vladimir Kulić)

memorial was so expensive and so visible that in many ways it sucked the air out of other memorialization efforts and became a "substitute" for all concentration camp memorial sites across the country. It came to represent the memory of WWII camps in the NDH, but also across Serbia and elsewhere.[76]

The Jasenovac memorial museum opened in 1968. The first exhibition was modest and displayed mostly inmates' items found during exhumations, letters, testimonies of resistance, and historical documents such as Ustasha deportation orders, as well as various weapons used to kill the prisoners.[77]

One of the last exhibitions at Jasenovac in the dying Yugoslavia opened in 1986 under the name *The Dead Opening the Eyes of the Living*. This was a completely revamped display, which now focused almost exclusively on extremely graphic images of Jasenovac victims. In fact, the main purpose of the exhibit was to demonstrate the gruesomeness and animalistic violence of the Ustasha. Its opening coincided with the start of the trial of the captured Ustasha leader Andrija Artuković and was meant to remind the Yugoslav (and first and foremost the Croatian) public of the horrors of the NDH in a context where Yugoslav authorities were increasingly concerned about how to contain the rising nationalism in the country.[78]

Memory Erasure after Communism

As communist Yugoslavia began to implode in the late 1980s, Croatia began to construct its new, post-Yugoslav national identity. This new identity was built on three stable security pillars: ethnic nationalism (security of the ethnic body politic), Europe (security of belonging to the European cultural space), and mnemonic security (security of the memory of its independence war, 1991–95). To stabilize these identities, postcommunist (therefore, post-Yugoslav) Croatia carried out multiple efforts at distinguishing itself from its former federation members, especially from Serbia. These efforts focused on the state goals of Croatization and Europeanization, and included such projects as determining the ethnic origin of Croats as proto-Aryans, with ancestral land in Iran and not in the Balkans, or officially distinguishing the Croatian language from the very similar Serbian language as a separate

76. Karge, "Sajmište, Jasenovac."

77. "Activities," Jasenovac Memorial Site, accessed February 10, 2019, http://www.jusp-jasenovac.hr/Default.aspx?sid=6560.

78. I thank an anonymous reviewer for clarifying these points.

linguistic family altogether.[79] The Croatian national question, therefore, became activated in the context of contemporary state insecurity.

These efforts were so heavy handed and ahistorical that they clearly reflected a deep sense of anxiety about what kind of polity postcommunist Croatia would be, but also anxiety over whether Croatia's significant others—the European Union, most importantly—would ever accept it as really, truly, European. This is why much of Croatian foreign policy after 1991 was dedicated to one single goal—accession to the European Union.

As was the case with other postcommunist states, Croatia joined the European cultural space after communism in many ways defined by the Western European foundational narrative of the Holocaust but also by an increasing openness on the part of Europe to delegitimizing communism as a totalitarian system akin to fascism. Croatia was well positioned to prove its European credentials on the carcass of communism. Destroying memories of communism and, with it, memories of communist, partisan, and antifascist struggle in WWII—was the first step in this process.

Destruction of Monuments

The first changes in the way in which Croatia remembered its communist past occurred in the early 1990s, when streets, schools, and public buildings that carried the names of famous partisans or communist leaders—as was the practice across communist Eastern Europe—were overnight changed to carry the names of famous precommunist Croatian public figures, including leaders of the NDH.[80] Communist-era monuments were replaced with statues of precommunist or anticommunist Croatian heroes, including public figures associated with the WWII Croatian fascist regime, while thousands of communist era monuments were vandalized, or completely destroyed.

In the hurricane of Croatian monument destruction in the 1990s, almost all communist-era monuments to WWII, including the few monuments that mentioned specifically Jewish victims, were fully removed or partially destroyed, vandalized, or desecrated. Often victims groups would put up a replica of the monument, only to see it disappear again, sometimes within

79. Jelena Subotić, "Europe is a State of Mind: Identity and Europeanization in the Balkans," *International Studies Quarterly* 55, no. 2 (2011): 309–30.

80. Dunja Rihtman-Auguštin, *Ulice moga grada: antropologija domaćeg terena* [The streets of my town: Anthropology of the local terrain] (Beograd: Biblioteka XX vek, 2000). The highest profile case was the renaming of Zagreb's central Victims of Fascism Square into Croatia's Nobles Square in 1990. In 1999, the conflict over the square's name led to violent slashes in the streets. The original name has since been returned in 2000 but is an issue of continuing contention and dispute.

FIGURE 4. Monument to civilians shot by Italian occupation forces in 1943, Bilice, Croatia, unveiled in 1977. The plaque with names of victims was removed in the 1990s and the monument in the shape of a red star vandalized (photograph by Vjeran Pavlaković)

twenty-four hours. Some monuments were simply replaced—in place of a monument to antifascist struggle, a new monument to Croatia's war of independence (1991–95) would spring up.

Many were desecrated by removing or destroying the red star and replacing it with a cross, or destroying the Cyrillic alphabet inscriptions commemorating Serb victims. Often, the inscription "Fallen for the People's Liberation Struggle" was replaced with "Fallen for Croatia." Yet at other monuments, names of Croats killed by partisans or in Croatia's war in the 1990s were added to the list of victims of fascism.[81] For example, on the site of the Stara Gradiška camp (part of the Jasenovac complex of camps), the Croatian government mounted a memorial plaque in 2011, memorializing "political prisoners, victims of the communist regime, who perished in the Stara Gradiška prison—on the occasion of August 23—Day of Commemoration of Victims of Totalitarian and Authoritarian Regimes." The use of the word prison and not camp is important because it directs remembrance to the prewar and postwar period, when the site was used as a prison, and not to the WWII-era

81. Hrženjak, *Rušenje antifašističkih spomenika.*

FIGURE 5. The crumbling remains of the Stara Gradiška concentration camp, Croatia. Of the three memorial plaques at the site, none indicates that this was a major camp during the Holocaust in Croatia (photograph by Vladimir Kulić).

Ustasha death camp, where more than twelve thousand Serbs, Jews, Roma, and other enemies of the NDH, including a very high number of women and children, were killed.

Some of the monuments were given explicitly opposite meanings. In 1999, the Croatian State Commission for Establishing War and Postwar Crimes submitted a report in which it claimed that the mass graves memorialized by the series of monuments at Dotršćina park—the burial site of some eighteen thousand Zagreb antifascists, as well as many Serb and Jewish civilians—were in fact graves of Croats killed by communists after the end of the war in 1945.[82]

The monuments that are important for the topography of the Holocaust in Croatia were also destroyed. One of the monuments in Tenja, the site of the Osijek ghetto, was destroyed, another desecrated with neo-Nazi graffiti. The monument at Jadovno was destroyed in an explosion in 1991.[83] A small monument built on the site of the Jasenovac sub-camp Krapje (which housed mostly Jewish inmates) was also destroyed. The monument on the site of the Sisak children's concentration camp was demolished in 1991. The monument on the site of the former Slana camp on the island of Pag—the execution site of thousands of Serbs and Jews—was destroyed multiple times, each

82. Šimpraga, "Najveći zločin."

83. It was replaced in 2011, but the memorial complex of which this monument was a part is still not complete—missing are memorial plaques with names.

attempt to replace it only to be destroyed again.[84] On the site of what was once the Đakovo concentration camp, today there is a gas station.[85]

Out of six thousand monuments memorializing WWII in Croatia, almost three thousand monuments, including more than seven hundred monuments of exquisite artistic or cultural value, were blown up with explosives, destroyed fully or in part in the post-independence decade, 1991–2000.[86] Not only was no one prosecuted for the destruction of cultural property, but in many locations it was the local chapter of the Croatian ruling political party—the Croatian Democratic Union (HDZ)—that organized the removal of the monuments.[87]

As Dejan Jović observes, the removal of the monuments symbolizes the end of a regime just as much as the literal toppling of a leader.[88] From the narrative perspective of the new Croatian state, the monuments to WWII had to be destroyed "because they represented a symbol of a different future," a vision of an international and domestic order Croatia no longer wanted and found threatening to its new national identity.[89]

However, it is important to emphasize the regional diffusion of this memory destruction—not all parts of Croatia were equally consumed by it. In regions with a strong culture of antifascist organizations—many of which have survived to this day—WWII monument destruction was minimal. In part, this explains the remarkable preservation of the expansive Kampor memorial complex on the island of Rab. The complex is maintained by the very active Antifascist Association of Rab, a group of WWII veterans and other interested citizens who take care of the site, organize lectures, seminar series, and have a publishing unit. But also, more deeply, Kampor was

---

84. Hrženjak, *Rušenje antifašističkih spomenika*; also, author correspondence with Vjeran Pavlaković, associate professor of cultural studies, University of Rijeka (February 13, 2018), and Sanja Horvatinčić, Institute of Art History, Zagreb (February 13, 2018).

85. Zvjezdan Živković, "Logor Đakovo: Sjećanje kao opomena" [Đakovo camp: Memory as warning], *Radio Slobodna Evropa*, November 8, 2013, https://www.slobodnaevropa.org/a/plp-zvjezdan-sjkecanje-na-logor-djakovo/25162294.html.

86. Hrženjak, *Rušenje antifašističkih spomenika*.

87. Some of the monuments were also removed by the rebel Croatian Serb paramilitary units. Tihomir Cipek, "Sjećanje na 1945: Čuvanje i brisanje—o snazi obiteljskih narativa" [Memory of 1945: Preserving and erasing—on the power of family narratives], in *Kultura sjećanja: 1945: Povijesni lomovi i svladavanje prošlosti*, ed. Sulejman Bosto and Tihomir Cipek (Zagreb: Disput, 2009), 155–66, here 161.

88. Dejan Jović, "'Official Memories' in Post-authoritarianism: An Analytical Framework," *Journal of Southern Europe and the Balkans* 6, no. 2 (2004): 97–108, here 100.

89. Gal Kirn and Robert Burghardt, "Jugoslovenski partizanski spomenici: Između revolucionarne politike i apstraktnog modernizma" [Yugoslav partisan monuments: Between revolutionary politics and abstract modernism], *Jugolink: pregled postjugoslovenskih istraživanja* 2, no. 1 (2012): 7–20, here 16.

never in the crosshairs of nationalist destruction because it commemorates an Italian camp, not a Croatian Ustasha camp, and so it is less contentious and much more easily explained away. The responsibility for the extensive crimes committed here can be deflected onto a foreign power and so it does not present a memory knot for the contemporary Croatian sense of self. This is why, at the peak of memorial cleansing in 1993, the Croatian Jewish Community could install, seemingly without much backlash, a memorial plaque at Kampor memorializing the fiftieth anniversary of the establishment of the Jewish Partisan Battalion, which, the plaque reads, "fought for its human dignity."

Other monuments were preserved—or at least the destruction was more isolated—if they were built in regions where there were limited or no violent clashes with Serb units during the 1990s war, such as, for example, in the northern Croatian region of Istria. This regional diversity points to very local ways of remembering that operate for reasons often detached from larger state narratives and can complicate memory politics after conflict.[90]

Normalization of the Ustasha

The legitimacy of postcommunist Croatia was built on a complete rejection of communism and a renewed connection to the precommunist, mythically nationally pure character of its statehood. This is why the new postcommunist elites insisted on rehabilitating many anticommunist public figures, including many profascist allies. The goal behind this national project was to sidestep the communist past as a legitimate period of the country's history and institute a clear historical connection with the precommunist state, creating an inspirational model for the contemporary manifestation of ethnic statehood and stabilizing Croatia's state identity through time. The problem, however, was that the only modern independent Croatia the new state could go back to for memorials and symbols was the fascist NDH and all the mnemonic baggage it brought with it.

The memory link between postcommunist Croatia and its WWII predecessor was not only in the adoption of state symbols—such as the checkerboard coat-of-arms on its flag and the new currency, the *kuna*—which were adopted from existing symbols of the NDH, with only minor alterations. It was also the fundamental commitment to anticommunism and the profound role of Catholicism in Croatia's postcommunist national identity that linked contemporary Croatia and the NDH. The Ustasha, who had

90. I thank Vjeran Pavlaković for clarifying these points.

been seen for the past fifty years as fascist criminals, were transformed into defenders of Croatian (and Catholic) identity from Serbs, partisans, and communists.[91]

The normalization of the Ustasha—from the reestablishment of the formerly banned pro-Ustasha Croatian Party of Rights and the formation of new Ustasha groups to the reintroduction of Ustasha visual symbols and iconography—started to emerge in the years leading up to the onset of the Croatian war in 1991 and has since remained mostly stable. Some of the first manifestations of Ustasha normalization were the public (although not officially sanctioned) commemorations of the establishment of the NDH on April 10. After 1945, these commemorations were the mainstay of Croatia's diaspora (many of whom were either themselves former Ustasha or their sympathizers or family members) and were organized regularly in Canada, Germany, and Australia. These commemorations were initially led by the Croatian Party of Rights, which also demanded that April 10 became a national holiday commemorating the establishment of independent Croatia. Over time, however, they have become less organized and more popular events that bring together a variety of loosely linked far-right and neofascist groups.[92]

The normalization of the Ustasha was also the central piece of the all-Croatian reconciliation ideology of Croatia's first post-independence president, Franjo Tuđman, which presupposed the unification of all Croatian people everywhere (Croatian communists, anticommunists, Ustasha sympathizers, and a vast Croatian diaspora), a joint nationalist effort in pursuit of Croatian statehood.[93] This reconciliation project viewed WWII as an unfortunate civil war among Croats, where Croatian partisans and Croatian nationalists both struggled for their version of the Croatian state. These divisions were real and ran through families, as it was not uncommon for members of the same family to join the partisans and the Ustasha, leading to difficult attempts at reconciliation after the war. These divisions between the red and black Croatia were painful and stark.

Part of Tuđman's plans for reconciliation included repurposing the Jasenovac memorial site, where, apparently inspired by the Valley of the

---

91. Sven Milekic, "Croatia: The Fascist Legacy," *Osservatorio Balcani e Caucaso*, September 3, 2015, https://www.balcanicaucaso.org/eng/Areas/Croatia/Croatia-the-fascist-legacy-163852.

92. Vjeran Pavlaković, "Opet *Za dom spremni*: Desetotravanjske komemoracije u Hrvatskoj nakon 1990. godine" [Again *Ready for the Homeland*: Commemorations of April 10 in Croatia after 1990], in *Kultura sjećanja 1941: Povijesni lomovi i svladavanje prošlosti*, ed. Sulejman Bosto, Tihomir Cipek, and Olivera Milosavljević (Zagreb: Disput, 2008), 113–32.

93. One of the many paradoxes of Franjo Tuđman was that he was a high-ranking general in the partisan forces during WWII.

Fallen, a similar reconciliation memorial built outside Madrid by Spain's General Francisco Franco, he proposed that the bodies of the Ustasha killed by the partisans in 1945 and Croatian soldiers killed in the 1990s war be buried together with remains of the victims of Jasenovac. This grotesque mixing of remains of perpetrators and victims was then rejected after much outcry in Croatia and abroad.[94]

The normalization of the Ustasha was also evident in Croatia's history textbooks. The retroactive normalization of the NDH was at its most extreme during the 1990s. Textbooks instructed students that the NDH represented Croatia's progress and independent statehood, listing its "cultural accomplishments" while completely ignoring its genocidal crimes. The Holocaust was not mentioned at all, while Croatia's genocide against the Serbs was presented as justified "because of [Serb] earlier hegemonic policies and because of the appearance of Chetniks and their atrocities in Croatia."[95] The lack of interest—and outright falsehoods—regarding the Holocaust in Croatia was so prevalent on the Croatian right that the far-right Croatian Liberation Movement party even claimed in 1995 that "the Jews in the NDH fared better than in any other European country that was involved in the war."[96]

The direct link between WWII's Ustasha and their modern-day followers became the paramilitary Croatian Defense Forces or HOS (Hrvatske obrambene snage), active during the 1990s war as the militia wing of the far-right Croatian Party of Rights. It also shares the acronym HOS with the WWII-era Croatian Armed Forces (Hrvatske oružane snage)—the armed forces of the Ustasha during the NDH. The open motivation for renewing the HOS was to continue the legacy of the Ustasha, and their members referred to themselves as the Ustasha and dressed the part (in black shirts, with Ustasha WWII insignia, etc.).[97] They even named one of their battalions after the Ustasha commander Rafael Boban, who had committed extensive crimes against humanity in WWII.[98]

---

94. Slavko Goldstein, "Otvoreno pismo predsjedniku Tuđmanu" [Open letter to president Tuđman], *Feral Tribune*, February 5, 1996.

95. Quoted in Ljiljana Radonic, "Croatia's Politics of the Past during the Tuđman Era (1990–1999)—Old Wine in New Bottles?," *Austrian History Yearbook* 44 (2013): 234–54, here 244.

96. *Globus*, December 1, 1995, quoted in Vjeran Pavlaković, "Flirting with Fascism: The Ustaša Legacy and Croatian Politics in the 1990s," in *The Shared History and the Second World War and National Question in ex-Yugoslavia* (Novi Sad: CHDR, 2008), 115–43, here 131.

97. Pavlaković, "Opet *Za dom spremni*." On the Serbian side, many paramilitary groups participating in the 1990s war appropriated Chetnik visual insignia and terminology.

98. Sven Milekic, "Croatia: Living the Past, Not Confronting It," *Erinnerungskulturen*, July 11, 2016, https://erinnerung.hypotheses.org/827.

The Croatian state has fully embraced this reintegration of the Ustasha legacy into its contemporary body politic. Croatian law allows for state pensions for members of the "Croatian Homeland Army from 1941 to 1945," which is a euphemism for Ustasha and Home Guard veterans.[99] At the same time, the Croatian far right coopted some specific NDH policies, such as the Croatian Party of Rights' claim that, after the 1990s war, there was no place in Croatia for Serbs, explicitly arguing for their expulsion.[100]

A state with European Union aspirations, however, could not openly glorify crimes of genocide and racial laws that led to the Holocaust. The narrative solution, then, was to deny—against all evidence—that the NDH was fascist, racist, anti-Semitic, and genocidal, but instead choose to memorialize it as a normal state that led in the path toward Croatia's independence.

Bleiburg as Croatia's Holocaust

And while the public memory of the Holocaust and genocide committed in the NDH was completely absent from the constitutive identity of the new state, a new public memory emerged that has since overtaken all other remembrance of WWII. This was the constructed memory of the massacre of Croatian soldiers—most of them Ustasha—by Yugoslav partisans at the end of the war in May 1945.

The details about what actually happened are murky. Beyond much dispute is the fact that a significant number of retreating Ustasha forces and other Croatian militiamen, along with remnants of other quisling forces (Serbian, Muslim, Slovene, and Montenegrin), some German soldiers, and many fleeing Croatian civilians, were captured by the Yugoslav partisan army at the very end of the war in May 1945 as they were retreating near the Austrian town of Bleiburg.[101] While the number of victims has been hotly disputed over the years, with many Croatian nationalists inflating the number killed to as many as half a million, scholarly consensus puts the number of killed somewhere near seventy thousand.[102] Historians have also struggled to determine the percentage of military casualties from firefights between the

99. In 2015 there were some nine thousand veterans receiving such pensions in Croatia. Milekic, "Croatia: The Fascist Legacy."

100. Pavlaković, "Opet *Za dom spremni*," 125–26.

101. While commemorations are held in the town of Bleiburg in today's Austria (where the British forces in May 1945 refused to receive surrendering Croatian troops and instead turned them over to Yugoslav partisans), the actual location of the "Bleiburg" massacre is elsewhere, at a number of sites, scattered across the Croatian, Slovenian, and Austrian border.

102. Pål Kolstø, "Bleiburg: The Creation of a National Martyrology," *Europe-Asia Studies* 62, no. 7 (2010): 1153–74, 1157.

partisans and the Ustasha during the fascist forces' retreat, in relationship to the percentage of those Croatian forces executed *after* they were captured by the partisans and should have received POW protection. Also difficult to establish is the number of civilian forces killed in the final rounds of fighting when compared to the executions afterwards.[103]

Throughout the communist era, the events of Bleiburg were not publicly discussed, and the only commemorations at the site were organized and attended by the Croatian diaspora. The attractiveness of the Bleiburg story to the anticommunist right is based in large part on the fact that Tito's regime suppressed any information on the massacre, and it therefore entered the realm of myths, half-truths, and legends. The Bleiburg story remained alive in the Croatian (often pro-Ustasha) diaspora, which over time developed its own version of the events and prepared it for public consumption in post-1991 Croatia, with great assistance and involvement by the Croatian Catholic Church.[104] With the resurgence of Croatian nationalism in the 1990s, the commemorations at Bleiburg became one of the central sites of Croatian nationalist mobilization. A previously submerged "archipelago of memory" suddenly resurfaced.[105]

While it was previously commemorated as the site of the communist army's massacre of Croatian (primarily Ustasha) *soldiers*, Bleiburg in the Croatian public consciousness since 1991 has begun to be seen and commemorated as a communist assault on the entire Croatian *nation*.[106] It has also gained very overt Christian overtones, as it began to be referred to as the Croatian Way of the Cross, implying martyrdom and Crucifixion of the Croatian nation.

Moving out of the realm of unofficial diaspora commemorations, Bleiburg ceremonies in post-Yugoslav Croatia have become fully state sanctioned, and the Croatian government has designated the Sunday closest to May 15 the Day of Bleiburg Commemoration, a day of memory of Croatian victims in the struggle for freedom and independence everywhere. But this new remembrance is not just a remembrance of a massacre. It became a memory of "the Holocaust"—with Croats as victims and not as perpetrators.

---

103. Milivoj Bešlin, "Mitologija, politika i istorija na blajburškom polju" [Mythology, politics and history on the field of Bleiburg], *Peščanik*, May 13, 2017, https://pescanik.net/mitologija-politika-i-istorija-na-blajburskom-polju/; Slavko Goldstein and Ivo Goldstein, *Jasenovac i Bleiburg nisu isto* [Jasenovac and Bleiburg are not the same] (Zagreb: Novi Liber, 2011).

104. Kolstø, "Bleiburg."

105. Author interview with Vesna Teršelič, director of Documenta—Center for Facing the Past, October 24, 2017, Zagreb.

106. Kolstø, "Bleiburg."

An early explicit use of the term "the Holocaust" for Bleiburg occurred at the fiftieth anniversary of the events in 1995, when the speaker of the Croatian parliament addressed the assembly and called Bleiburg "the Holocaust of Croatian martyrs."[107] The appropriation of the Holocaust both for Bleiburg specifically and for the larger Croatian historical suffering has since become ubiquitous.[108] The claim that Bleiburg was "the Holocaust of Croatian Catholics" has fully entered the Croatian public narrative and goes mostly unchallenged in the public sphere.[109] Public Holocaust remembrance in Croatia, therefore, has been retold as a history of Croat suffering that excludes most stories of Croats perpetrating atrocities.

Croatian nationalists used Bleiburg to build a seamless narrative connecting the events of WWII and those of the war of the 1990s, making the recent war seem historically predetermined and inevitable and using tenuous historical analogies to provide a particular interpretation of the most recent past. For example, one of the frequent chants at annual Bleiburg commemorations is "Ante, Ante!"— not in memory of Ante Pavelić, the leader of the NDH, but instead of Ante Gotovina, the Croatian general indicted—and ultimately acquitted—of war crimes against the Croatian Serb population in 1995.[110]

The commemorations at Bleiburg, however, have not occurred in an international vacuum. In fact, much of Croatia's contemporary memorialization follows the narrative framework laid out in the 2008 EU Prague Declaration. The declaration's statement on "two totalitarianisms" is referred to whenever a discussion arises about proper remembrance of Croatia's fascist legacies.[111] At the 2011 Bleiburg commemoration, Andrija Hebrang, a member of the Croatian parliament, said, "Bleiburg is the biggest symbol of Croatian suffering that levels fascism and communism. Communism becomes worse than fascism, it becomes the world's biggest evil, because it turns into the system of killing everyone who thought differently."[112]

---

107. Banjeglav, "Sjećanje na rat," 109.

108. For example, a pseudoacademic history of Bleiburg is titled "The Croatian Holocaust: Documents and Testimonies on Afterwar Massacres in Yugoslavia," John Ivan Prcela and Dražen Živić, eds., *Hrvatski Holokaust: Dokumenti i svjedočanstva o poratnim pokoljima u Jugoslaviji* (Zagreb: Hrvatsko društvo političkih zatvorenika, 2001).

109. Nicolas Moll, "Fragmented Memories in a Fragmented Country: Memory Competition and Political Identity-Building in Today's Bosnia and Herzegovina," *Nationalities Papers* 41, no. 6 (2013): 910–35, here 920.

110. Kolstø, "Bleiburg," 1163.

111. Teršelič, interview.

112. "Andrija Hebrang: Komunizam je na Bleiburgu postao gori od fašizma" [Andrija Hebrang: Communism at Bleiburg became worse than fascism], *Nacional*, May 14, 2011.

Some of these memory practices have already caused a rift between Croatia and its traditional allies, most contentiously with Austria. Bleiburg commemorations—which are supported by the Croatian state but take place on the territory of Austria—have begun to cause great consternation and unease within this country, as the commemorations have over time become a large assembly of Europe's fascists and neo-Nazis—mostly Croatian, but also many coming from all over Europe just to attend this gathering.

Obviously, Austria has its own highly contested relationship with the Holocaust and the annual reminder of fascist symbols, insignia, and chants that the Bleiburg commemorative carnival brings to town is a cause of significant embarrassment and discomfort. Austria also holds the unique distinction of being the only European Union member state ever to be sanctioned for issues related to Holocaust remembrance, when in 2000 the EU froze diplomatic relations with Austria in the aftermath of the electoral success of the Freedom Party, a far-right party with Nazi roots.[113]

Keenly aware of the symbolic and political importance of disassociating Austria from fascist groups (and preserving the legal teeth of Austria's own laws criminalizing anti-Semitism and hate speech), a political and civil society coalition has formed in Austria to try and ban the Croatian Bleiburg commemoration, calling it "the largest neo-Nazi congregation in Europe" and "the largest meeting of revisionists, neo-Nazis and followers of a fascist state."[114] However, in the absence of any EU mechanism for—or seemingly, interest in—policing this fascist normalization among its member states, it appears that once Croatia won EU membership, "the black shirt could be put back on" with impunity.[115]

It is in this political context that in 2002 Croatia first notified the Auschwitz Memorial Museum that it wanted the Yugoslav exhibition dismantled and demanded permission to establish its own national exhibit, to keep control over its own Holocaust narrative, which would exclude any mention of antifascist struggle, outside or inside the camp. The Auschwitz Museum, however, rejected this proposal and notified individual Yugoslav successor states that the only allowable renovated exhibit would have to be a joint

---

113. Stefan Seidendorf, "Defining Europe against Its Past: Memory Politics and the Sanctions against Austria in France and Germany," *German Law Journal* 6, no. 2 (2005): 439–64. It is worth pointing out that the electoral success of the Freedom Party in 2017 and its induction into the ruling coalition as a junior partner has not led to similar EU punishment.

114. Sven Milekic, "Austrians Seek to Ban Croatian WWII Commemoration," *Balkan Insight*, May 11, 2017, http://www.balkaninsight.com/en/article/austrians-seek-banning-croatian-controversial-wwii-commemoration-05-11-2017.

115. Author interview with Vjeran Pavlaković, November 9, 2017, Chicago.

effort of all Yugoslav successor states. Since no joint effort was produced, in 2009 the museum closed the Yugoslav pavilion and sent the exhibited objects to the Museum of the History of Yugoslavia in Belgrade for safekeeping. Block 17 in the Auschwitz Memorial Museum remains empty, with a sign for visitors that exhibitions are being "redone." The twenty thousand Yugoslav victims at Auschwitz are no longer represented at the museum, the memory of their lives and deaths disappearing with the disappearance of the state in which they once lived.[116]

The Mnemonic Transformation of the Jasenovac Memorial Site

During the Croatian war of independence (1991–95), the Jasenovac site became a location of armed conflict between Croatian Serb paramilitaries and the Croatian army.[117] The Jasenovac site was occupied by Serb rebels and seriously damaged in the fighting, the main damage to the site inflicted deliberately by Croatian forces in 1991. The terrain was littered with land mines, which seriously hampered postwar reconstruction.[118] The documentary material—some 7,700 museum exhibits—was removed and taken by Serb forces to Republika Srpska, the Serb entity in Bosnia-Herzegovina.[119] Some of this material was taken to Belgrade, where it was displayed at the Museum of Genocide Victims in the 1994 exhibition *Jasenovac—a System of Ustasha Death Camps*. At the height of the Croatian war, this exhibit was meant to demonstrate "the genocidal tendencies of the Croatian people"—and had tremendous public appeal in Serbia at the time.[120] Until 1997, two years after the end of the Croatian war, there were

116. For a full account of the history and dismemberment of the Yugoslav national exhibition at Auschwitz, see Jelena Subotic, "Political Memory after State Death: The Abandoned Yugoslav National Pavilion at Auschwitz," *Cambridge Review of International Affairs* (forthcoming, 2019).

117. It was not just the Serb paramilitaries and the Croatian Army that displayed disregard for the historical significance of the site during the Croatian war. The UN peacekeeping mission, UNPROFOR, also stockpiled confiscated heavy ammunition in one of the complex buildings. Mataušić, *Jasenovac*.

118. Another major camp from the Jasenovac network—Stara Gradiška—was used by Croatian Serb rebels as a prison for detained Croatian soldiers and was also heavily damaged in the war.

119. "Renovation of Jasenovac Memorial Site," Jasenovac Memorial Site, accessed February 10, 2019, http://www.jusp-jasenovac.hr/Default.aspx?sid=6484. Although the transport of the archival material to Republika Srpska can be described as looting, there is widespread recognition by scholars today that much of this material would not have survived had it remained in Jasenovac at the time of the Croatian military operation Flash in May 1995. I thank an anonymous reviewer for this observation.

120. Rob Van der Laarse, "Beyond Auschwitz? Europe's Terrorscapes in the Age of Postmemory," in *Memory and Postwar Memorials: Confronting the Violence of the Past*, ed. Marc Silberman and Florence Vatan (New York: Springer, 2013), 71–92, here 81.

no commemorations of any kind at the site and Jasenovac did not exist as a commemorative space in Croatia.

Repairs on the Jasenovac site began in 1998. The return of removed objects required lengthy negotiations between Croatia and Republika Srpska, and involved direct mediation by the US Holocaust Memorial Museum. According to museum estimates, a full third of the items were lost in the war, destroyed, or stolen.[121] The remaining 70 percent were finally returned to Jasenovac in 2001, and the Bogdanović flower memorial was repaired in 2002.

The center-left government of then prime minister Ivica Račan (2000–2003) made the reopening of Jasenovac a priority, partly out of its political commitment to fighting right-wing revisionism, but also as part of its EU accession strategy. Successive Croatian governments also did not oppose the rebuilding of Jasenovac and in fact continued to support its construction quite generously. With the change in government in 2003, however, and the return of the right-wing HDZ to power, this commitment to Jasenovac became much less clearly about remembering the Holocaust or the genocide against the Serbs, and even less about criminalizing the NDH. Instead, it became a commitment to use the genocide of WWII to mnemonically interpret the more recent war of the 1990s as a genocide against Croats. For example, addressing the 2005 commemoration event at Jasenovac, then Croatian prime minister Ivo Sanader said, "We should not forget the aggression that Croatia endured because we too were victims of a terrible madness of Nazism and fascism, and we, Croatian citizens, Croats, know the best what it is like to suffer from aggression."[122] What the prime minister obviously ignored was the fact that the memorial site at Jasenovac was itself a commemoration of Croatian fascist crimes and not of Croatian victimization. Sanader then repeated this speech during his visit to Yad Vashem in 2005, de facto "identifying Croatians as the 'new Jews' and Serbs as 'the new fascists,'" and thus firmly affixing the memory of the Holocaust to Croatia's victimization, first during WWII and then during the war of Yugoslav succession in the 1990s.[123]

As Croatia moved toward the European Union and especially since obtaining EU candidate status in 2004, it has had to adapt to EU remembrance expectations, including an expectation to commemorate the Holocaust and denounce its fascist past. Croatia joined the International Holocaust

121. Mataušić, *Jasenovac*.

122. Banjeglav, "Sjećanje na rat," 115.

123. Ljiljana Radonić, "Univerzalizacija holokausta na primjeru hrvatske politike prošlosti i spomen-područja Jasenovac" [Universalization of the Holocaust exemplified in the Croatian politics of the past and the Jasenovac Memorial site], *Suvremene teme* 3, no. 1 (2010): 53–62, here 56.

Remembrance Alliance in 2005—the first of the former Yugoslav states to do so—and this intensified international pressure to reopen the Jasenovac museum.[124]

The new permanent exhibition at Jasenovac was inaugurated in 2006. In a complete departure from the exhibits during the communist era, the new display was hypermodern, with white plasma screens scrolling the names of victims. The exhibition focused on individual victims and presented their personal artifacts, stories about their prewar life, a few objects found in excavating the destroyed camp site. The documentary material displayed included various NDH orders that set the genocidal policies in place, as well as photographs from the period—including, significantly, a photograph of a 1941 meeting of the NDH leader Ante Pavelić with Adolf Hitler.

The exhibition was immediately met with significant domestic controversy. The first problem was that Serb victims groups were concerned that Jasenovac would be "just a Holocaust museum" (presumably due to the consulting assistance provided by the US Holocaust Memorial Museum and Yad Vashem) and would ignore the majority non-Jewish victims—Serbs, Roma, and Croatian antifascists.[125] Another question was whether victims should be identified by ethnicity and date of birth, a pretty standard and important marker of who was targeted and why; this, however, was resisted by the Jasenovac exhibition authors, who instead favored a generic victim-focused (rather than ethnic-focused) display.[126] In the end a compromise was reached, by which victims' ethnicity was not displayed in the exhibition, but victims were categorized by ethnicity in the museum's searchable database.

The permanent exhibition also chose not to present a fuller picture of the horrors at Jasenovac by not displaying the many preserved instruments of death. Some of these decisions were made in the context of the early 2000s, when the memories of the Croatian war were still fresh, and the authors felt that gruesome images of the dead would serve to further generate interethnic hatred.[127] In fact, almost completely missing in the exhibit is the narrative of what, exactly, *happened* at Jasenovac, an absence further compounded by the fact that there exist no material remains of the camp, so the Jasenovac past had to be completely reconstructed and reimagined. To an uninformed visitor, the memorial appears as a tribute to the many lives lost, but without a

---

124. Author interview with Andriana Benčić, curator at the Jasenovac Memorial Site, October 25, 2017, Zagreb.

125. Banjeglav, "Sjećanje na rat," 118.

126. Author interview with Nataša Mataušić, Croatian History Museum, the author of the 2006 Jasenovac permanent exhibition, October 24, 2017, Zagreb.

127. Mataušić, interview.

full historical context and without the emotional punch that the description of the camp's machinery of death would provide. The exhibition's exclusive focus on the victims, while poignant and respectful, therefore missed the opportunity to tell the story of what exactly happened to them at the camp, why, and how.[128] The consequence of this curatorial choice is that the Jasenovac exhibit is devoid of meaning and of historical interpretation, making it an exhibition of mnemonic emptiness.[129]

Other, larger problems with the Jasenovac memorial remained. Perhaps most troubling was the presentation of the NDH as a puppet Nazi state, with limited independence and closely following Hitler's orders. The displayed photograph of a July 1941 meeting between Pavelić and Hitler is captioned: "On this occasion Hitler gave Pavelić full support for the genocidal policies against the Serbian population." This interpretation, however, is misleading as the NDH pursued its anti-Serb policies largely autonomously from Nazi Germany and, as stated earlier, often to the chagrin of German authorities, who were annoyed at the backlash and resistance it was generating among the Serbs. A further paradox of the Jasenovac exhibit is that in the exclusive focus on victims the role of the perpetrators (and their portrayal and identification) is almost completely absent, creating an impression that Jasenovac somehow just happened; the exhibit is thus dehistoricized from the genocidal policies of a homegrown Croatian regime.[130]

The exhibit also missed the opportunity to offer a teachable moment on anti-Semitism. Next to the display of an anti-Semitic poster from 1941 accusing the Jews of the "destruction of Croatia" the Jasenovac exhibit organizers placed a list of Jewish architects who had literally *constructed* Zagreb—in their attempt to rebut the anti-Semitic poster, the exhibit organizers instead perpetuated a narrative of "deserving Jews" and completely missed the point of both anti-Semitism and a pedagogic approach to fighting it.[131]

The Jasenovac Memorial Museum is also rather sparsely visited today. Its peak popularity was in the 1970s, when between three hundred thousand and four hundred thousand visitors would arrive annually, with many schools across communist Yugoslavia making a visit to Jasenovac a part of the curriculum. When the museum was reopened and revamped in 2006, it

128. Author interview with Ognjen Kraus, president of the Zagreb Jewish Community, October 24, 2017, Zagreb, Croatia.

129. Ana Kršinić Lozica, "Između memorije i zaborava: Jasenovac kao dvostruko posredovana trauma" [Between memory and oblivion: Jasenovac as a doubly mediated trauma], *Radovi Instituta za povijest umjetnosti* 35 (2011): 297–308.

130. Radonić, "Univerzalizacija holokausta."

131. Radonić, "Univerzalizacija holokausta," 58.

had only eight thousand annual visitors, and the number has since settled at around twelve thousand, of whom seven thousand are visitors from Croatia and five thousand are foreigners, mostly from neighboring Slovenia and Bosnia-Herzegovina.[132]

But for the purposes of the main political narratives in Croatia, Jasenovac remained a site of opportunity to link the atrocities of WWII—including the Holocaust—with Croatian contemporary political needs: to secure the memory of its war of independence in the 1990s, to signal Croatia's readiness to join the European memory space, and to delegitimize communism. At the official inauguration of the Jasenovac Memorial Museum in 2006, then prime minister Ivo Sanader made all three connections:

> We need the truth about Jasenovac and its victims because, let's not forget, it was the lies about Jasenovac and exaggerated numbers that were part of the justification for Greater Serbian aggression against Croatia. We need the truth in the broader region of this part of Europe so we can turn to the modern values of Europe, which has overcome its old divisions and conflicts. . . . In the Homeland War we have overcome all these divisions, strengthened our antifascist foundations, but also condemned that other communist totalitarianism, raised the paradigm of a new united and reconciled Croatia, and that is our commitment in the new Europe.[133]

It was at Jasenovac that Sanader coined the phrase "Antifascism yes—communism no!," a way of constructing contemporary Croatian identity that denies communism its historical role as the primary antifascist force, decouples it from the legacy of WWII, and subsequently fully delegitimizes and criminalizes it.[134] Again, Croatia here was only following the larger EU template of remembrance.[135] In 2006 Croatia passed a Declaration Condemning the Crimes Committed during the Totalitarian Communist Regime in

132. Željka Godeč, "Muzej Holokausta u Zagrebu: Projekt koji ne smatraju svi Židovi dobrom idejom" [The Holocaust museum in Zagreb: A project that not all Jews consider a good idea], *Jutarnji list*, November 18, 2017.

133. Government of Croatia, "Jasenovac: otvoren Memorijalni muzej i Obrazovni centar" [Jasenovac: Memorial museum and education center opens], November 27, 2006, https://vlada.gov.hr/vijesti/jasenovac-otvoren-memorijalni-muzej-i-obrazovni-centar/5524.

134. Sanader spoke at the unveiling of the reconstructed Bogdanović stone flower monument. "Ne smijemo dopustiti zaborav ustaških zločina" [We must not allow forgetting of Ustaša crimes], *Večernji list*, March 17, 2004.

135. Ana Milosevic and Heleen Touquet, "Unintended Consequences: The EU Memory Framework and the Politics of Memory in Serbia and Croatia," *Southeast European and Black Sea Studies* 18, no. 3 (2018): 381–99.

Croatia 1945–1990, which was passed "in accordance with" the 2006 Council of Europe Parliamentary Assembly Resolution 1841, which condemned "crimes of totalitarian communist regimes."[136] Since 2011 Croatia began to officially commemorate August 23 as the Day of Remembrance of All Totalitarianisms, while progressively disregarding January 27, International Holocaust Remembrance Day.[137]

But it was especially the new Jasenovac memorial that presented a great opportunity for the realization of Croatia's EU ambitions. The memorial director was proud that the new exhibit was designed "to meet the standards of the Council of Europe and the EU."[138] Croatian media also approved of this European turn via Jasenovac, editorializing, for example, that "if this rhetoric had emerged earlier and been perpetuated longer, our image in the world would have been much more positive. This would also have eased our entry into the European community."[139]

And yet, Jasenovac today remains a site of divided memory—while most of the site is on the territory of Croatia, a smaller part of the memorial is in Donja Gradina, just across the river Sava, which, since 1995, is on the territory of Bosnia's Republika Srpska. Here the Serbian narrative prevails. Commemorations at Donja Gradina are designed to present an alternative narrative of Jasenovac to the one at the main site, and always include the greatly exaggerated Serbian number of seven hundred thousand killed in the camp. Donja Gradina commemorations are big state affairs, often with the presidents of Republika Srpska and Serbia in attendance. At the 2017 commemoration, the Serbian president Aleksandar Vučić used the occasion to make an impassioned defense of Serbia's borders against "Albanian expansionism" (a reference to Kosovo's 2008 declaration of independence that Serbia did not recognize). The role of Jasenovac in nationalist mobilization, on both banks of the river Sava, continued.

Croatia Back in Europe—Holocaust Revisionism under the EU Flag

Croatia joined the European Union in 2013, to the great relief of its political elites and a mix of joy and skepticism of its citizens. Croatia's late entry meant that it joined the EU at a time when Europe's own practices of remembrance

136. *Narodne novine*, 76/2006, July 10, 2006.
137. Benčić, interview.
138. *Vjesnik*, August 18, 2004.
139. *Novi list*, April 25, 2005.

had dramatically changed, influenced by previous rounds of Eastern enlargement, finally settling on the narrative of the "two totalitarianisms" of the twentieth century. Croatia's own remembrance practices fit perfectly into this EU mold. The problem, however, was with Croatia's strengthened far right, which had begun to openly defy some of the canons of European WWII and Holocaust remembrance to mostly silence and shrugs from its EU partners.

These revisionist remembrance practices have only increased since Croatia's EU accession, and have started to become fully mainstreamed into major Croatian institutions since 2016 with the formation of a new center-right government.[140] Instead of serving as a politically stabilizing force, the EU instead has provided the Croatian far right opportunities both to network with like-minded groups (politically through the European People's Party in the European Parliament and more broadly through associations with other European far-right networks) and also to model its practices after successful far-right movements in Hungary and Poland.[141] Now that Croatia was safely in the EU, the EU lost what leverage it had during the accession process. This has allowed Croatia free rein in this arena, and the Croatian far right has certainly taken advantage of this permissive international environment, creating a state of permanent crisis over how Croatia deals with its contested past.

Croatia's Far-Right Surge

While the sharp tilt to the right in Croatia has been more noticeable since 2016, an earlier indication of the strengthening of Croatia's far right was the election of Tomislav Karamarko as the head of the largest party—HDZ—in 2012. Anti-Serb sentiment in the country had been on the rise ever since the Serbian minority installed street signs in the Cyrillic (Serbian) alphabet in Vukovar in 2013, a move that outraged Croats as Vukovar was the site of some of the worst anti-Croat atrocities by Serb forces in 1991.[142]

The personnel choices of the new government immediately indicated a new radicalization in Croatia's attitudes toward its past, especially the legacy of the Ustasha. While Ustasha sympathies existed in Croatia throughout the

---

140. Author interview with Ivo Goldstein, October 23, 2017, Zagreb.

141. Marija Ristic, Sven Milekic, Maja Zivanovic, and Denis Dzidic, "Far-Right Balkan Groups Flourish on the Net," *Balkan Insight*, May 5, 2017, http://www.balkaninsight.com/en/article/far-right-balkan-groups-flourish-on-the-net-05-03-2017.

142. Tamara Opacic, "Selective Amnesia: Croatia's Holocaust Deniers," *Balkan Insight*, November 24, 2017, http://www.balkaninsight.com/en/article/selective-amnesia-croatia-s-holocaust-deniers-11-16-2017.

postwar period, in the new 2016 coalition these views penetrated into the heart of government. Most alarming was the appointment of Zlatko Hasanbegović as Croatia's minister of culture—the position in charge of the entire culture of memory, including monuments, memorials, and street names.

Hasanbegović is a revisionist historian with a history of inflammatory statements regarding the role of the Ustasha, the Holocaust, and the NDH. He denied that Jasenovac was a death camp and advocated that the state stop financing Jasenovac commemorations.[143] In the mid-1990s, he wrote an article for a profascist newsletter, *The Independent State of Croatia*, in which he referred to the Ustasha as "martyrs and heroes."[144] He was a member of the Croatian Pure Party of Rights—the far-right pro-Ustasha party; he called the partisan antifascist victory in WWII "the biggest loss in Croatia's history."[145] Because of his long history of such views, scholars have called him "an unabashed and strong-willed fascist."[146] But Hasanbegović was hardly alone. Croatia's science and education minister—in charge of the school curricula and textbooks—expressed similar views.[147] This was the new Croatian elite in charge of its memory politics.

And while the far right was gaining steam, the new government also signaled a political environment of impunity—if not encouragement—for overt glorification of Croatia's fascist past. In November 2016, a group of Croatian war veterans affiliated with the HOS paramilitary erected a memorial plaque with the unit's call to arms, "Za dom spremni!" (Ready for the homeland!), etched into the HOS coat of arms displayed on the plaque. The plaque was then mounted in the town of Jasenovac, near the memorial site.[148] The problem was that "Za dom spremni!" was also the official, main rallying cry of the Ustasha. Such a plaque outside Jasenovac

143. Milekic, "Croatia: Living the Past."

144. Hrvoje Simicevic, "What were the Ustasa for Minister Hasanbegovic?," *Balkan Insight*, February 12, 2016, http://www.balkaninsight.com/en/article/what-were-the-ustasa-for-minister-hasanbegovic-02-12-2016.

145. Milekic, "Croatia: Living the Past."

146. Paul Hockenos, "Croatia's Far Right Weaponizes the Past," *Foreign Policy*, May 6, 2016, http://foreignpolicy.com/2016/05/06/croatias-far-right-weaponizes-the-past-ustase-hasanbegovic/.

147. Sven Milekic, "Croatian Minister Praised WWII Fascist Official," *Balkan Insight*, October 28, 2016, http://www.balkaninsight.com/en/article/croatian-minister-praised-ustasa-minister-in-science-paper-10-28-2016.

148. According to the veterans' groups, the plaque was mounted to honor eleven soldiers from the HOS paramilitary unit killed in the 1990s Croatian war. Hrvoje Šimičević, "Usred Jasenovca podigli ploču s ustaškim pozdravom" [A plaque with the Ustaša salute mounted in the center of Jasenovac], *Novosti*, December 4, 2016, https://www.portalnovosti.com/fotogalerija-usred-jasenovca-podigli-plocu-s-ustaskim-pozdravom.

was as offensive as would be a plaque with the words "Sieg Heil!" placed outside of Auschwitz.[149]

Ustasha symbols, however, are not banned in Croatia, and the ruling coalition faced an internal rebellion after the public outcry over the new memorial plaque. While Croatia's president Kolinda Grabar-Kitarović downplayed the use of the slogan, referring to it simply as an "old Croatian salute," the minority Independent Democratic Serb Party (SDSS) and the liberal Croatian People's Party (HNS) threatened to leave the government if the plaque was not removed, while various war veteran associations—on whose support the ruling HDZ party had historically relied—insisted that it remain.[150] The government collapse was averted when the plaque was moved a few miles down the road to the city of Novska and the government announced the formation of a special Council for Dealing with Consequences of the Rule of Non-Democratic Regimes, which was to provide the final ruling on acceptable memorialization of both fascism and communism.[151]

After a year of deliberations, in February 2018 the council came up with what it presented as a compromise solution. The "Za dom spremni!" slogan was, indeed, unconstitutional, but it should still be permitted. The council squared this circle by arguing that, while clearly a slogan used by the Ustasha during WWII and thus an unconstitutional glorification of fascism, it could be used in a more limited context, such as to commemorate HOS militia units that operated during Croatia's independence war. In such a context, the council argued, the slogan should be allowed because it memorialized HOS in the 1990s and not HOS in the 1940s.[152] One of the members of the council explained, "The slogan was *cleansed* through the Homeland War"—meaning that its memory was now attached to the "unproblematic" war of the 1990s and not to the problematic WWII.[153] That HOS units in the 1990s also committed extensive crimes against humanity against non-Croat civilians and that the use of the same slogan was a purposeful continuation of

149. Author interview with Tvrtko Jakovina, professor of history, University of Zagreb, October 24, 2017, Zagreb.

150. Opacic, "Selective Amnesia."

151. Sven Milekic, "Croatia Removes Fascist Slogan Plaque from Jasenovac," *Balkan Insight*, September 7, 2017, http://www.balkaninsight.com/en/article/croatian-wwii-fascist-chant-plaque-from-jasenovac-09-07-2017.

152. Sven Milekic, "Croatian Fascist Slogan Deemed Unconstitutional but Allowable," *Balkan Insight*, February 28, 2018, http://www.balkaninsight.com/en/article/croatian-fascist-slogan-deemed-unconstitutional-but-permitted-02-28-2018.

153. "Lučić: Pozdrav ZDS pročišćen je kroz Domovinski rat" [Lučić: 'Ready for the Homeland' salute cleansed through the Homeland war], *HRT*, February 28, 2018, http://vijesti.hrt.hr/431550/otvoreno-treba-li-u-hrvatskoj-zabraniti-ikonografiju-totalitarnih-rezima (emphasis added).

the legacy of the Ustasha, and not a coincidence, was left completely outside of the contemporary Croatian interpretation of its past. Not only, then, was Croatia's fascist legacy not delegitimized, but it was further normalized, mainstreamed, and weaponized.

Other examples of historical revisionism abound. In April 2017, the city of Zagreb awarded the prestigious annual City Award to Jakov Sedlar, director of the documentary *Jasenovac—The Truth*. This documentary—shown in Zagreb in front of an overflowing audience—claims that the story of Jasenovac was "overblown" and that its high death toll was fabricated by Yugoslav communist and later Serbian nationalist propaganda. The film's biggest "smoking gun" is the alleged revelation that after the Ustasha abandoned the camp in April 1945, Yugoslav communist partisans moved in and turned it into a "place of mass execution" of ethnic Croats, which is why Jasenovac should properly be remembered as a communist, and not a fascist camp.[154]

The documentary is almost comical in its amateurish forgery. It features an image of an apparent facsimile of a *Vjesnik* newspaper front page from 1945, with a headline stating that bodies from Jasenovac were turning up on the banks of the Sava in Zagreb (which is located upstream from Jasenovac). The image was exposed as a forgery. A photograph of apparently happy and content Jasenovac inmates was found to be, in fact, a photograph of a 1978 football team. Newspaper clippings were doctored, with new photographs replacing the originals.[155]

To rebut growing Jasenovac revisionism and especially the claim that Jasenovac was a communist camp, the Jasenovac Memorial Site published a comprehensive book with more than seven hundred photographs from the Jasenovac site between 1945 and 1947, demonstrating that the site was abandoned and in ruins, and not a location of any camp, during this period.[156] The epistemic problem, however, is that in the world of "alternative facts," a professional rebuttal may mean very little after the false narrative has entered the public sphere.[157] The extent to which the basic historical facts about Jasenovac are now subject to revisionism is evident in the 2018 call by Grabar-Kitarović for the creation of an international commission to determine the truth about the camp between 1941 and 1945 "but also

154. Sven Milekic, "Dishonour for Zagreb over 'Alternative Facts' about Holocaust," *Balkan Insight*, April 21, 2017, http://www.balkaninsight.com/en/article/dishonour-for-zagreb-over-alternative-facts-about-holocaust-04-21-2017.

155. Mataušić, interview.

156. Đorđe Mihovilović, *Jasenovac 1945.–1947.: Fotomonografija* [Jasenovac 1945–1947: Photomonograph] (Jasenovac: Javna ustanova Spomen-područja Jasenovac, 2016).

157. Jakovina, interview.

after"—indicating that the narrative that Jasenovac was a communist camp after the war is now accepted at the top seat of power.[158]

Routine, overt, and habitual use of Ustasha chants and insignia has become ubiquitous. Marko Perković-Thompson, one of Croatia's most popular rock singers, performs regularly dressed in Ustasha gear, riling his supporters into Ustasha chants. At soccer games—hotbeds of racism across Europe—the fans often break into the Ustasha salute, calling out "Za dom spremni!" or "Let's go Ustasha!" This happened at a March 2016 soccer match against Israel, with Israel's ambassador to Croatia in attendance.[159] It took a visit of the US special envoy for the Holocaust a month later to coax Croatia's president and prime minister into explicitly condemning Ustasha crimes.[160]

There are also increasingly loud voices in support of the Ustasha and the NDH coming from within the Croatian Catholic Church. In a well-publicized case in 2016, a priest in a popular televised Sunday sermon discussed with nostalgia the NDH and asked, "Whom have we really ever killed outside our borders?"[161] His question, then, assumed that there was nothing wrong with killing *inside* NDH's borders. This normalization of the Ustasha within the Church is not isolated, but in fact quite institutionalized. The Church is one of the main transmitters of Ustasha normalization, based on the simple logic that the Ustasha were Catholics and anticommunists and therefore deserving of Church's support.[162]

Croatia's far-right surge and especially its increasingly problematic official memory of WWII have begun to destabilize its relationships with its traditional allies and friends. Israel's ambassador to Croatia wrote an open letter of protest against Sedlar's film.[163] The United States publicly condemned Croatian government's toleration of the "Za dom spremni!" plaque outside of Jasenovac. The US State Department envoy for the Holocaust warned

---

158. Hina, "Predsjednica o Jasenovcu" [The President on Jasenovac], *Jutarnji list*, April 24, 2018.

159. Goran Penić, "S osječkih tribina se orilo 'Za Dom Spremni' i 'Ajmo, Ustaše'" [The stands in Osijek roar with "Ready for the Homeland" and "Let's go Ustaša" chants], *Jutarnji list*, March 24, 2016. The same thing happened at a Croatia-Israel soccer match in 2012. Dario Brentin, "Ready for the Homeland? Ritual, Remembrance, and Political Extremism in Croatian Football," *Nationalities Papers* 44, no. 6 (2016): 860–76.

160. Lajla Veselica, "Croatia's Jews Fear Growing Intolerance under Conservatives," *Times of Israel*, April 29, 2016, https://www.timesofisrael.com/croatias-jews-fear-growing-intolerance-under-conservatives/.

161. Quoted in Nebojša Blanuša, "Trauma and Taboo: Forbidden Political Questions in Croatia," *Politička misao* 54, nos. 1–2 (2017): 170–96, here 180.

162. Goldstein, interview.

163. Sven Milekic, "Croatian Director Reported for Jasenovac Camp Film," *Balkan Insight*, July 15, 2016, http://www.balkaninsight.com/en/article/croatian-director-reported-for-jasenovac-camp-film-07-15-2016.

Croatia, "It is especially offensive to the Holocaust survivors and their family members. . . . It is hard, especially for the Holocaust survivors, to watch those symbols."[164]

Since 2016, in response to the growing normalization of fascism in Croatia, Serbian and Jewish communities have boycotted the annual memorial events at the Jasenovac site. Instead, they have each organized their own, separate memorials, some at Jasenovac, some at different locations.[165] The community also asked that the Jasenovac exhibition be overhauled: "In 2006, when the Jasenovac exhibition was first opened, displaying the knife and the mallet was not necessary. Now, in the environment of Holocaust revisionism, now it is necessary."[166]

There is increasing general anxiety in the Croatian Jewish community about Holocaust revisionism and denial.[167] "When fascist events start happening in a society, this brings about a sense of uneasiness among Jews. But when institutions don't react, this causes fear because you don't know where that really can lead us," explained Sanja Zoričić Tabaković, a judge and representative of the Jewish community in Zagreb, voicing a common concern within the community.[168] Daniel Ivin, a well-known Croatian Holocaust survivor said, "We know that with the new government we don't have a future, but in recent times, they are starting to take our past."[169]

Memory Divergence: "Holocaust Yes, Genocide No"

Remembrance of crimes of WWII—and, within it, crimes of the Holocaust—as crimes *against* Croats and not *by* them was one mnemonic strategy Croatia

164. Sven Milekic, "US Holocaust Envoy Warns Croatia About Fascist Symbols," *Balkan Insight*, March 24, 2017, http://www.balkaninsight.com/en/article/us-holocaust-envoy-warns-croatia-of-offensive-symbols-03-24-2017. Especially ironic, then, was the February 2017 rally in Croatia's capital Zagreb, when the Croatian far-right party A-HSP marched with the American flag, apparently recognizing in American president Donald Trump a possible ideological ally. AP, "US Embassy Condemns Far-right March with US Flag in Croatia," *Times of Israel*, February 28, 2017, https://www.timesofisrael.com/us-embassy-condemns-far-right-march-with-us-flag-in-croatia/.

165. Sven Milekic, "Boycott Overshadows Croatian Concentration Camp Memorial," *Balkan Insight*, April 22, 2016, http://www.balkaninsight.com/en/article/boycott-overshadows-memorial-for-croatia-wwii-victims-04-22-2016.

166. Goldstein, interview.

167. Kraus, interview.

168. Quoted in Opacic, "Selective Amnesia."

169. Quoted in Sven Milekic, "Croatia Govt Criticised at WWII Death Camp Commemoration," *Balkan Insight*, April 23, 2016, http://www.balkaninsight.com/en/article/alternative-concentration-camp-commemoration-criticizes-croatian-govt-04-23-2016-1. Daniel Ivin is the brother of Slavko Goldstein. He changed his last name in honor of his murdered father Ivo. Daniel survived the Holocaust by joining the partisans at the age of ten. As of 2018, he was recognized by the Imperial War Museum in London as the youngest living WWII partisan anywhere in Europe.

employed in securing its postcommunist identity. The second, in many ways more interesting path was to completely separate NDH genocidal crimes against the Jews from those against the Serbs and Roma and reserve Holocaust memorialization for Nazi (not Croatian) crimes against the Jews while completely erasing NDH crimes against the Serbs and Roma from any remembrance at all.[170]

This strategy can be partly explained by the narrative possibility available to Croatia of simply deflecting the responsibility for the Holocaust to Nazi Germany and placing it within a larger European story of the Holocaust, a story to which, in this reading, Croatia had very little if anything to contribute; this is a strategy also used by other Eastern European states, perhaps most explicitly by Hungary and Poland.

This strategy is also manifest in Croatian contemporary history textbooks, which dutifully, albeit briefly, report on the horrors of the Holocaust but focus this discussion almost exclusively on the larger Holocaust of European Jews, with only one textbook discussing the Holocaust in Croatia in any meaningful detail. If they mention Jasenovac at all, the textbooks always emphasize that its victims were also ethnic Croats (not only Serbs, Jews, and Roma), so as not to escape the reader's attention.[171]

This strategy of memory divergence has played out in a seemingly endless string of controversies, such as the banning of the Anne Frank exhibition in the city of Šibenik in January 2017. The director of the high school where the exhibition was to be displayed did not object to the story of Anne Frank, which he agreed was an important one to be told. What he objected to vociferously were six exhibition panels that, as is the practice with the traveling Anne Frank exhibit (organized by the Anne Frank House in Amsterdam), explained the local context of the Holocaust in the country the exhibition was visiting.[172] "We wanted an exhibition on Anne Frank and the Holocaust, not the Ustasha and the partisans," explained the director, as he took umbrage to the negative depictions of the Ustasha. The paradox of his complaint was that the controversial panels did not discuss the partisans at all but told the stories of three Jewish children in the NDH—Lea Deutsch, who died, and Vojko Šterk and Oto Konstein, who both lived—and

170. Jakovina, interview.

171. Tamara Pavasović Trošt, "War Crimes as Political Tools: Bleiburg and Jasenovac in History Textbooks 1973–2012," in *(Mis)Uses of History: History as a Political Tool in the Western Balkans 1986–2012*, ed. Srdjan M. Jovanović and Veran Stančetić (Belgrade: CSDU Press, 2013), 13–47, here 30.

172. Sven Milekic, "Croatian School Removes Anne Frank Exhibition," *Balkan Insight*, January 20, 2017, http://www.balkaninsight.com/en/article/croatian-school-shocks-by-cancelling-anne-frank-exhibition-01-20-2017.

the heroic effort of Righteous Gentile Diana Budisavljević to save children from Ustasha concentration camps. In this case, providing a Croatian context for the Holocaust, including NDH crimes against Jews and Serbs, was unacceptable.[173]

Other attempts to historicize the NDH and its crimes during WWII were also met with violent rejection. A project in the town of Sisak—the site of the horrific concentration camp for children—to rename a public park after Diana Budisavljević was initially blocked because the term "Ustasha concentration camp" was used to describe where the children perished. A district history competition for high school students held in Sisak disqualified a submission by a group of students who wrote about the Sisak children's camp, judging its content to be "anti-Croatian."[174] An Israeli TV crew was chased off the island of Pag in 2015 by local citizens who were angry that the crew was preparing a film about camps for Jewish and Serbian women located on the island—events that the locals claimed "never happened."[175]

Perhaps even more notable has been the apparent choice to memorialize Jewish victims of the Holocaust pursued by the same groups who have denied the actual history of the Holocaust in Croatia, especially the central location of mass atrocity, Jasenovac. For example, Jakov Sedlar, the same documentary filmmaker who produced the revisionist film that denied Ustasha crimes at Jasenovac, has also made numerous emotional films about the fate of Croatian Jews, including stories about Croatian survivors of Auschwitz and other camps.[176]

Similarly, a pseudo-academic institute established in 2015, the Society for Research of the Threefold Jasenovac Camp, admits that "a number of Jews, excluded from deportations to Germany, were interned at Jasenovac *on German orders*" (emphasis added).[177] But the society goes on to claim that

---

173. Milekic, "Croatian School Removes Anne Frank Exhibition"; AFP, "Anger at Croatian School's Snub of Anne Frank Exhibit," *Times of Israel*, January 24, 2017, https://www.timesofisrael.com/anger-at-croatian-schools-snub-of-anne-frank-exhibit/.

174. Saša Kosanović, "Gdje nestaše ustaše" [Where did the Ustaša go?], *Novosti*, October 30, 2017.

175. "Policijom na Izraelce zbog TV snimanja o konc-logorima" [Dispatching the police against the Israelis for making a TV show about concentration camps], *tportal.hr*, September 6, 2015, https://www.tportal.hr/vijesti/clanak/policijom-na-izraelce-zbog-tv-snimanja-o-konc-logorima-20150906/print.

176. Sven Milekić, "Falsifikator među narodima" [A forger among nations], *Novosti*, September 11, 2016, www.portalnovosti.com/falsifikator-medju-narodima.

177. The designation "threefold" refers to the revisionist argument that the Jasenovac camp had three distinct functions: during WWII as a labor (not death) camp where some 1,500 inmates died of exhaustion, between 1945 and 1948 as a concentration and death camp for Ustasha and other Croatian quislings run by communists, and between 1948 and 1951 as a labor camp for political opponents of the communist regime. None of this corresponds to the historical record. Slavko

Jasenovac was only a detention camp for political prisoners, and that it only turned into a death camp once communists took over in 1945, as a post-war camp for the destruction of Croatian patriots and the German national minority, and the majority of crimes allegedly occurred in that period until the camp's closure in 1951. This narrative then directly uses the camp in which the Holocaust and genocide occurred to criminalize communism. Again, this revisionist history is not carried out in an international vacuum—the society explicitly notes that "the research on Jasenovac camps, especially the period after 1945, is in accordance with the 2006 Council of Europe Resolution on the need for international condemnation of crimes of totalitarian communist regimes."[178]

Igor Vukić, one of the society's leaders, expressed this mnemonic strategy of divergence quite explicitly: "Of course we don't deny the Holocaust. . . . When it comes to Jewish people, nobody who is serious, nobody who is smart can deny or fail to be compassionate with that." However, Vukić said, "When it's about genocide, it is often linked to Serbs. If it's about that, we do deny it."[179]

This strategy has been pursued from the very top. President Grabar-Kitarović paid a visit to Yad Vashem in 2015, and in an emotional statement apologized for crimes against the Jews committed by Croatian fascists during WWII.[180] The same year, however, she refused to attend the annual commemoration at Jasenovac.[181]

In another example of Croatia's attempt to resolve its fundamental narrative inconsistency, the city of Zagreb in 2017 announced plans for the construction of the Museum of the Holocaust in Zagreb. The museum, however, would not focus primarily on victims of the Holocaust in Croatia (in fact, the Croatian Jewish community was never consulted on any phase of the project and learned about it in the media), but would instead be dedicated to all six million Jews who perished in the Holocaust. The obvious

---

Goldstein, *Jasenovac—tragika, mitomanija, istina* [Jasenovac—tragedy, mythomania, truth] (Zaprešić: Fraktura, 2017).

178. "O nama" [About us], Društvo za istraživanje trostrukog logora Jasenovac, accessed March 15, 2019, https://drustvojasenovac.wordpress.com/about/.

179. Quoted in Opacic, "Selective Amnesia." Other members of the society are closer to outright Holocaust denial. The society's president Stjepan Razum, a Catholic priest, has on multiple occasions publicly approved of statements by prominent European Holocaust deniers (Opacic, "Selective Amnesia").

180. Sven Milekic, "Croatian President Apologises for Nazi Regime Deaths," *Balkan Insight*, July 23, 2015, http://www.balkaninsight.com/en/article/croatian-president-apologizes-for-holocaust-in-yad-vashem.

181. Sven Milekić, "Holokaust da, genocid ne," February 1, 2016, article on file with author.

strategy here was to plug the Croatian narrative of the Holocaust into the larger European narrative, while at the same time completely avoiding the memory work necessary to be done at home. This is why the president of the Zagreb Jewish community objected to this project, arguing, "If Croatia considers it should build a monument to the victims of the Holocaust, I believe a monument should be built to all victims of the Ustasha terror in Croatia," meaning to Serbs, Roma, and other enemies of the Ustasha state.[182]

And while the Holocaust is recognized—although never taken responsibility for—the very notion that the NDH committed genocide against the Serbs is taboo, especially within the rightist circles in Croatia, where the "word genocide cannot cross the lips," and the genocide is often referred to in Croatian historiography euphemistically as the "Serbian question in Croatia."[183] This denial of the true character of the NDH, especially its persecution of the Serbs, is further deepened by the complete transformation of the ethnic makeup of Croatia following the 1995 war and the exodus of some three hundred thousand Serbs from the state. It is this historically new ethnic homogeneity of Croatia that is silencing minority voices and creating a vision of the past that is for Croats only. The refusal to memorialize the genocide against the Serbs is also the result of the still very raw perception of Serbs as aggressors during the 1990s war, and as such not worthy of empathy. But more directly, it allows for the continuing discrimination against Croatia's Serb minority, evident in problems with refugee return, the denial of Serb Cyrillic script in public places, and a general tendency to conceptualize of Croatia as a state of *Croatians*, and not Croatian *citizens* (which would include Serb and other minorities).[184]

This particular kind of Holocaust remembrance, which some in Croatia have called "Holocaust yes, genocide no," also serves as a form of screen memory, which absolves Croatia from both the NDH crimes of the Holocaust and the more recent war crimes against Croatia's Serb minority in the 1990s.[185] This removal of Serbs as possible victims of any Croatian atrocity then also serves other Croatia's ontological security needs: it further legitimizes Croatia as an ethnic homeland and it removes the bad past from its state-building project, stabilizing Croatia's view of self and its place in the European society of states.

---

182. Godeč, "Muzej Holokausta u Zagrebu."

183. Goldstein, interview.

184. Dejan Jović, *War and Myth: The Politics of Identity in Contemporary Croatia* (Zaprešić: Fraktura, 2017).

185. Milekić, "Holokaust da."

Contemporary Jewish Life and Non-state Remembrance

In the statewide census carried out in 2011, only 536 citizens of Croatia self-identified as Jews.[186] The community is too small to have its own representation as a national minority in the Croatian Parliament, and it is represented by proxy by a Roma MP. However small, the community is quite active and organizes many Holocaust remembrance projects independently, often completely outside of state purview and without state support. The Zagreb Jewish community hosts the annual Shoah Academy, which educates around three thousand students each year on the Holocaust, trying to compensate for the extremely scarce public education about the Holocaust in Croatian schools.[187] Since 2007, there has been an annual Jewish Film Festival, since 2012 a Department of Jewish Studies at the University of Zagreb, and the Bet Israel Jewish community hosts a Jewish K–8 school and a daycare center in Zagreb.[188]

The Jewish community has also taken upon itself to erect new memorials at various Holocaust sites across Croatia, including replacing memorials that were demolished in the wave of monument destruction in 1990–2000. In 2004, the Jewish community erected a monument in Tenja, the site of the Osijek ghetto. In 2013, a memorial to Holocaust victims was unveiled at the cemetery in Đakovo, the work of Israeli artist Dina Gross Merhav, herself a Croatian Holocaust survivor.[189] Merhav also donated a large collection of her art to her hometown of Vinkovci with the vision of creating a sculpture park in memory of her family.[190]

These independent activities, as well as remembrance projects by civil society groups such as Documenta and the Center for Holocaust Research and Education, are taking place in a political and legal environment at best disinterested and often hostile to the memory of the Holocaust.[191] Perhaps

186. Opacic, "Selective Amnesia." The Zagreb Jewish community counts 1,300 members. Kraus, interview.

187. Boris Pavelić, "Kraus: O Muzeju Holokausta nitko ništa nije pitao Židove" [Kraus: Nobody asked the Jews about the Holocaust museum], *Novi list*, October 6, 2017.

188. Goldstein, interview.

189. "Peace in Heaven, 2013, Iron 260x340x155 cm," Dina Merhav, Sculptress, accessed February 10, 2019, http://ein-hod.info/artists/dina/exhibition/zakovo/zakovo.htm.

190. "Closing a Life Circle, Vinkovci July 2013; Flying Birds, Exhibition in the Town Gallery," Dina Merhav, Sculptress, accessed February 10, 2019, http://ein-hod.info/artists/dina/exhibition/vinkovci/vinkovci.html.

191. Documenta maintains a website that discusses memorialization of the Dotršćina mass grave site. It also runs an oral history project, which includes oral histories of Holocaust survivors. Belgrade-based CHRE has worked with Croatian partners from the University of Rijeka to create a comprehensive map of killing sites in the NDH, at "Killing Sites: The First Stage of the Holocaust in Serbia and Croatia," accessed February 10, 2019, www.killingsites.org.

the most pressing continuing problem facing the small remaining Jewish community is the absence of any restitution law that would govern the return of Jewish property "Aryanized" during WWII. The very limited legislation that does exist only allows claimants in the first order of succession (surviving children or grandchildren, but not brothers and sisters and their descendants) and the deadline for applications is only six months, which is far too short of a period to allow for such complex historical claims. The highest amount that can be claimed for compensation is 500,000 Euro, which would immediately disqualify major property claims, such as whole buildings in downtown Zagreb taken from Jewish families and businesses during the Holocaust.[192]

This legal framework therefore denies the historical realities and consequences of the Holocaust. As it was often entire families who were murdered, the point of restitution laws is to allow relatives—however distant—to claim property, an issue of justice that is a staple of international restitution policies. In cases of unclaimed property, the best practice is for property to be returned to the local Jewish community to dispense with as it chooses; this was the spirit of the 2009 Terezin Declaration on Holocaust Era Assets, of which Croatia was a signatory.[193]

But the most significant—and political—problem with Holocaust restitution in Croatia is that Croatia does not recognize the NDH as its legal predecessor, and only claims socialist Yugoslavia as its state parent, allowing limited restitution only for property seized after the communist takeover in 1945, when the Holocaust was over. According to the 1997 Law on Restitution/Compensation of Property Taken during the Time of the Yugoslav Communist Government, only the property confiscated by Yugoslavia can be returned to its owners, but not property confiscated by the NDH during the "Aryanization of property" phase of the Holocaust.[194] The ugly paradox of this law is that members of the Ustasha regime and their families can claim property confiscated by the communist Yugoslavia after May 15, 1945,

192. Ljiljana Dobrovšak, "Restitution of Jewish Property in Croatia," *LIMES plus: časopis za društvene i humanističke nauke* 7, no. 2 (2017): 65–88, here 75; Haris Dajč, "Jews of Former Yugoslavia and Their Decline after Wars in Yugoslavia: Legal and Material Positions in Serbia, Croatia and Bosnia & Herzegovina 1991–2016," *Belgrade Historical Review* 8 (2017): 117–36.

193. "Terezin Declaration," World Jewish Restitution Organization, accessed March 15, 2019, https://wjro.org.il/our-work/international-declarations-resolutions/terezin-declaration/.

194. Sven Milekic, "Croatians Struggle to Regain Property Confiscated in WWII," *Balkan Insight*, December 6, 2017, http://www.balkaninsight.com/en/article/croatians-struggle-to-regain-property-confiscated-in-wwii-12-05-2017.

but Jewish families whose property was confiscated by the NDH between 1941 and 1945 can claim nothing at all.[195]

Croatia is a state in crisis. The obvious crisis is economic, where high unemployment rates and a dropping standard of living have been a rude awakening after the high expectations following accession to the European Union in 2013.[196] But more deeply, Croatia is a state acutely divided about its past, its role in WWII, its place in the larger history of Europe, its status as a full member of the EU, and its relationship to the multilayered legacies of fascism, communism, and the ethnic war of the 1990s.

This crisis can best be understood as a feeling of profound ontological insecurity, insecurity about Croatia's identity, its view of self, and even its state biography. Croatia's political memory, especially its memory of the Holocaust and of communism, is deeply contested, and the cleavage between the red and black Croatia is the crack at the state's foundation.

Croatia's transition from communism into the European embrace has produced tremendous narrative rewriting, relaxing some of the most established historical canons of the twentieth century and creating a political environment fertile for mnemonic challenges, disruptions, and revisions. Croatia's narratives about its past have become "islands of memory."[197] The memories of the Holocaust exist, contained within the remembrance practices of the ever-dwindling Jewish community, but isolated from the larger narrative arc of Croatia's WWII. The memories of the NDH genocide against the Serbs—in many ways the principal genocidal effort of the NDH—are almost completely suppressed, existing on the margins within an ethnic minority that increasingly feels unwelcome and disenfranchised. The overwhelming public narrative of the past is one of Croatia's suffering, first by Yugoslav communists in 1945, and then—in a linear narrative direction—by the Serbs in 1991.

To secure this new narrative, Croatian principal memory actors—right-wing political parties, the intellectual elite, the media, historical commissions—have engaged in sustained historical revisionism that directly attributed to communists the atrocities committed (often against them) by Croatian fascists. This long-term systematic effort to criminalize the communist regime and retroactively burden it with fascist crimes has been an incredibly successful

195. Dobrovšak, "Restitution of Jewish Property in Croatia."

196. Sinisa Bogdanic and Sead Husic, "Rude Awakening for Croatia after EU accession," *Deutsche Welle*, April 15, 2014, http://www.dw.com/en/rude-awakening-for-croatia-after-eu-accession/a-17559492.

197. Pavlaković, interview.

effort of delegitimizing not only the entire legacy of Yugoslav socialism but also its biggest achievement—Yugoslav multiculturalism. This has then provided further legitimacy for Croatia's construction of its postcommunist identity as an ethnically homogenous and Catholic state.

All of this revisionism has happened not in spite, but as a result of the EU's own practices of remembrance, especially its reductionist interpretation of the twentieth century as an era of two totalitarianisms, equal in their criminal nature. The EU's youngest member turned out to be a quick study.

Chapter 4

The Long Shadows of Vilna

Unlike Serbia and Croatia, which both had historically small Jewish communities, the Jews in Lithuania had a remarkably long and rich history and on the eve of World War II comprised at least 7 percent of Lithuania's population as the country's largest ethnic minority. Lithuanian Jews—Litvaks—developed a distinct regional culture with a special Yiddish dialect. For centuries, Lithuania was the center of Yiddish cultural life in Europe. In the Jewish world, Vilnius (Vilna in Hebrew)—the home to 150 various Jewish organizations—was known as the Jerusalem of the north, the cultural epicenter of Jewish life in Eastern Europe. It was in Vilnius that the famous YIVO Institute for Jewish Research was founded in 1925 to study all aspects of Jewish life—language, history, religion, and culture, while the first Jewish museum in Lithuania was established as early as 1913.[1]

At the end of World War I, Lithuania established an independent state, following a series of wars of independence in which more than two thousand

1. Both Poland and Lithuania claimed Vilnius at the end of World War I. Poland occupied the city in 1920 and kept it under its hold until the Soviet occupation of Poland in 1939, after which the USSR transferred it—briefly—to Lithuania. Vilnius was at least 30 percent and by some estimates as high as 45 percent Jewish before the war. The majority population was in fact Polish, with Lithuanians a distinct minority.

Jews fought side by side with Lithuanians.[2] Newly independent Lithuania granted ethnic minorities citizen rights, and Jews had elected representatives in the Lithuanian parliament. Jews also had a modicum of self-rule through the Jewish National Council, which elected a Jewish representative to serve in the Lithuanian government as the minister for Jewish affairs. This period (1918–24) represented a high mark for Jewish civil liberties in Lithuania, a period of Jewish civic representation in the high ranks of the government, the military, and the police. The Ministry of Jewish Affairs was abolished in 1924 amid a growing sense among ethnic Lithuanians that Jewish autonomy was running counter to efforts at creating strong Lithuanian national identity, unity, and loyalty.[3]

As the 1930s approached, anti-Semitism was on the rise in Lithuania, diffused from elsewhere in Europe. It was also the result of increasing resentment by ethnic Lithuanians of the perceived economic progress and higher economic status of Lithuanian Jews.[4] The Jews were beginning to be seen as an economic threat. One of the most virulent anti-Semitic organizations in the 1930s was the Lithuanian Businessmen's Association, which called for mass boycotts of Jewish businesses.[5] Geležinis Vilkas (Iron Wolf), another anti-Semitic organization, advocated "Lithuanian struggle for liberation from Jewish economic slavery" but through non-excessive, "humane" means.[6]

By the late 1930s anti-Semitic incidents were also on the rise. Anti-Semitism was becoming more common and more prominent in newspapers and academic publications. Jewish students were attacked at Kaunas University in 1938. In 1939, Jews were not allowed to compete in the World Lithuanian Olympics, a major Lithuanian sporting competition at the time. These incidents, however, were mostly renounced by the Lithuanian government,

2. Saulius Sužiedėlis and Šarūnas Liekis, "Conflicting Memories: The Reception of the Holocaust in Lithuania," in *Bringing the Dark Past to Life: The Reception of the Holocaust in Post-Communist Europe*, ed. Joanna B Michlic and John-Paul Himka (Lincoln: University of Nebraska Press, 2013), 319–51, here 321.

3. Saulius Sužiedėlis, "The Historical Sources for Antisemitism in Lithuania and Jewish-Lithuanian Relations during the 1930s," in *The Vanished World of Lithuanian Jews*, ed. Alvydas Nikžentaitis, Stefan Schreiner, and Darius Staliūnas (Amsterdam: Brill, 2004), 119–54, here 124.

4. By 1936, Jews owned more than half of Lithuania's small businesses. By 1937, more than 40 percent of Lithuania's doctors and lawyers were Jewish, although almost no Jews were employed in public service or the military. Sužiedėlis, "Historical Sources," 125.

5. Anatol Lieven, *The Baltic Revolution: Estonia, Latvia, Lithuania, and the Path to Independence* (New Haven: Yale University Press, 1993), 145.

6. Sužiedėlis, "Historical Sources," 131.

and in general Lithuania's treatment of its Jews compares very favorably to that of Poland, where anti-Semitism was deeper and more pronounced.[7]

But Lithuania was a society profoundly ethnically divided—Lithuanians and Jews spoke mostly different languages, attended different social events, and lived largely in social isolation from each other. It is the tragic paradox of the size, vibrancy, success, and self-sufficiency of the prewar Lithuanian Jewish community that it did not feel compelled to integrate—as was the case with much smaller communities in the former Yugoslavia—and this lack of integration in part precipitated its destruction.[8]

Soviet Occupation 1940–41

In August 1939, the Soviet Union and Nazi Germany signed the Molotov-Ribbentrop non-aggression pact. On September 19, the Red Army entered Vilnius, and a few weeks later the agreement was made that would return Vilnius to the still independent Lithuania. For a few months, thousands of Polish Jews who were fleeing the Nazi occupation of Poland moved to Lithuania, swelling the Lithuanian Jewish numbers to some two hundred sixty thousand, or 10 percent of Lithuania's population. Until June 1940, Vilnius was a hotbed of Jewish political activity and a center of documentation and information about the persecution of Jews already underway in Nazi-occupied Europe.[9]

On June 15, 1940, the Soviet Union invaded Lithuania, which became the first of the three Baltic states to fall. A new Soviet puppet government was formed, headed by a Lithuanian communist, Justas Paleckis. The new government held show elections and unanimously "voted" to turn Lithuania into a Lithuanian Soviet Socialist Republic and join the Soviet Union. The annexation of Lithuania to the USSR was complete.[10]

In the immediate aftermath of the annexation, Soviet authorities embarked on an extensive process of Sovietization in Lithuania. This involved the

7. For example, the Lithuanian government never instituted the *numerus clausus* anti-Jewish laws that many other governments, including the government of Yugoslavia, did in this period. Sužiedėlis, "Historical Sources," 145.

8. On the larger relationship between Jewish prewar integration and chances of survival, see Evgeny Finkel, *Ordinary Jews: Choice and Survival during the Holocaust* (Princeton, NJ: Princeton University Press, 2017); Jeffrey S. Kopstein and Jason Wittenberg, *Intimate Violence: Anti-Jewish Pogroms on the Eve of the Holocaust* (Ithaca, NY: Cornell University Press, 2018).

9. Yad Vashem, "Overview," *The Jerusalem of Lithuania: The Story of the Jewish Community of Vilna*, accessed February 16, 2019, https://www.yadvashem.org/yv/en/exhibitions/vilna/overview.asp.

10. Timothy Snyder, *The Reconstruction of Nations: Poland, Ukraine, Lithuania, Belarus, 1569–1999* (New Haven: Yale University Press, 2003), 83.

nationalization of all land, the breaking up of large farms, and their redistribution. Also nationalized were banks, large companies, and all real estate. The massive disruption of the economy produced chaos and food shortages. Sovietization was also political—all religious, cultural and political organizations were prohibited, the Communist Party the only one allowed. Arrests of "enemies of the people" followed. Then came the deportations—in June–July of 1940 alone, twenty thousand people (mostly former public and military officials, as well as members of the intellectual elite and their families) were deported to Siberia.[11] In another massive wave of deportations in June 1941, another ten to twenty thousand Lithuanians were forcibly removed from the country.[12] Many died in Siberian camps from exposure, disease or exhaustion.

Significantly, however, these deportations were political and not ethnic in nature—Soviet documents indicate that the purpose of the deportations was a form of social class destratification—the elimination of the bourgeoisie but also the squelching of any nascent anti-Soviet resistance.[13] In fact, not only were the deportations not aimed to repopulate the Baltics with Russians (as became the Lithuanian nationalist narrative), but it was the Jews who bore the brunt of the deportations, on account of their class status and involvement in private business enterprise.[14]

Sovietization and deportations created a further crack in Lithuanian-Jewish relations. There was widespread belief among Lithuanians that Jews welcomed the USSR as the Jewish socialist organizations in Lithuania were strong, and many Jews were no doubt attracted to a multicultural communist utopia that the Soviet Union promised.

But, contrary to Lithuanian perception of Soviet favoritism of the Jews, Soviet occupation stopped Jewish political and cultural organizing in its tracks. Jewish educational and cultural programs were shut down and banned.[15] Zionists, religious groups, and Jewish businesses were treated especially harshly (57 percent of all nationalized businesses in Lithuania were Jewish

11. Dovilė Budrytė, "'We Call it Genocide': Soviet Deportations and Repressions in the Memory of Lithuanians," in *The Genocidal Temptation: Auschwitz, Hiroshima, Rwanda, and Beyond*, ed. Robert S. Frey (Lanham: University Press of America, 2004), 79–101, here 82.

12. Alexander Statiev, *The Soviet Counterinsurgency in the Western Borderlands* (Cambridge: Cambridge University Press, 2010), 167–68.

13. Dovilė Budrytė, *Taming Nationalism?: Political Community Building in the Post-Soviet Baltic States* (Aldershot: Ashgate, 2005).

14. Statiev, *Soviet Counterinsurgency*.

15. "Overview," *Jerusalem of Lithuania*.

owned).[16] The use of Hebrew was prohibited (but Yiddish was allowed). Some 1,700 Lithuanian Jews deemed "class enemies" were deported to the Far East in the wave of deportations.[17]

The Soviets did institute some Jewish-friendly policies that further alienated ethnic Lithuanians. For example, prior university enrollment restrictions for Jewish students were lifted, and Jews were allowed to advance to supervisor positions in public administration.[18] These inconsistent policies fueled the already growing anti-Semitism and fostered a perception among the Lithuanians that it was the *Jews* who were the principal agents of Soviet repression. This created a sense—which exists in large part until this day—that the Jews welcomed the Soviets, that they prospered under them, and that they gleefully enjoyed the Soviet repression and deportation of Lithuanians. It is in this context that the onset of the Holocaust, the Lithuanian welcome of Nazi Germany, and the subsequent Lithuanian participation in the extermination of their fellow citizens needs to be understood.

The Holocaust in Lithuania

Nazi Germany's invasion of the Soviet Union—Operation Barbarossa—began on June 22, 1941. Within weeks, the Red Army withdrew and Germany occupied the Baltics, including Lithuania. Relieved to see the Soviets out, many Lithuanians welcomed the Germans as liberators.[19] There was considerable expectation that Germany would grant Lithuania its independence back. Indeed, in the first weeks of the occupation, Germany allowed the establishment of the Lithuanian Provisional Government, and there were indications that Germany would let Lithuania organize a form of self-rule, akin to the Independent State of Croatia.[20] These hopes were squashed after a few months when Germany took full control and established Reichskommissariat Ostland in July.

16. Dov Levin, *The Litvaks: A Short History of the Jews in Lithuania* (Jerusalem: Yad Vashem, 2000), 194.

17. Violeta Davoliūtė, "Multidirectional Memory and the Deportation of Lithuanian Jews," *Ethnicity Studies/Etniskumo Studijos* 2 (2015): 131–50, here 134.

18. Levin, *Litvaks*.

19. Dina Porat, "The Holocaust in Lithuania: Some Unique Aspects," in *The Final Solution: Origins and Implementation*, ed. David Cesarani (London: Routledge, 1994), 159–74, here 166; Budrytė, "'We Call it Genocide,'" 82.

20. Author interview with Andžej Pukšto, chair of the Department of Political Science, Vytautas Magnus University, February 3, 2018, Vilnius.

Pogroms and Collaboration

As the Soviets retreated, the Lithuanian Activist Front (LAF), a Lithuanian militia group, mounted an insurgency against the Soviets (the so-called June Uprising) and managed to take control of two major cities, Vilnius and Kaunas (Kovno), for about a week before the Wehrmacht took full control of the country. Too small and weak to fight the Red Army by themselves—the LAF had no more than sixteen to twenty thousand members—the militia joined forces with the advancing German troops to drive the Soviets out. As the Germans took control, they disbanded the LAF, reorganized some units into police battalions, and sent them out to begin the extermination of Lithuanian Jews.

But the LAF harbored anti-Semitic views even before it was weaponized by the Nazis to become one of the main tools of the Holocaust in Lithuania. The LAF manifesto, *What Are the Activists Fighting For?*, states, "The Lithuanian Activist Front, by restoring the new Lithuania, is determined to carry out an immediate and fundamental purging of the Lithuanian nation and its land of Jews, parasites and monsters . . . [this] shall be one of the most essential preconditions for starting a new life."[21]

The first pogroms of Jews happened against the background of the chaotic Soviet retreat on June 22 and the German arrival on June 24–25.[22] While Lithuanian mainstream historiography continues to deny that it was pro-German Lithuanian nationalist militia who began the killing even before the Germans arrived, there is strong evidence that points to Lithuanians—not Germans—carrying out the first pogroms both immediately before and immediately after the German troops arrived.[23] There is evidence that smaller-scale murderous attacks against the Jews happened in at least forty locations before the arrival of German troops.[24] Lithuanian militia wearing white armbands patrolled the cities, hunted the Jews, robbed and humiliated

21. Quoted in Yitzhak Arad, "The Murder of the Jews in German-Occupied Lithuania (1941–1944)," in *The Vanished World of Lithuanian Jews*, ed. Alvydas Nikžentaitis, Stefan Schreiner, and Darius Staliūnas (Amsterdam: Brill, 2004), 175–204, here 191.

22. In some places, the Germans did not establish full administrative control until a few days or more later, and the anti-Jewish violence stretched until July. Author correspondence with Dovid Katz, professor, Department of Philosophy and Communications, Vilnius Gediminas Technical University, July 2, 2018.

23. Arad, "Murder of the Jews," 177–80; Porat, "Holocaust in Lithuania," 163; United States Holocaust Memorial Museum, "Lithuania," accessed February 16, 2019, https://www.ushmm.org/wlc/en/article.php?ModuleId=10005444; Yad Vashem, "Kovno," accessed February 16, 2019, http://www.yadvashem.org/righteous/stories/kovno.html.

24. Levin, *Litvaks*, 218.

them, and often shot them.[25] They attacked panicked fleeing Jewish refugees.[26] Holocaust survivors refer to these days of chaos and violence prior to the German arrival as "the first week," distinguishing them in their memory from what came after.[27] The violence was so extensive that some Jews even met the subsequent establishment of German administrative control with a dose of relief, hoping the worst was over.[28] This is an issue of responsibility that is at the core of Lithuania's contemporary Holocaust memory knot.

The first big pogrom began in Kaunas on June 25, where Lithuanian mobs—LAF partisans and Lithuanian civilians—killed hundreds of Jews in the city. The violence was gruesome (beheadings, mutilations, clubbing) and it happened in front of cheering crowds. The most infamous of these attacks was the Lietūkis garage massacre in Kaunas on June 27, which occurred in a festive atmosphere. There was much clapping as each Jew was killed, and the Lithuanian killers played popular songs on the accordion after the job was done.[29] Between June 25 and 27, a massive pogrom occurred in the predominantly Jewish Vilijampolė neighborhood where Lithuanian militia, joined by some students, killed about a thousand Jews.[30]

In Lithuanian historiography much has been made of the fact that the German forces were present in the vicinity or at the location of some of these pogroms, and so Lithuanians cannot be deemed responsible for acting out, presumably out of fear of German reprisal. Lithuanian historians also point to the report by the SS-Brigadier General Franz Walther Stahlecker, who in October 1941 reported back to his superiors, "To our surprise it was not easy at first to set in motion an extensive pogrom against Jews."[31] There is also the argument that Jews were targeted as communists, not Jews per

25. Christoph Dieckmann and Saulius Sužiedėlis, *The Persecution and Mass Murder of Lithuanian Jews during Summer and Fall of 1941* (Vilnius: Margi Rastai, 2006), 120.

26. Dieckmann and Sužiedėlis, *Persecution and Mass Murder*, 102.

27. Interviews by Dovid Katz of Lithuanian Holocaust survivors who describe violence in "the first week" prior to the arrival of the Germans are available at Dovid Katz, "Holocaust in Lithuania: The First Week," YouTube playlist, last modified July 3, 2018, https://www.youtube.com/playlist?list=PLA2BAA3ADC43CC101&feature=plpp.

28. Tomasz Szarota, *On the Threshold of the Holocaust: Anti-Jewish Riots and Pogroms in Occupied Europe—Warsaw, Paris, The Hague, Amsterdam, Antwerp, Kaunas* (New York: Peter Lang, 2015), 170.

29. Ernst Klee, Willi Dressen, and Volker Riess, *"The Good Old Days": The Holocaust as Seen by Its Perpetrators and Bystanders* (New York: Free Press, 1991), 31.

30. Dieckmann and Sužiedėlis, *Persecution and Mass Murder*, 123.

31. Report by Stahlecker on the activities of Einsatzgruppe A until October 15, 1941, in Office of United States Chief of Counsel for Prosecution of Axis Criminality, *Nazi Conspiracy and Aggression*, Vol. 7 (Washington, DC: United States Government Printing Office, 1946), 984, available via the Library of Congress website, accessed February 16, 2019, http://www.loc.gov/rr/frd/Military_Law/pdf/NT_Nazi_Vol-VII.pdf. In another part of the report, however, Stahlecker writes, "The active antisemitism which flared up quickly after the German occupation did not falter. Lithuanians

se. However, in their study of the actual mechanics of anti-Jewish pogroms on the eve of the Holocaust, Jeffrey Kopstein and Jason Wittenberg point to a very different dynamic—one that is driven by local ethnic resentment and the majority violently suppressing Jewish minorities who were increasingly considered politically threatening.[32] And because local nationalists constructed the Jews as communists—regardless of how few Jews in fact were communist—"while Germans wanted the locals to act against the Jews, they stopped well short of forcing the issue. Therefore, the German presence does not automatically absolve civilian populations of responsibility."[33] The virulence of local anticommunism, blended with local anti-Semitism, was enough for the violence to erupt.

Over the next few weeks, pogroms spread to the Lithuanian countryside—by early July, between seven and eight thousand Jews were killed in this first Holocaust wave.[34] Lithuanian militiamen searched for Jews and communists indiscriminately, while anti-Semitic proclamations blasted from the government radio, inciting the population to take justice in their own hands and eliminate the enemy within.[35] The Lithuanian nationalist government considered the Jews to be, quite simply, enemies, based on their supposed sympathies with the Soviet Union. They not only did not protect the Jews, but they adopted the Nazi extermination goal as their own.[36]

Special killing squads, the *Einsatzgruppen*, followed the advance of the Wehrmacht and immediately began organizing the full-scale murder of Lithuanian Jews.[37] The first systemic killing by the Nazis occurred as early as June 24, when around two hundred male Jews were shot in the town of Gargždai.[38] The *Einsatzgruppen* worked through Lithuanian auxiliaries, primarily the Lithuanian Security Police. They received full support from the

---

are voluntarily and untiringly at our disposal for all measures against Jews: sometimes they even execute such measures on their own" (989).

32. Kopstein and Wittenberg, *Intimate Violence*.

33. Kopstein and Wittenberg, *Intimate Violence*, 46.

34. Arad, "Murder of the Jews," 180.

35. Michael MacQueen, "Nazi Policy toward the Jews in the Reichskommissariat Ostland, June–December 1941: From White Terror to Holocaust in Lithuania," in *Bitter Legacy: Confronting the Holocaust in the USSR*, ed. Zvi Y. Gitelman (Bloomington: Indiana University Press, 1997), 91–103, here 97.

36. Arūnas Bubnys, "Holocaust in Lithuania: An Outline of the Major Stages and Their Results," in *The Vanished World of Lithuanian Jews*, ed. Alvydas Nikžentaitis, Stefan Schreiner, and Darius Staliūnas (Amsterdam: Brill, 2004), 205–22, here 215.

37. Porat, "Holocaust in Lithuania," 159.

38. Vilna Gaon State Jewish Museum, "The First Mass Execution of the Jews of Gargždai," *Holocaust Atlas of Lithuania*, accessed February 16, 2019, http://www.holocaustatlas.lt/EN/#a_atlas/search//page/1/item/173. Also see Konrad Kwiet, "Rehearsing for Murder: The Beginning of the Final Solution in Lithuania in June 1941," *Holocaust and Genocide Studies* 12, no. 1 (1998): 3–26.

Lithuanian municipal authorities and attracted mass participation by Lithuanian police units, who were drafted into these auxiliary German forces.[39] On occasion, German commanders reported that the enthusiasm of Lithuanian units surpassed that of the SS.[40]

Some of the Lithuanian operatives were affiliated with Iron Wolf, others with the Lithuanian Labor Guard.[41] Lithuanian troops hunted the Jews, prepared the logistics of the executions, drove trucks to the shooting sites, buried the bodies—and did the actual shooting.[42] By the end of August 1941, most Jews in Lithuania's countryside—approximately sixteen thousand, mostly men—had been shot.

By mid-August, the *Einsatzgruppen* expanded their actions to now include all Jews, indiscriminately—women, children, the elderly—on the direct orders of Heinrich Himmler.[43] This coincided with the establishment of Jewish ghettos across Lithuania—with the biggest ones in Vilnius (Vilna ghetto), Kaunas (Kovno ghetto), and Šiauliai (Shavli ghetto). The ghettos were split into two—the labor ghetto where able bodied Jews were put to work as slaves, and the non-working ghetto from which Jews deemed unfit for work were regularly taken in large groups and shot. Some ghettos were liquidated immediately—almost all Jews of the Kovno and Vilna non-working ghettos were shot in October 1941. In Kovno alone the German *Grossaktion* left ten thousand Jews from the ghetto dead in one day—October 29.[44]

In December 1941, SS Colonel Karl Jäger, the commanding officer of Einsatzkommando 3, wrote back to his supervisors that the objective of "clearing Lithuania of Jews" was "virtually completed" thanks to the "cooperation of the Lithuanian Partisans and Civil Authority."[45]

---

39. Arad, "Murder of the Jews," 182.

40. Porat, "Holocaust in Lithuania," 164.

41. Porat, "Holocaust in Lithuania," 162; Michael MacQueen, "The Context of Mass Destruction: Agents and Prerequisites of the Holocaust in Lithuania," *Holocaust and Genocide Studies* 12, no. 1 (1998): 27–48.

42. There are many first-hand accounts of the killing operations by Lithuanian perpetrators themselves. Some of the most powerful accounts were presented in the exhibition *Some Were Neighbors* at the US Holocaust Memorial Museum in Washington, DC, in 2013. Video testimonies are available at the exhibition website, accessed February 16, 2019, http://somewereneighbors.ushmm.org.

43. Arad, "Murder of the Jews," 184.

44. United States Holocaust Memorial Museum, "Kovno," accessed February 16, 2019, https://www.ushmm.org/wlc/en/article.php?ModuleId=10005174; United States Holocaust Memorial Museum, "Vilna," accessed February 16, 2019, https://www.ushmm.org/wlc/en/article.php?ModuleId=10005173.

45. Dieckmann and Sužiedėlis, *Persecution and Mass Murder*, 113.

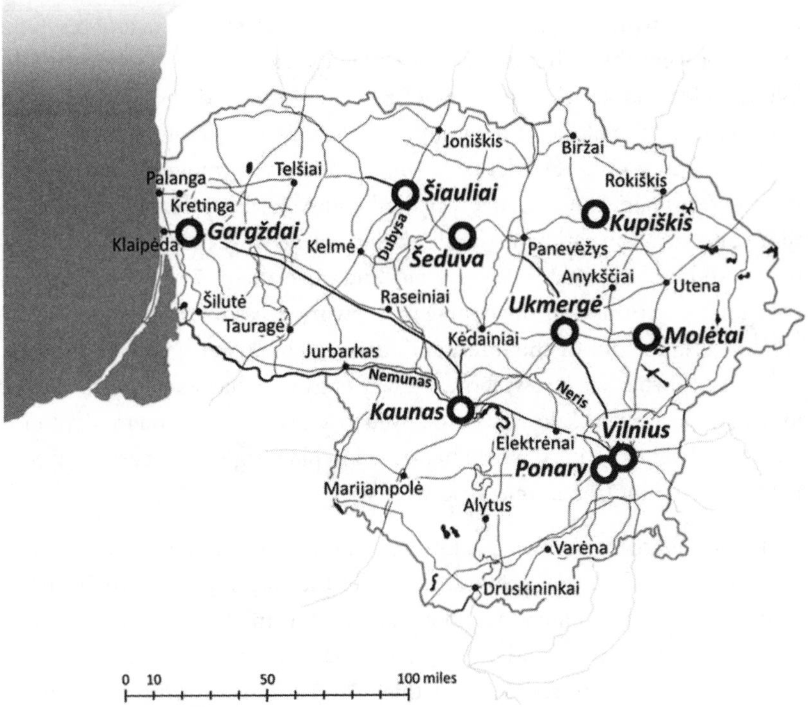

MAP 3. Ghettos and execution sites in Lithuania (map by Aleksandar Stanojlović)

The Executions at Ponary

The biggest shooting site was at Ponary (Paneriai in Lithuanian), a forest just outside of Vilnius and a popular weekend destination before the war. Starting in July 1941 and continuing until August 1944, Jews, mostly from the Vilna ghetto but also brought in from elsewhere, were taken in groups of a few dozen to the edge of death pits. There they were ordered to take off their clothes and hand over any valuables, and then they were shot. The Ponary executions were carried out by Lithuanian units, the Special Squad (Ypatingasis būrys, also known as "white armbanders"), under the command of the German Security Police and the SS.

As the executions at Ponary continued—by August 1944, at least seventy-two thousand Jews had been murdered in the forest—local Lithuanians who lived in nearby villages sold and resold abandoned Jewish clothes and valuables, cooked meals for the Special Squad, and went on with their lives, even though mass death was obvious to all as the unmistakable stench of corpses enveloped the forest.[46] Lithuanian women waited for the trucks to be brought back from the killing fields. They would then weed out the dresses stripped off of Jewish women, cut out the sewn in Star of David patch, and resell the dresses or wear them themselves.[47] A few helped a rare Jew who escaped the killing fields and knocked on the door begging for food and clothes, while many ignored the pleas for help until they heard the final gunshots.[48]

In 1944, as part of Sonderaktion 1005, aimed at removing the traces of mass extermination, Germans recruited eighty Jewish prisoners from Stutthof concentration camp into *Leichenkommando* (corpse units) whose job was to dig up bodies buried in Ponary pits and burn them. In an extraordinary coordinated action, over the course of a few months twelve of these prisoners dug a tunnel out of the forest and managed to escape.[49]

Much of what we know about Ponary is from a diary kept by the Polish journalist Kazimierz Sakowicz, who lived in a nearby town and meticulously recorded daily shootings, which happened in plain sight. In a passage typical for its flat, unemotional tone, Sakowicz writes,

> The Lithuanians throw the clothing onto a pile; suddenly one of the Lithuanians pulls out a child from under the clothing and throws him into the pit; again a child, and again another. In the same way—into the pit. One of the Lithuanians stands over the pit and shoots at these children, as we can see. What is this? The desperate mothers thought that in this way "they had saved" the lives of the children, hiding under the clothing. Evidently, they expected that when the clothing was collected the children hidden in that way might be saved. Unfortunately.[50]

---

46. Also killed at Ponary were eight thousand Poles, as well as thousands of Lithuanians, Roma, and Soviet POWs. Timothy Snyder, "Neglecting the Lithuanian Holocaust," *New York Review of Books*, July 25, 2011, http://www.nybooks.com/daily/2011/07/25/neglecting-lithuanian-holocaust.

47. Author interview with Faina Kukliansky, chairwoman of the Lithuanian Jewish Community, February 2, 2018, Vilnius.

48. For stunning video testimony from rare Jewish survivors of Ponary as well as from local Lithuanian bystanders and helpers, see the 2003 Israeli documentary *Out of the Forest*.

49. One of these escapees, engineer Yudi Farber, gave one of the first direct testimonies about the Holocaust to Vasily Grossman and Ilya Ehrenburg as they were preparing the *Black Book* of the Holocaust in 1945. Only in 2016 did an international team of archaeologists find evidence of the tunnel and present it to the survivors' children. This discovery is the subject of the 2017 PBS NOVA documentary *Holocaust Escape Tunnel*.

50. Sakowicz hid his diary in lemonade bottles and buried them in his yard. He was killed in 1944. When the diaries were discovered after the war they remained relatively unknown. They were painstakingly reconstructed by Rachel Margolis, a Lithuanian Holocaust survivor, and were first published in Polish only in 1999, and then in 2005 in English as Kazimierz Sakowicz and Yitzhak Arad, *Ponary Diary, 1941–1943: A Bystander's Account of a Mass Murder* (New Haven: Yale University Press, 2005).

By the end of 1941, most of Lithuania's Jews—some one hundred sixty-five thousand—had already been killed.[51]

Life in the Ghettos

Between 1942 and the spring of 1943, there was a brief respite in killings, as the Germans used the remaining Jews as labor in the military effort.[52] Life in the ghettos went on. In the Kovno ghetto, an underground school operated. For almost a year, there was a ghetto orchestra, a children's choir, a ballet studio, and a court of justice.[53] There is remarkable photographic evidence of life in the Kovno ghetto. One of the ghetto prisoners, George Kadish (Hirsh Kadushin), took meticulous photographs daily with a hidden camera through the buttonhole of his coat and a special camera he built to wear on his trouser belt. His vast surviving collection represents some of the most detailed evidence of life in the ghettos during the Holocaust anywhere in occupied Europe.[54]

The Vilna ghetto was set up in the old Jewish quarter, in the heart of the old city. The ghetto had a remarkable cultural life, difficult to fathom under the circumstances of daily threat of extermination.[55] Cultural activities centered on the Mefitze Haskole Library—the house of culture—which had a collection of forty-five thousand books as well as a reading room, archive, science room, museum, post office, and sports ground.[56] There were literary clubs for youth and prizes given for best submissions, and a magazine, *Folksgezunt*, published in Yiddish. The ghetto set up three elementary schools, a secondary school, a nursery, and an orphanage. There was a music school and a symphony orchestra.[57]

---

51. The majority of the Lithuanian Roma population (around five hundred, but definitive numbers are difficult to ascertain) was also killed.

52. Bubnys, "Holocaust in Lithuania," 215.

53. Vilna Gaon State Jewish Museum, *Catalogue of the Holocaust Exhibition* (Vilnius: Vilna Gaon State Jewish Museum, 2011); Porat, "Holocaust in Lithuania," 170.

54. Kadish escaped the ghetto in July 1944. He lived until 1997. United States Holocaust Memorial Museum, "George Kadish," accessed February 16, 2019, https://www.ushmm.org/wlc/en/article.php?ModuleId=10008201.

55. It also had a very well run health department, which managed to keep infections and contagion at bay in unimaginably difficult conditions. Mckenna Longacre, Solon Beinfeld, Sabine Hildebrandt, Leonard Glantz, and Michael A Grodin, "Public Health in the Vilna Ghetto as a Form of Jewish Resistance," *American Journal of Public Health* 105, no. 2 (2015): 293–301.

56. Michael Robert Marrus, *The Holocaust in History* (Hanover, NH: University Press of New England, 1987), 121.

57. Shirli Gilbert, *Music in the Holocaust: Confronting Life in the Nazi Ghettos and Camps* (Oxford: Oxford University Press, 2005).

Theater groups put up plays in Yiddish and Hebrew, including new works written in the ghetto—a total of 111 performances were delivered, and 34,804 tickets sold by January 1943.[58] The last ghetto theater production was *Der mabl* (The flood), and it opened in the summer of 1943, just a few weeks before the ghetto was destroyed. It was a story of a group of people brought together during a time of peril.[59]

We know much about life in the Vilna ghetto from a diary kept by Yitzchak Rudashevski, a Vilna teenager who participated in the ghetto social and cultural life and was a member of its literature, poetry, and history clubs. Describing club activities, the sixteen-year-old Yitzchak wrote,

> In our group two important and interesting things were decided. We create the following sections in our literary group: Yiddish poetry, and what is most important, a section that is to engage in collecting ghetto folklore . . . I feel that I shall participate zealously in this little circle, because the ghetto folklore which is amazingly cultivated . . . must be collected and cherished as a treasure for the future.[60]

Resistance

In addition to maintaining this extraordinarily vibrant cultural and social life, the Lithuanian ghettos were also sites of armed resistance. In 1943, a Kovno ghetto resistance group called Death to the Occupiers facilitated the escape of some three hundred resistance fighters from the ghetto to join the Soviet partisans.[61] In the Vilna ghetto another resistance group fought against the Germans as they entered to begin deportations in September 1943. After this operation failed—in part because the ghetto Jewish Council (*Judenrat*) cooperated in the deportations hoping to avoid greater bloodshed—some resistance fighters managed to escape through the sewers and also join the partisans in the nearby forests.[62] Some of the leading

58. Solon Beinfeld, "The Cultural Life of the Vilna Ghetto," *Simon Wiesenthal Center* 1 (1997), accessed February 16, 2019, http://motlc.wiesenthal.com/site/pp.asp?c=gvKVLcMVIuG&b=394971#0.

59. Beinfeld, "Cultural Life of the Vilna Ghetto." Theater productions of the Vilna Ghetto have themselves been memorialized in a play. *Ghetto*, by Joshua Sobol, was first performed in New York City in 1989.

60. Yitskhok Rudashevski, *The Diary of the Vilna Ghetto, June 1941–April 1943* (Tel Aviv: Ghetto Fighters' House, 1973), 80–81.

61. United States Holocaust Memorial Museum, "Kovno." For a vivid memoir by a member of the Kovno resistance, see Sara Ginaitė-Rubinsonienė, *Resistance and Survival: The Jewish Community in Kaunas, 1941–1944* (Oakville: Mosaic Press, 2005).

62. United States Holocaust Memorial Museum, "Vilna."

writers in the ghetto—Avraham Sutzkever and Abba Kovner are the most well known—were also the leaders of the Vilna ghetto resistance. It was in Vilna ghetto that on January 1, 1942, 150 members of the youth movement gathered to hear the manifesto written by Abba Kovner, probably the first Jewish public statement that understood Hitler's plan as total extermination. It read, in part:

> Hitler is scheming to annihilate all of European Jewry.
> The Jews of Lithuania were tasked to be first in line.
> Let us not go like sheep to the slaughter!
> It is true that we are weak and defenseless, but resistance is the only response to the enemy!
> Resist! To the last breath.[63]

Resistance was also cultural. Vilna Jews realized that part of the Nazi extermination agenda was the destruction of Jewish material artifacts and the annihilation of all traces of Jewish prewar life. A special Nazi unit was established to plunder YIVO and other Jewish libraries for various cultural valuables that would be then displayed in a German Institute for the Study of the Jewish Question to be opened in Frankfurt. All other materials were to be destroyed.

The Germans ordered a group of Jewish ghetto residents to carry on this project. Instead, calling themselves the Paper Brigade, they hid books and valuables in various places in the ghetto and homes of non-Jewish allies. They buried papers under the floors, hid them in walls and special underground hiding spots.[64]

One of these papers resurfaced in a cache of one hundred seventy thousand pages discovered in Vilnius in 2017. It was a poem by the great Yiddish poet Avraham Sutzkever:

> Death is rushing, riding on a bullet-head
> To tear apart in me my brightest dream.[65]

---

63. Yad Vashem, *Jerusalem of Lithuania*. For a comprehensive biography of Abba Kovner, including details of his multiple failed plots to kill six million Germans after the war, see Dina Porat, *The Fall of a Sparrow: The Life and Times of Abba Kovner* (Stanford: Stanford University Press, 2010).

64. After the war, the few survivors helped track these materials. Many were hidden in the basement of a church in Vilnius, only to be discovered in 1991. Today they constitute the bulk of the rich YIVO archives of Jewish life and culture, which have been reconstituted in New York. "YIVO during WWII," YIVO Institute for Jewish Research, accessed February 16, 2019, https://yivo.org/YIVO-During-WWII.

65. Joseph Berger, "A Trove of Yiddish Artifacts Rescued From the Nazis, and Oblivion," *New York Times*, October 18, 2017.

Liquidation

In September 1943, the remaining ghettos were liquidated. In Vilna, German, Lithuanian, and Estonian soldiers participated in the *Aktion* and removed Jews from their houses. Panic spread in the ghetto and people began to hide in the sewers. Of the remaining ten thousand Jews who were still alive in the Vilna ghetto, about five thousand were taken to the gas chambers at Majdanek or Sobibor death camps, some were shot in death pits, and some were transported to labor camps in Estonia and Latvia, where most of them were killed.[66] Yitzchak Rudashevski and his family went into hiding. Two weeks later, they were discovered and taken to Ponary, where they were shot.[67]

In October 1943, of the 3,500 remaining Jews in the Kovno ghetto 2,700 were removed—those able to work sent to Estonian labor camps, women and the elderly to Auschwitz. On July 9, 1944, the Germans closed the ghetto—which had now become a concentration camp—and deported the remaining Jews to Dachau and Stutthof. As the Soviet army approached, the Nazis burned the ghetto to the ground—at least two thousand Jews were burnt alive in these very last days before liberation.[68]

The Red Army took over Vilnius on July 13, 1944, Kaunas on August 1. Also marching in were Jewish partisans, who searched for their loved ones in the rubble of their homes. A few thousand Jews survived by hiding in the forests or in the ghetto sewers. One of the partisans wrote,

> Three days after the town was liberated, terrified figures of Jews hesitantly come out of hiding. They slip away along the streets . . . including those that had hidden in the sewers for almost a year, in the realization that above the ground no Jews had survived, only those that had been beneath it. . . .[69]

By the time of liberation, 95 percent of Lithuanian Jews—the highest rate of extermination of any Jewish group during the Holocaust—was no more.

---

66. Snyder, *Reconstruction of Nations*, 86; United States Holocaust Memorial Museum, "Vilna"; Vilna Gaon State Jewish Museum, *Catalogue*.

67. Yad Vashem, "The Diary of Yitzchak Rudashevski," https://www.yadvashem.org/education/educational-materials/artifacts/diary.html.

68. United States Holocaust Memorial Museum, "Kovno."

69. Rozka Korczak, *Lahavot Baefer* (Flames in the dust, 1965), 311, quoted in Yad Vashem, "Commemoration of the Vilna Community after the War," *The Jerusalem of Lithuania: The Story of the Jewish Community of Vilna*, accessed February 16, 2019, https://www.yadvashem.org/yv/en/exhibitions/vilna/after/index.asp.

The Soviet Period: Remembrance Interrupted

Summer of 1944 was liberation for the Lithuanian Jews, but it was the beginning of another occupation of Lithuania. With agreement of the victorious Allied forces at Yalta and Potsdam in 1945, the Soviet Union claimed Lithuania and incorporated the Lithuanian Soviet Socialist Republic into the union.

Stalinist terror began immediately. The Soviet authorities continued with massive deportations to forced settlements in Siberia and further in the Soviet east. Between 1944 and 1953, one hundred twenty thousand people (5 percent of the entire Lithuanian population) were deported. Thousands were imprisoned. Large Lithuanian anti-Soviet resistance continued in the forests, but ultimately unsuccessfully and with high rates of death and deportation.[70] While the Holocaust completely destroyed the Litvak community, considerably more ethnic Lithuanians died after WWII than during the war.[71] Again, the historical experience of the Jews and the Lithuanians diverged.

The Soviet Union encouraged immigration of non-Lithuanians—particularly Russians—into Lithuania. The Lithuanians greatly resented these demographic policies and considered them aimed at diluting the ethnic identity of Lithuania. Historical evidence, however, indicates that the intent of this Russification was integration of Lithuania into the USSR and further industrial development—not necessarily ethnic destruction. In fact, Lithuania experienced Russification at levels much lower than did other Soviet republics.[72]

What the Soviets were interested in, and what the Lithuanians came to benefit from, was the Lithuanization of Lithuania—the social and cultural rebalancing of the country which now put Lithuanians on top and large Polish minorities, formerly higher in status, education, and urbanization, on the bottom of the social scale.[73] Vilnius—now empty of its Jews—became more Lithuanian as the urban Poles were moved to the countryside and Lithuanians moved into the city in large numbers. The Lithuanian language was standardized, a university where classes were taught in the Lithuanian language was opened, and more generally schools taught in Lithuanian at higher rates than at any other time in Lithuanian history.[74] And yet Lithuania largely

70. Snyder, *Reconstruction of Nations*, 95.

71. Sužiedėlis and Liekis, "Conflicting Memories," 325.

72. Snyder, *Reconstruction of Nations*, 93.

73. Theodore R Weeks, "Remembering and Forgetting: Creating a Soviet Lithuanian Capital. Vilnius 1944–1949," *Journal of Baltic Studies* 39, no. 4 (2008): 517–33.

74. Snyder, *Reconstruction of Nations*, 95.

functioned as a Soviet republic, experiencing agricultural collectivization, property nationalization, political repression, and international isolation.[75]

A wave of new deportations, aimed at crushing resistance to collectivization and Soviet occupation and providing cheap labor to remote Soviet areas, followed. These deportations were much more massive than the first wave in 1940–41. Particularly large were deportations in 1948 and 1949, when thirty-nine thousand and thirty-two thousand Lithuanians were deported to the east, respectively. About twenty thousand Lithuanian resistance fighters were killed and eighteen thousand arrested; thousands of their family members were deported.[76]

The total number of Lithuanian civilians deported between 1944 and 1953 is estimated, at the minimum, at one hundred six thousand.[77] After Stalin's death in 1953 and some thawing in the USSR, gradually—well into the 1970s—about seventy thousand Lithuanian deportees returned.[78] The total number of Lithuanian deportees, however, conceals their great diversity—these were family members of resistance fighters and other opponents of the regime, farmers, and ethnic Poles, but also a large number of German collaborators and anti-Soviet partisans. This diversity is largely absent in Lithuanian national memory of this period. But in the memory wars in postcommunist Lithuania it is the memory of these deportations that has decidedly won over the memory of the Holocaust.

Suppressed Holocaust Remembrance

In the very first years after the war, a significant number of Lithuanian Jews found themselves in West Germany, where they briefly regrouped after relocation from various displaced persons' camps or release from the Soviet Union. One of the groups that had been set up in the displaced persons' camps was the Association of Lithuanian Jews, which served as an ad hoc support group for displaced survivors and organized their emigration, mostly to Palestine and the United States. The association saw not only memorialization but also providing testimonies of members' suffering as key parts of their activities. At its first conference in the spring of 1947 in

75. John Hiden and Patrick Salmon, *The Baltic Nations and Europe: Estonia, Latvia and Lithuania in the Twentieth Century* (London: Longman, 1994).

76. Alexander Statiev, "Motivations and Goals of Soviet Deportations in the Western Borderlands," *The Journal of Strategic Studies* 28, no. 6 (2005): 977–1003, here 992.

77. Statiev, "Motivations and Goals," 987.

78. Budrytė, "'We Call it Genocide,'" 83.

Munich, the association issued a declaration that explicitly implicated Lithuanians in the Holocaust:

> We, the few remnants of Lithuanian Jewry, are living testimony of the Lithuanians' cruelty to their Jewish neighbors. Each one of us can recount many facts concerning the unspeakable murders of innocent and helpless Jews perpetrated by the Lithuanian people during the occupation. . . . Every part of Lithuanian society (intelligentsia, bureaucracy, peasants, craftsmen, and proletariat) actively collaborated with the murderers in the destruction of Lithuanian Jewry, particularly in the provinces.[79]

For those survivors who were in Lithuania—and these were mostly former partisans—one of the first missions was to establish state schools for Jewish children; one was opened in Vilnius, another one in Kaunas.[80] Another priority was to reestablish the Jewish Museum—the only Jewish museum anywhere in the Soviet Union. Neither the local Lithuanian population nor Soviet authorities had any interest in such an institution; after all, the Soviet Union repressed ethnic diversity, persecuted overt religiosity, and was suspicious of Jews asserting their culture.[81] Remarkably, however, the Jewish Museum was allowed to open in 1944 and was placed under the authority of the Soviet Lithuanian Ministry of Culture. Having no allocated space, the museum opened in the apartment of its first director, Shmerl Kaczerginski, who was one of the members of the Jewish Paper Brigade and had saved hundreds of documents from destruction.[82]

For the first few years after the war, the museum served as a Jewish community center, fielding hundreds of inquiries from all across the world from survivors asking about the fate of their relatives. The replies almost never brought good news. When the museum finally found a permanent location in early 1945 in the former ghetto library and jail buildings, the surviving cultural objects hidden throughout the country in basements, attics, and walls were brought in for display. Many documents, however, were destroyed by the Soviet authorities and recycled as used paper. The first exhibition at the Vilnius Jewish Museum was titled *The Brutal Destruction of the Jews during the German Occupation*. It was soon followed by exhibitions on the Vilna and Kovno ghettos, the Ponary execution site, and Jewish literature.[83]

---

79. Quoted in Levin, *Litvaks*, 238.

80. Levin, *Litvaks*, 238.

81. Levin, *Litvaks*, 238.

82. Vilna Gaon State Jewish Museum, "History of the Jewish Museum," accessed February 16, 2019, http://www.jmuseum.lt/en/about-the-museum.

83. Vilna Gaon State Jewish Museum, "History of the Jewish Museum."

In June 1949, the Council of Ministers of Soviet Lithuania ordered the Jewish Museum reorganized into the Vilnius Local History Museum, de facto closing the institution. The ethnographic material on Jewish life remained at the museum, but political artifacts and documents were moved to the State History and Revolution Museum, art objects to the Art Affairs Board, and books to Soviet Lithuania's Book Chamber. The building that housed the museum was placed under the authority of the Committee for Cultural and Educational Institutions. The Jewish Museum ceased to exist.[84]

The Vilnius Jewish school was closed in 1946, the Kaunas school in 1950.[85] The old Jewish cemetery in Vilnius was paved over so that a sports arena and pool and athletic fields could be built on its site, even though there was plenty of available adjacent construction space. The Old Vilnius Synagogue was razed. Across the country, surviving synagogues were used for storage. Much of the old Jewish quarter in Vilnius was reconstructed—narrow streets widened and renamed, new promenades built.[86] The Vilna ghetto remained completely unmarked and unmemorialized. Jewish gravestones were used to build street sidewalks and repair damaged buildings and to construct the stairs to the popular Vilnius city vista, Tauras Hill, as well as those to the Evangelical Reformed Church, the main front steps of which still show clearly visible Hebrew letters today.[87] The immediate postwar political window that had allowed for some Jewish remembrance was quickly closed.

The city of Vilnius went on, the memory of its old residents completely erased. In a poem remembering Vilna, Abba Kovner wrote,

A Town
A Town
How does one eulogize a town
Whose residents are dead
but who still live on in one's heart[88]

---

84. Vilna Gaon State Jewish Museum, "History of the Jewish Museum."

85. Levin, *Litvaks*, 239.

86. Weeks, "Remembering and Forgetting."

87. Eglė Rindzevičiūtė, "Institutional Entrepreneurs of a Difficult Past: The Organisation of Knowledge Regimes in Post-Soviet Lithuanian Museums," *European Studies*, no. 30 (2013): 63–95, here 76; Rod Nordland, "Where the Genocide Museum Is (Mostly) Mum on the Fate of Jews," *New York Times*, March 30, 2018. The use of destroyed Jewish places of worship for construction material was rampant across the country. For example, a staircase in Šiauliai was constructed in part from tombstones from the nearby Jewish cemetery. Andrew Higgins, "Nazi Collaborator or National Hero? A Test for Lithuania," *New York Times*, September 10, 2018.

88. Abba Kovner, *Achoti Ktana* (My little sister, 1967), quoted in Yad Vashem, "Commemoration of the Vilna Community."

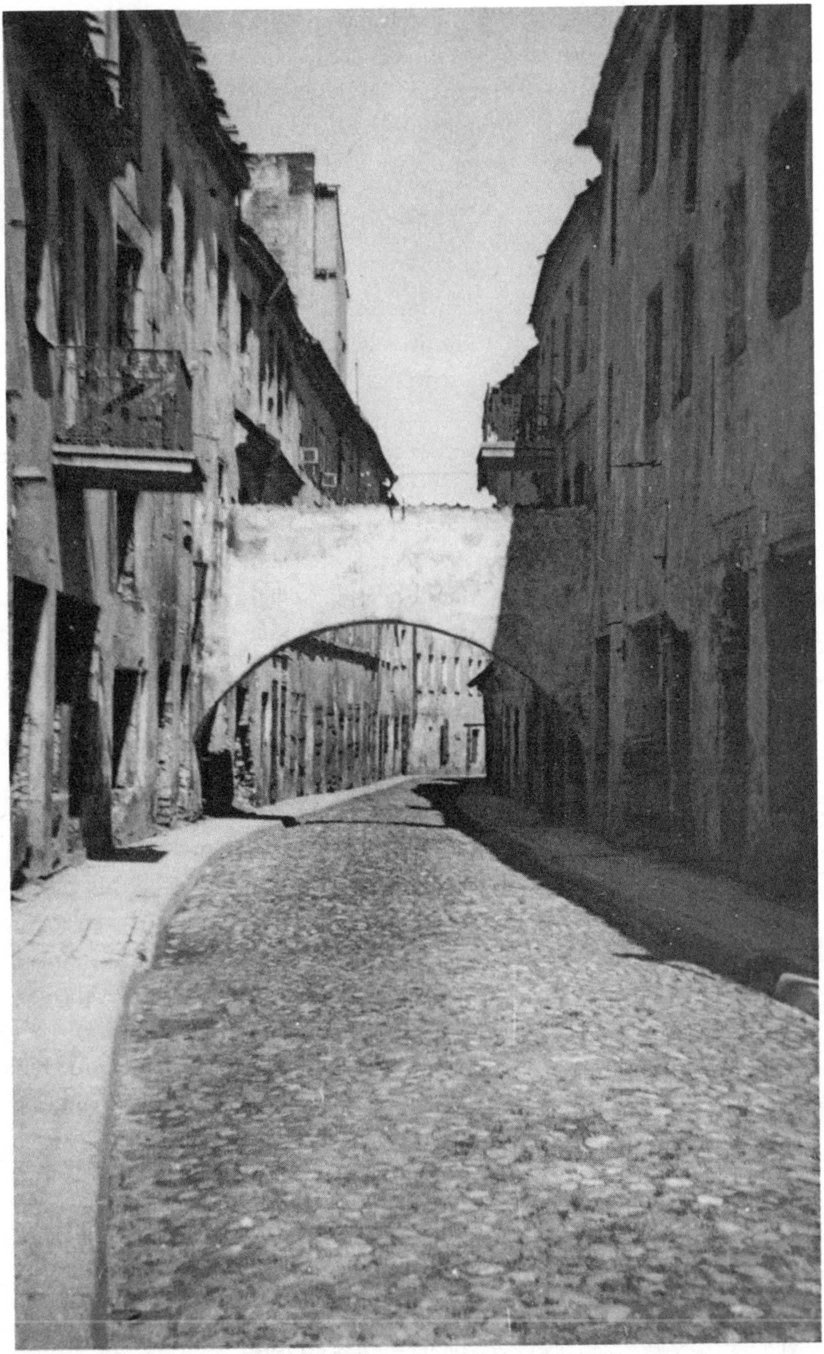

FIGURE 6. Vilna ghetto after the war, 1945/46 (photograph by George Kadish/Zvi Kadushin, reprinted courtesy of the US Holocaust Memorial Museum)

For most Jews, there was no life in Lithuania any more—the country had become a haunted gravesite. As Liuba Segal, one of the survivors, described her visit after the war to her hometown of Utena, now completely empty of its large prewar Jewish community, "It seemed to me there with every step that blood is soaking from under the ground."[89]

Memory Allowed

While the Holocaust was certainly not discussed as a discrete historical phenomenon with unique dynamics, it is also not quite the case that it was not discussed at all. Among a great variety of Soviet historical interpretations of the Holocaust, a fundamentally Marxist unifying theme—a master narrative—subsumed the Holocaust under the larger narrative of fascism, which was viewed as an extension of capitalism.[90] It was also a narrative that suppressed nationality and ethnicity under one USSR and did not allow space for separate national experiences. Since there was no understanding of "Lithuania" as such other than it being a Soviet republic, there was no understanding of the Holocaust in Lithuania other than as an event that was part of the larger world war, which the Soviet army fought against the Nazis.[91] But within this narrative, there was still some room for Holocaust accounts, however inconsistent, contradictory, incomplete, and fragmented.

Already in June 1945, Holocaust survivors organized to erect a monument at the Ponary execution site with inscriptions in Yiddish and Russian. As the Soviet authorities became increasingly hostile to Jewish remembrance, however, in 1952 the monument at Ponary was destroyed. In its place a more modest obelisk was placed, adorned with the Soviet red star and an inscription in Lithuanian and Russian that commemorated only "victims of fascism."[92] In 1960, a small museum was opened at Ponary, part of the state Museum of the Revolution. The Soviet Lithuanian authorities, however, also placed a military garrison with barracks at the mass execution site and built a railroad over the site—seemingly oblivious to the semiotic significance of trains and railroad tracks to the visual imagery of the Holocaust.[93]

89. Quoted in Davoliūtė, "Multidirectional Memory," 143. Liuba survived because she was one of the 1941 Soviet deportees to the Far East.

90. Zvi Gitelman, "History, Memory and Politics: The Holocaust in the Soviet Union," *Holocaust and Genocide Studies* 5, no. 1 (1990): 23–37; Thomas C. Fox, "The Holocaust under Communism," in *The Historiography of the Holocaust*, ed. Dan Stone (London: Palgrave Macmillan, 2004), 420–39.

91. Pukšto, interview.

92. Weeks, "Remembering and Forgetting," 529.

93. Rindzevičiūtė, "Institutional Entrepreneurs," 76.

While institutionalized Jewish memory was abolished, a few memorials were allowed to continue and offer some, if vague, reference to the Holocaust. Most of the memorials did not mention the Jews at all but instead commemorated the suffering of "victims of fascism," "peaceful Soviet citizens," or "local inhabitants." And yet many monuments to the Holocaust were erected during the Soviet period—of the total 231 Holocaust memorials in Lithuania cataloged by the Vilna Gaon Jewish Museum, at least forty-five were constructed before 1991.[94]

Most often Jews were completely erased from memorial sites. At the site of the Steponys forest executions of Jews and communists in the summer of 1941, a memorial was erected in 1958, with the Lithuanian inscription, "Here lie buried 981 citizens of the Soviet Union, shot by bourgeois nationalists on June 27 and August 14, 1941."[95] At the site of the Kaunas Seventh Fort prison and execution site, a memorial plaque was erected in 1968, which said, "The Hitlerian occupiers murdered about 8,000 people here in the months of June and July, 1941" (Lithuanian only). At the site of the 1941 massacres of some thousand Jews at Batiškės, a memorial was placed in 1957 that read, "At this place, in 1941–1944, German fascists and Lithuanian bourgeois nationalists murdered about four thousand innocent residents of Šakiai District." The inscription was in Lithuanian, Russian, and Yiddish, which was the only subtle indication that the victims were Jews.

But some early memorials did indicate that they were Holocaust memorials. At the site of the execution of one thousand Jews in Kupiškis in 1941, a memorial was erected in 1952 with two separate inscriptions: "In eternal memory of the Jews of Kupiškis. Here lie men, women and children brutally murdered by the Nazis and their collaborators in the summer of 1941: May God grant their souls eternal life and eternal peace" (in Lithuanian, Yiddish, Hebrew, and English); and, "At this place, Nazi executioners and their helpers murdered about 1000 people of Kupiškis in 1941; the majority of the victims were Jews" (in Yiddish and Lithuanian).[96]

Another early memorial was built in 1953 at the site of the massive Ukmergė massacres where around seven thousand Jews were killed by Lithuanian militia between July and September 1941. This memorial explicitly narrates the

---

94. Vilna Gaon State Jewish Museum, *Holocaust Atlas of Lithuania*, accessed February 16, 2019, http://www.holocaustatlas.lt.

95. Vilna Gaon State Jewish Museum, *Holocaust Atlas of Lithuania*.

96. In this period, occasional transcriptions in English indicate that they were likely put up by the English-speaking Jewish diaspora, mostly from the United States. In postcommunist Lithuania, English transcriptions may indicate an attempt to place Lithuanian Holocaust remembrance within larger, European memory.

story of the Holocaust: "Here, in 1941, 10,239 innocent Lithuanian citizens—sons and daughters of the Jewish nation, little babies and the elderly—were struck by the bullets of Hitler's henchmen and their local collaborators. May their innocent blood wake everyone's conscience, so that people would never be killed again" (in Yiddish, Hebrew, and Lithuanian).

Some memorials had completely different inscriptions in Hebrew and Lithuanian. The 1958 memorial to two hundred Jews shot at Šiaudviečiai says in Hebrew:

> Here lie buried in Eternal Memory the Martyrs of the Community of Nayshtot, may God avenge their blood, murdered and annihilated by the Germans and their local assistants, may their names be blotted from memory, in the year 5701–1941, the day of memory is the twenty-fourth of Tammuz. Their sacred memory will forever be in our midst. May their souls be tied to the lands of the living.

Under this inscription is this one in Lithuanian: "Here lie buried Soviet people, shot by German occupants and bourgeois nationalists in 1941."[97]

And yet some memorial sites show the progression of the Holocaust narrative. At Ylakiai, where hundreds of Jews were killed by local Lithuanian "white armbanders" in July 1941, the 1965 memorial inscription says, "People, while the heart is beating hot, remember the dear price of freedom for their lot. In memory of the victims of fascism, shot in 1941" (in Lithuanian). The new monument erected in 1988 instead says, "Hitler's murderers and their local helpers murdered 446 Jews, 25 Samogitians and 4 Karaites here in 1941. May the memory of the victims remain sacred" (in Lithuanian, Yiddish, and Hebrew).

After Stalin

After Stalin's death in 1953, the situation for the Jews improved somewhat—some limited cultural activities, such as plays, readings, and lectures in Yiddish, were allowed. Jews from elsewhere in the Soviet Union (mostly Belarus, Ukraine, and Russia) began relocating to Lithuania, attracted to its higher living standards. There were also more vocal Jewish demands for emigration to Israel in the late 1960s, including a demonstration organized by Lithuanian Jews outside the Communist Party headquarters in Moscow and Vilnius. It is in this period that *Mass Murders in Lithuania,* the first publication to directly

97. Vilna Gaon State Jewish Museum, *Holocaust Atlas of Lithuania.*

address the Holocaust—and Lithuanian participation in it—was published as a two-volume project, in 1965 and 1973.[98] Also published at this time were a history of resistance in the Kovno ghetto, an account of Lithuanian Gentile rescuers of Jews, and a few memoirs of Jewish resistance fighters—some of the first publications that explicitly narrated the Holocaust.[99] These publications all portrayed the Lithuanian public as willingly and bravely helping the Jews, while Lithuanian collaborators were presented in class terms as "members of the nationalist bourgeoisie" who have since either emigrated to the West or have joined the anti-Soviet partisans—a move that then justified fierce Soviet retaliation.[100]

At Kaunas, the first exhibition about Nazi crimes at the Ninth Fort (the location of the October 1941 shooting of ten thousand Jews) was opened in 1958 at the Museum of Revolution History. Research and excavation on the site began in 1960, as did negotiations over artistic rendering of a memorial, which took thirteen years to complete. The new memorial complex was opened in 1984. It was a thirty-two-meter monument dedicated to "victims of fascism" and grouped in three separate giant sculptures—Death, Hope, and Liberation. New pedestrian pathways were constructed and a new museum building opened.[101] The inscription on the monument says, "This is the place where Nazis and their assistants killed more than thirty thousand Jews from Lithuania and other European countries" and is displayed in Lithuanian, Russian, English, and Yiddish.[102]

At the same time, in mid 1980s, the Ponary memorial was renovated. The exhibition was completely overhauled in 1985 and a new museum opened. The site now added new pathways, renovated burial pits, and erected commemorative stones—but in Russian and Lithuanian only, continuing to evoke only "Soviet citizens."[103] This provoked some open Jewish resistance. Occasionally, Israeli flags would appear at the monument, only to be removed and then again replaced.[104]

98. Levin, *Litvaks*, 241–42.

99. Sužiedėlis and Liekis, "Conflicting Memories," 326.

100. Sužiedėlis and Liekis, "Conflicting Memories," 326.

101. Kauno IX forto muziejus, "The Museum," accessed February 17, 2019, http://www.9fortomuziejus.lt/istorija/muziejus/?lang=en.

102. Vilna Gaon State Jewish Museum, "Kaunas IX Fort" *Holocaust Atlas of Lithuania*, accessed February 17, 2019, http://www.holocaustatlas.lt/EN/#a_atlas/search//page/22/item/24/.

103. Vilna Gaon State Jewish Museum, "Memorial Museum of Paneriai," accessed February 17, 2019, http://www.jmuseum.lt/en/exposition/i/198/.

104. Zvi Gitelman, "The Soviet Politics of the Holocaust," in *The Art of Memory: Holocaust Memorials in History*, ed. James Edward Young (New York: Prestel-Verlag, 1994), 139–47.

In 1988, in the waning years of Soviet Lithuania, a big exhibition, titled *The Art of Lithuania's Jews*, was opened in Kaunas and Vilnius. It was the first public display of Jewish culture anywhere in the Soviet Union. That same year, the Lithuanian Jewish Cultural Association (in 1991 reorganized and renamed the Lithuanian Jewish Community) was formed, and on September 25 the association organized a march to commemorate the liquidation of the Vilna ghetto.[105]

Holocaust Remembrance in Post-Soviet Lithuania

By the late 1980s, the Soviet Union was experiencing a full-blown legitimacy crisis. The Baltic states were at the forefront of anti-Soviet organizing and used the openings provided by Gorbachev-era *glasnost* and *perestroika* to push first for reform and soon for full independence. In 1988 a group of Lithuanian intellectuals formed Sąjūdis, the Reform Movement of Lithuania, which proposed a broad platform of democratic changes and called for a national reawakening from decades of Soviet multinational flattening. Lithuanian communist leadership adopted some of these reforms, including introduction of a multiparty system, annulment of the 1940 pact that put Lithuania under Soviet control, and restoration of the national flag and anthem. On March 11, 1990, Lithuania proclaimed independence from the Soviet Union, the first of the Soviet republics to do so. The crumbling USSR tried to prevent Lithuanian independence through sabotage and a coup, but these attempts ultimately failed. Lithuania was free.

The Production of a New Lithuanian Identity

Lithuanian post-Soviet identity was constructed on the full-scale rejection of Soviet legacy, culture, politics, and historiography, and a creation of a new, ethnically Lithuanian identity that looked for its place in the cultural sphere of Western, not Eastern, Europe. While scholarly assessments of Soviet national policies in the Baltics have made the case that quite a large space existed for Baltic national self-awareness, including the extensive process of Lithuanization described earlier, the public perception—elite and popular—of the Soviet period is uniformly one of national suppression and ethnic destruction.[106] This narrative is based on the deep memory of massive waves

105. Rindzevičiūtė, "Institutional Entrepreneurs," 78.

106. Budrytė, *Taming Nationalism?*

of deportations, arrests, and forced migration to the Soviet east. But they are also rooted in an equally deep resentment of the Soviet policy of Russification or forced repopulation of the Baltics with ethnic Russians.[107]

For much of the Soviet era, it was the Lithuanian anticommunist diaspora that preserved a fossilized version of the Lithuanian past—a memory of its pre-Soviet independence and a strong resentment of Lithuanian victimization at the hands of Soviet communists, first during the war and especially in the postwar years. This new memory was actively resuscitated through the activities of the Commission for Investigation of Stalinist crimes, created by Sąjūdis in 1988, which collected data about deportations and killings during the Stalinist era. This process itself then became part of nationalist political mobilization and consolidation.[108] This was followed by mass rallies, commemorative events, pilgrimage visits to former labor camps in Siberia, new monuments to anti-Soviet partisans, and a proliferation of memoirs from survivors of deportations.

Many families repatriated the remains of their relatives who died in exile and reburied them back in Lithuania with massive public participation in what Dovilė Budrytė has called "sorrow tourism."[109] The memory of Soviet repression in general was—similarly to the Croatian case—thickly overlaid with Catholic motifs, especially those of Christian martyrdom, reinforcing Lithuanian victimization as uniquely Catholic and leaving no room for non-Christian (namely Jewish) victims.[110] Lithuanian nationalists also very early on began to use the term "the Lithuanian Holocaust" for the Soviet occupation.[111] Just like in Croatia, the concept of "the Holocaust," its visual imagery, and its mnemonic markers began to be used to denote a completely different historical event—in Lithuania, Soviet repression.

Missing from this newly constructed memory was recognition that a very high percentage of 1941 Soviet deportations to Siberia included Jews in addition to ethnic Lithuanians (and that post-1945 deportations included no Jews because by that point there were no Jews left in Lithuania to deport). The anti-Jewish Soviet policies were a storyline that simply did not fit into the

107. In Latvia and Estonia, the demographic consequences of Russification were most pronounced. The percentage of Russian population increased from 8 to 20 percent in Estonia, and from 9 to 27 percent in Latvia. In Lithuania, however, the demographic shifts were less dramatic—the already small Russian population (2.5 percent) increased to 9 percent by 1953. Budrytė, *Taming Nationalism?*, 43.

108. Davoliūtė, "Multidirectional Memory."

109. Budrytė, "'We Call it Genocide,'" 87.

110. Davoliūtė, "Multidirectional Memory."

111. Budrytė, *Taming Nationalism?*

emerging Lithuanian historical narrative, and therefore remained mostly absent from the memory repertoire.

The uniqueness of the twentieth-century Baltic experience also manifests itself in a very different conceptualization of WWII and even its established timeline. While in the West, WWII signifies a discrete period of global war with Nazi Germany and its allies between 1939 and 1945, a war in which the West—critically, with the help of the Soviet Union—prevailed and saved Western civilization, in the Baltic states, the world war is just a backdrop to a much larger disaster, which was the Soviet terror after 1945, and especially the Stalinist period, 1945–53. The Western narrative of WWII is, therefore, incomplete from the Baltic point of view. This has immediate consequences, of course, for how WWII is remembered and why the unique and distinct catastrophe of WWII—the Holocaust—does not have the emotional or mnemonic impact in the Baltics that it does in the West. It is often seen as a "Western obsession" with little or nothing to do with Lithuanian national memory.[112] It is simply not seen as the central event in Lithuanian history—for Jews and non-Jews alike.

The Lithuanian rejection of the Soviet narrative of WWII that divided participants into fascists (Nazis and their collaborators, including local collaborators) and victims ("Soviet citizens," including the Jews) has particularly significant consequences for Holocaust remembrance. The rejection of this Soviet matrix—what the Baltic states have referred to as the "de-Sovietization of history"—produces an inversion of WWII where local collaborators are praised for their anti-Soviet resistance and the victims become newly suspect.[113]

Constructing the "Soviet Genocide"

It is within this interpretive context that the Soviet period began to be referred to in the Baltics—and most strongly in Lithuania—as the "Soviet genocide." It was not just the repression and deportations that constituted "genocide" in Lithuanian national memory; it was also the demographic changes and the perceived Russification of Lithuania that created a sense that Lithuania was not Lithuanian any more, but that it was first politically and then demographically occupied by the Soviet Union, and particularly by Russians. The Soviet presence and policies were seen as an existential threat to the very survival of the Lithuanian nation. In this understanding of

112. Sužiedėlis and Liekis, "Conflicting Memories," 326.
113. Budrytė, *Taming Nationalism?*, 181.

Lithuania's recent past there was mnemonic space for only one genocide—and it was going to be the "genocide" against Lithuanians, not the genocide against the Jewish others who were never truly considered part of the Lithuanian body politic.

While the term "genocide" was used in the diaspora to refer to the Soviet occupation as early as the late 1940s, the official renaming of the Soviet period as "Soviet genocide" began in October 1992, when the Lithuanian Parliament established the Center for Genocide and Resistance Research with the mandate to investigate the "Soviet genocide."[114] This term has remained in use ever since and has become hegemonic, transmitted through a proliferation of memoirs of victims of Soviet deportations that started to come out in the late 1980s and throughout the 1990s, and through the mass production of newspaper articles and other media representations of the deportations.[115] It is used routinely to denote the Soviet rule, and has become institutionalized in a series of major government projects including, most prominently, the Museum of Genocide/Occupation (on which much more, below).

"Soviet genocide" moved from interpretation to legislation later in 1992, when Lithuania passed the Law on the Liability for Genocide against the People of Lithuania (often referred to as the Genocide Law), the purpose of which was to prosecute those who perpetrated atrocities against Lithuanian citizens during the Soviet occupation. In using the word "genocide" in the title of the law, the Lithuanian government greatly expanded the 1948 United Nations Genocide Convention definition to now include persecution on social and political grounds—which would then include Soviet crimes of deportations of farmers and intelligentsia to Siberia.[116] Based on the law, thirty-one people were convicted of crimes during the Soviet occupation, and eight of these were convicted of "genocide"—the killing of anti-Soviet Lithuanian partisans. The prosecution successfully argued that membership in Soviet NKVD antiresistance units was enough grounds to prove "genocidal intent" against the Lithuanian nation. Amendments to the law adopted in 1997–98 further expanded the war crimes provisions to now also include deportations.[117]

---

114. Budrytė, *Taming Nationalism?*, 181.

115. Budrytė, *Taming Nationalism?*, 181.

116. Tomas Balkelis and Violeta Davoliūtė, "Legislated History in Post-Communist Lithuania," in *The Palgrave Handbook of State-Sponsored History After 1945*, ed. Berber Bevernage and Nico Wouters (New York: Springer, 2018), 121–36. Ironically, of course, it was the Soviet Union that insisted in 1948 that the UN Convention not include persecution on social and political grounds.

117. Eva-Clarita Pettai, "Prosecuting Soviet Genocide: Comparing the Politics of Criminal Justice in the Baltic States," *European Politics and Society* 18, no. 1 (2017): 52–65, here 56–57.

Jewish Remembrance in the New Lithuania

While the hegemonic narrative of the "Soviet genocide" was solidifying in Lithuania, Jewish remembrance was developing on a separate track. The political opening provided by late Soviet *glasnost* and especially the democratization of Lithuania after 1991 also opened up space for existing Jewish institutions to try to reestablish their presence. In 1989, the Jewish Museum reopened in Vilnius. Strapped for cash in the poor Lithuanian post-Soviet economy, the museum relied on volunteers, mostly Holocaust survivors, and focused on literary collections (especially those in Yiddish), Holocaust remembrance, and engagement with survivors. While local support certainly increased after independence, much of the memorialization activities were gifts from donors, including many from abroad.

The museum was allocated two spaces—the modest Green House on the edge of Vilnius Old Town (to house the Holocaust exhibition) and the Ponary memorial site, where a new small exhibition was opened in 1990. Gradually, the Jewish Museum expanded to include a building in Vilnius Old Town that housed the Jewish cultural center in the interwar period, now turned into the Tolerance Center Museum, as well as a separate building for administration and inventory. In 1997, the museum was renamed the Vilna Gaon State Jewish Museum.

Lithuanian independence also created an opening for cultural rendering of the Holocaust to some, however limited, popular impact. The first Lithuanian adaptation of Joshua Sobol's *Ghetto* play was performed in Vilnius in 1990, and in 2005 it was made into a film. A documentary on Vilna, *Goodbye, Jerusalem*, was shown in 1994. An international art festival in remembrance of the fifty-fifth anniversary of the Vilna ghetto theater was organized in 1997.[118]

As part of this new political opening, many sites of Holocaust massacres were newly rememorialized with plaques and memorials indicating the Jewish identity of the victims. Some of these monuments were newly built, but many had already existed and were now renarrated with new, more complete, inscriptions. For example, next to the 1968 monument at the Kaunas Seventh Fort, which initially memorialized the killing of unspecified "people," a new inscription was added in 1991 that read, "In 1941 here at the Seventh Fort the Nazis and their local collaborators murdered about 3,000 people, most of them Jews from Kaunas" (in Lithuanian and Yiddish).[119]

118. Sužiedėlis and Liekis, "Conflicting Memories," 337.

119. Vilna Gaon State Jewish Museum, *Holocaust Atlas of Lithuania*.

The new memorials constructed after 1991 also needed to be renegotiated in the new Lithuanian political landscape. The execution site at Ponary has proved particularly difficult because it is a site of central importance for the Holocaust of Lithuanian Jews—more than seventy thousand Jews were shot in Ponary forest—but it is also the site of clear Lithuanian participation—the shooters at Ponary were Lithuanians. In the newly open political space after independence, one of the survivors, Yeshayahu Epstein, lobbied the Lithuanian government to allow construction of a new, more appropriate memorial at Ponary, which would be financed by private donations, mostly from abroad. The inscription was to read: "Here in the Ponary forest, from July 1941 to July 1944, the Hitlerite occupiers and their local assistants murdered 100,000 people, of whom 70,000 were Jews—men, women, and children." The Lithuanian authorities, however, rejected this inscription because of the phrase "their local assistants" and the project was for a while at a standstill. Eventually a compromise was reached—the inscription would remain in full, but only in Yiddish and Hebrew, and a redacted version without mention of local collaboration would be placed in Lithuanian, so as not to cause offense to Lithuanian visitors.[120] The Lithuanian inscription has since been replaced to include the full sentence.

New Lithuania Encounters the Holocaust

In the first decade after Lithuania's independence, there was great enthusiasm and expectation among the remaining Lithuanian Jews as well as the Lithuanian Jewish diaspora that the new, postcommunist, "European" Lithuania would acknowledge Jewish suffering and begin serious Holocaust research and remembrance. The assumption was that Holocaust remembrance was suppressed under the Soviet Union and memories could now flow freely.[121]

But this recognition of the Holocaust—its full recognition, with dignity, and its integration into the central narrative arc of Lithuania's modern history—did not happen after 1991. Instead, one of the very first actions of the new Lithuanian parliament was the rehabilitation of those Lithuanians convicted of collaboration with the Nazis during the Soviet regime. In just

120. Gitelman, "Soviet Politics," 143–44; Dov Levin, "Lithuanian Attitudes toward the Jewish Minority in the Aftermath of the Holocaust: The Lithuanian Press, 1991–1992," *Holocaust and Genocide Studies* 7, no. 2 (1993): 247–62, here 250.

121. David Brook, "Double Genocide," *Slate*, July 26, 2015, http://www.slate.com/articles/news_and_politics/history/2015/07/lithuania_and_nazis_the_country_wants_to_forget_its_collaborationist_past.html.

a few months after it was passed in May 1990, the new Law on the Reconstitution of Legal Rights of the People Repressed for the Resistance to Occupation Regimes rehabilitated over fifty thousand people, including those who directly participated in the Holocaust.[122] A major street in Vilnius was renamed after Kazys Škirpa, prime minister in the Lithuanian interim government, which fully collaborated with the Nazi occupation. Jonas Noreika, who signed deportation orders to confine Jews to the ghettos, was declared a national hero of Lithuania—all in the very first months of post-Soviet independence.[123] All these moves indicate that, as Budrytė documents, "the Holocaust did not exist or 'almost did not exist' in the collective memory of Lithuanians."[124]

As Lithuania opened itself toward the rest of Europe, however, its nationalist narrative was suddenly confronted with a very different Jewish and Western narrative that looked at Lithuania as the site of some of the worst anti-Jewish violence in all of WWII. Independence also brought with it freedom of speech and an enlarged public space for Jewish dissent.

Slowly, Jewish voices began to emerge, objecting to the "Soviet genocide" narrative on legal, historical, and moral grounds. Lithuanian Jews were joined in this objection by international organizations as well as some liberal Lithuanian diaspora intellectuals, Tomas Venclova being the most prominent. Lithuania was increasingly pressured to revisit the Holocaust, start research into local complicity of Lithuanians in the annihilation of the Jews, and begin serious Holocaust memorialization.

The Lithuanian Parliament issued its first official statement of admission of Lithuanian participation in the Holocaust in 1990, passing the Declaration on the Jewish Genocide in Lithuania. In 1994, September 23 (the day of the Vilna ghetto liquidation) was declared National Memorial Day for the Genocide of Lithuanian Jews, and it has since been officially commemorated every year at Ponary.[125]

---

122. Violeta Davoliūtė and Dovilė Budrytė, "Entangled History, History Education, and Affective Communities in Lithuania," in *Transitional Justice and the Former Soviet Union: Reviewing the Past, Looking toward the Future*, ed. Cynthia M. Horne and Lavinia Stan (New York: Cambridge University Press, 2018), 323–44, here 327. As a result of international pressure, in 1995 the law was amended and rehabilitation of some one hundred individuals, with clearly documented participation in the Holocaust, was revoked. See Balkelis and Davoliūtė, "Legislated History."

123. Benas Gerdziunas, "Decades after Soviet Terror, Lithuania Confronts Its Holocaust," *Politico*, August 30, 2017, https://www.politico.eu/interactive/decades-after-soviet-terror-lithuania-confronts-holocaust.

124. Budrytė, *Taming Nationalism?*, 184.

125. Davoliūtė and Budrytė, "Entangled History."

In 1995, during his visit to Israel, then Lithuanian president Algirdas Brazauskas issued an official state apology "for the actions of those Lithuanians who mercilessly murdered, shot, deported and robbed Jews."[126] Brazauskas later explained that the motivation for the apology was both a need for atonement for Lithuanian collaboration and a need to present Lithuania as being in line with Western values: "I did not want to keep to the ostrich policy while in the West the legal, moral, and economic issues of the Holocaust [were] solved."[127] This apology, however, was much criticized by the media and the intellectual elite at home, some of whom demanded that the Jews apologize "in return" for their alleged collaboration with the Soviets.[128]

It is in this context of defensiveness that the argument about the "double genocide" was born. The revisionist narrative of the "double genocide" claims that the Lithuanian collaboration in the Holocaust was, if perhaps regrettable, still an understandable response to the "genocide" perpetrated against Lithuanians by communist Jews as agents of the Soviet Union during the first Soviet occupation in 1940–41. This narrative is then a Baltic take on the old "Judeo-Bolshevik alliance" anti-Semitic canard that was at the root of the Nazi's extermination program and that was propagated vigorously by Nazi authorities throughout the occupied Soviet Union.[129]

From the beginning, in an attempt to bridge the domestic narrative of Lithuanian victimization with the increasingly present Jewish (and international) narrative of the Holocaust and Lithuanian complicity in it, Lithuania's official efforts at dealing with its past operated within a single framework—the Holocaust and the Soviet occupation were to be studied together, the crimes of the Nazi and Soviet regimes were to be analyzed together, the victims of the Nazi and Soviet terror were to be tallied together.

The problem here is not one of historical timelines—it certainly makes sense to take the long view and explain the historical context of the Soviet occupation, the early deportations, and the rise of anti-Semitism and ethnic resentment, without which local collaboration with Nazi occupation authorities after 1941 cannot be fully understood. The problem, however, is in contextualizing the 1940–41 and 1945–53 Soviet periods and the Stalinist terror that produced mass deportations from the Baltics within the framework of the Holocaust. The only reason to conceptualize of the Holocaust and the

126. Quoted in Suižedėlis and Liekis, "Conflicting Memories," 330.

127. Quoted in Alexander Karn, *Amending the Past: Europe's Holocaust Commissions and the Right to History* (Madison: The University of Wisconsin Press, 2015), 134.

128. Sužiedėlis and Liekis, "Conflicting Memories," 330.

129. Sužiedėlis and Liekis, "Conflicting Memories," 330.

postwar Soviet deportations together is to elevate Soviet crimes to the level of the Holocaust, which minimizes both the uniqueness of the Jewish disaster and the massive local collaboration by Lithuanians.

Much of the state effort Lithuania expended on Holocaust remembrance in the years following independence was, in fact, an attempt to educate the West about the horrors of the Soviet occupation, which the Baltic states perceived as being ignored, minimized, and drowned out by the "obsessive" focus on the Holocaust. As the Baltic states increasingly started to be viewed as viable candidates for European Union membership, this "re-education" of Europe became more urgent for them.[130] But to get its grievances heard, Lithuania first had to get in line with European expectations regarding Holocaust remembrance.

Holocaust Remembrance at the Gates of the EU

Lithuania's major strategic goal after independence was European Union and NATO membership. This desire to become fully—and again—European was shared across the political spectrum and across all levels of society. It is really within this context of Lithuania's European ambition that the flurry of activities regarding Holocaust remembrance in the late 1990s and early 2000s needs to be understood.

International pressures on Lithuania, as well as on other Baltic states, were not subtle. The United States made a connection with Holocaust remembrance direct and unconditional if the Baltic states were to join NATO:

> All NATO aspirants need to do more to better prepare themselves for membership so that they are ready and able to contribute to European security in tangible ways. For the Baltic States, this means hard work—not just words, but concrete action on complex domestic issues like dealing with the history of the Holocaust . . .[131]

The US then followed up by establishing a special envoy for Holocaust issues in Central and Eastern Europe, whose purview included the Baltics.[132]

---

130. For a related argument, see Maria Mälksoo, "The Memory Politics of Becoming European: The East European Subalterns and the Collective Memory of Europe," *European Journal of International Relations* 15, no. 4 (2009): 653–80.

131. Heather Conley, Deputy Assistant Secretary for European and Eurasian Affairs, Remarks to Stockholm Security Conference, Stockholm, Sweden, April 24, 2002, https://2001-2009.state.gov/p/eur/rls/rm/2002/9753.htm.

132. Doyle Stevick, "The Holocaust in the Contemporary Baltic States: International Relations, Politics, and Education," *Holocaust: Study and Research* 1, no. 5 (2012): 87–103.

In addition, the European Union required the Baltics to begin proper commemoration of the Holocaust and to return seized Jewish property to survivors or existing Jewish communities.[133] This perception that Holocaust remembrance "had to be done" then had an impact on how Lithuanians understood and internalized its significance and its moral import.[134]

As part of its preparation for an EU membership bid, Lithuania actively sought membership in the ITF / IHRA, the main international institution that coordinated such activities. Also as part of this bid, Lithuanian institutions joined international partnerships, including a critical partnership in 2000 with the United Kingdom to create a Liaison Project, in which UK experts on Holocaust memorialization, education, and history would mentor their Lithuanian counterparts. As part of this project, the period 2000–2005 saw a burst in activity in Holocaust memorialization, primarily in teacher workshops and the development of various educational materials for Holocaust education, but also in the mentoring of existing and largely marginalized Lithuanian Holocaust institutions, such as the small Green House Holocaust exhibition.[135]

A major institutional development in 1998 was the establishment of a historical commission to investigate the crimes of the Holocaust (but also, as will become significant shortly, the crimes of the Soviet occupation); at the same time, two other Baltic states, Latvia and Estonia, established similar commissions. The timing of the commission's opening was clearly a part of Lithuania's desire to join NATO and the EU.[136]

This pre-EU period also saw a rise in Lithuanian civil society's interest in Holocaust remembrance. There were a series of documentaries, including powerful interviews with Lithuanian perpetrators in Saulis Beržinis's 2002 film, *The Lovely Faces of the Murderers*. There was a Holocaust education series by the nongovernmental organization Center for School Improvement, as well as the establishment of a remembrance center, House of Memory, which published a series of oral testimonies by Lithuanian witnesses of the Holocaust, titled *Our Grandparents' Jewish Neighbors*.[137]

---

133. Christine Beresniova, "'Unless They Have To': Power, Politics and Institutional Hierarchy in Lithuanian Holocaust Education," in *As the Witnesses Fall Silent: 21st Century Holocaust Education in Curriculum, Policy and Practice*, ed. Zehavit Gross and E. Doyle Stevick (Cham: Springer, 2015), 391–406.

134. Beresniova, "'Unless They Have To,'" 394.

135. Larissa Allwork, "Intercultural Legacies of the International Task Force: Lithuania and the British at the Turn of the Millennium," *Holocaust Studies* 19, no. 2 (2013): 91–124.

136. Karn, *Amending the Past*.

137. Dovid Katz, "The Extraordinary Recent History of Holocaust Studies in Lithuania," *Dapim: Studies on the Holocaust* 31, no. 3 (2017): 285–95, here 290.

These activities, however, were also couched as part of Lithuania's European ambitions: "As we head for European Union membership this becomes increasingly important. . . . An open discussion of the Holocaust is the starting point in showing the world that this is a tolerant society," documentary filmmaker Vaidotas Reivytis, one of the founders of the House of Memory, said in 2000.[138]

Institutions of Sanctioned Memory

In 1998, then Lithuanian president Valdas Adamkus established the International Commission for the Evaluation of the Crimes of the Nazi and Soviet Occupation Regimes in Lithuania. Emanuelis Zingeris, a respected Jewish Lithuanian politician, was appointed head of the commission, which initially included a broad cross-section of scholars from the United States, Israel, Germany, and Russia, as well as Lithuania. As has become established practice in Lithuania, the commission's mandate was to study both occupations simultaneously. This did not sit well with international experts, who worried about the motivation to level the Nazi and Soviet crimes. In response, the commission created two separate units to investigate the Holocaust and the Soviet occupation independently.

The Lithuanian commission's Holocaust division was initially quite active, organizing a series of international conferences on the Holocaust in Lithuania—including in 2002 the largest conference on the Holocaust held in any of the Baltic states.[139] It published important Holocaust scholarship and prepared educational materials for Holocaust education in Lithuanian schools.[140] Its work, however, was torpedoed by the actions of the Lithuanian judiciary in 2007, which opened an investigation into one of the commission's leading members, the renowned Holocaust scholar Yitzhak Arad, for war crimes (much more on this case below), a political blow from which the commission has never quite recovered.

In addition to the commission, the other major state institution that narrates and disciplines official Lithuanian political memory of the twentieth century is the Genocide and Resistance Research Centre. Established in 1992, it has also nominally undertaken Holocaust research, but, again, it has contextualized it in tandem with the Soviet occupation. The "genocide

---

138. Darius James Ross, "House of Memory," *Baltic Times*, September 14, 2000, https://www.baltictimes.com/news/articles/2544.

139. Sužiedėlis and Liekis, "Conflicting Memories," 335.

140. A very important publication was Dieckmann and Sužiedėlis, *Persecution and Mass Murder*.

and resistance" from the institution's name do not refer to the Holocaust and Jewish or Lithuanian anti-Nazi resistance, but instead to the "genocide" of Soviet occupation and Lithuanian anti-Soviet resistance.[141] According to the center's director, "the inclusion of the word 'genocide' in its title had nothing to do with the Holocaust but reflected a strong emotional impulse to signal the suffering of the Lithuanian nation at the hands of the Soviet occupying power."[142] This approach is evident in the most visible state institution that is under the center's direct control—the Museum of Genocide/Occupation.

Museum of Genocide/Occupation

The Museum of Genocide/Occupation in Vilnius was opened in 1992, only a year into Lithuania's independence, in a building in the city center that carried its own memory baggage. Built initially as a courthouse, the building was taken over in 1940 by the Soviet authorities, who placed the secret service (NKVD, later to become KGB) headquarters there. During the Nazi occupation from 1941 to 1944, it was the headquarters of the Gestapo and a site of torture and murder. After the Soviet reoccupation in 1944, the building was again repurposed as a prison for political opponents, a grim place that included torture rooms, solitary confinement, and a host of other oppressive measures. It remained the KGB headquarters until the collapse of the Soviet Union. In 1997 it was placed under the control of the Genocide and Resistance Research Centre, which transformed it into Vilnius's top tourist destination and the main vehicle of "educating the West" on the horrors of the Soviet occupation.

The Museum of Genocide/Occupation is the most elaborate mnemonic representation of the "Soviet genocide" narrative. It presents a story of Soviet repression of Lithuanians, especially Lithuanian "freedom fighters"—nationalist partisans who fought the Soviets. The museum describes its object of representation as "genocide performed by the Soviet occupiers against the Lithuanian inhabitants"; it also "demonstrates the methods and

141. While an overwhelming majority of the center's publications are on the Soviet occupation, the center has also published some important Holocaust research. In addition to Holocaust monographs by the historian Arūnas Bubnys, in 2012 it published Sakowitz's *Panerių dienoraštis 1941–1943* (Paneriai Diary 1941–1943), and in 2017 *Mes nežudųme* (*We Did Not Murder*) by Arkadijus Vinokuras, a collection of interviews with descendants of Lithuanian perpetrators in the Holocaust. Genocide and Resistance Research Centre of Lithuania, "Publications in Lithuanian," accessed February 17, 2019, http://genocid.lt/centras/en/1980/a.

142. Davoliūtė and Budrytė, "Entangled History," 326.

extent of resistance to the occupying regime, and commemorates genocide victims and freedom fighters."[143] The point here, obviously, is to generalize Soviet violence to Lithuanian "inhabitants"—not to specific political or economic classes but all Lithuanians—making the narrative link with what the visitor may understand as "genocide" more direct. But another objective is to glorify Lithuanian anti-Soviet resistance and place it within a larger narrative of Lithuanian independence from foreign occupation—independence rooted in a strong national identity based on ethnic kin. The museum therefore constructs an image of a persecuted Lithuanian nation and nurtures an "environment of collective pity."[144]

The curatorial choice of the museum is to emphasize the gruesome nature of the Soviet regime by showing some of the most violent images of execution or torture of anti-Soviet activists, clearly instilling a sense in the visitor of extreme brutality of the Soviet regime against those the museum represents as national heroes. The building itself is presented as "largely intact" from the days of the KGB, with dilapidated wall paint, rusted gates, and scratched-in walls. The impression the museum gives is that this "terror house" has only just closed.

That, in the view of the museum curators, the Soviet terror was what really qualified as "genocide" is evident in the fact that between the opening of the museum in 2002 and 2011 there was no mention of the Holocaust at all in the permanent exhibition. By 2011, however, museum authorities were coming under increasing pressure (much of it from foreign governments) to include the Holocaust in its exhibit. In 2011, a single small room was repurposed as the "Holocaust exhibition." The Lithuanian government made much of this addition, and its opening was a prominent cultural and political affair, with the Lithuanian prime minister in attendance.[145]

But this diplomatic success is not matched by the actual museum product. The new room addition is emotionally bland, displaying mostly documents and reports and a small screen video of a documentary about exhumations at Ponary, a rather technical story about new archaeological methods used by Lithuanian scientists to identify Ponary victims. The question of Lithuanian collaboration is dismissed in half a sentence: "Although the persecution

---

143. Genocide and Resistance Research Centre of Lithuania, Museum of Occupations and Freedom Fights, accessed February 17, 2019, http://genocid.lt/muziejus/en/708/c.

144. A. Craig Wight and J. John Lennon, "Selective Interpretation and Eclectic Human Heritage in Lithuania," *Tourism Management* 28, no. 2 (2007): 519–29, here 528.

145. Dovid Katz, "The New Holocaust Room in a Basement Cubicle of the Genocide Museum in Vilnius," *Defending History*, November 21, 2011, http://defendinghistory.com/%20genocide-museum-new-holocaust-room-in-the-basement.

and executions of Jews were organized by Nazi Germany, in most occupied countries, and Lithuania is no exception, the Nazis managed to involve some of the local residents in these crimes." The panel then goes on to state: "The occupants also tried to mobilize Lithuanian youth to military and police units. However, the attempt of the Germans in February and March 1943 to form a Lithuanian SS legion failed. Lithuanian youth did not want to join the legion and boycotted the military mobilization and work duties announced by the Germans."[146] The message here is clear—the conscience of the nation is clean.

While the added-on Holocaust room is bland and unemotional, the real gore, pathos, and emotional punch the museum reserves for its true object of interest—Soviet occupation and Lithuanian victimization. The depth of contrast between how the "two genocides" are presented is also visible even before the visitor enters the building. Hundreds of names of Lithuanian anti-Soviet partisans are etched into the façade of the museum. There are no names of any victims of the Holocaust.

The museum is extremely popular and is often touted in tourist brochures as the "number one attraction in Vilnius." And indeed, the troves of visitors—eighty thousand a year according to the museum's records—prove that point.[147] And while the main purpose of the museum may be international, to "educate the West" regarding Soviet terror, the Lithuanian state also uses it to instill a sense of national loyalty and pride, as well as "collective pity," in its own citizens by organizing regular visits by Lithuanian schoolchildren, students, and the military.[148] The museum has been under international pressure to change its name, but the domestic opposition to the change has been strong.[149] In May 2018, the Genocide and Resistance Research Centre announced that the museum's name had been changed to the Museum of Occupations and Freedom Fights.

146. Museum of Genocide/Occupation, Vilnius, panels displayed as of February 2018, observed by author.

147. This very high number of visitors has grown exponentially over the years and the museum has only become more popular. In 2003, for example, it had twelve thousand visitors a year. A. Craig Wight, "Lithuanian Genocide Heritage as Discursive Formation," *Annals of Tourism Research* 59 (2016): 60–78, here 63.

148. On the day I visited the museum in February 2018 there was a line to get in, but the museum was especially busy as a military regiment was there on what seemed an official group visit.

149. While Lithuanian historians were aware of international objections to the institution's name, the biggest obstacle to changing it came from former Soviet deportees and political prisoners who were instrumental in the museum's establishment and ongoing curation. Author interview with Monika Kareniauskaitė, senior historian with the Genocide and Resistance Research Centre, February 2, 2018, Vilnius.

Disciplining the Past at Lithuania's Sites of Memory

In addition to the museum, other memorial locations in Lithuania have also demonstrated the problematic treatment of the Holocaust, especially Lithuanian complicity in it, and the overlapping narratives of the Soviet occupation, the Lithuanian anti-Soviet resistance, and the Holocaust.

In 1994, the government established a commission to investigate the Soviet executions of political enemies and their burial in the mass grave in Tuskulėnai, outside of Vilnius. The Tuskulėnai site soon became another location of Lithuanian martyrdom as the extent of the Soviet executions and numbers (more than 700) of victims became public. In 1998, Tuskulėnai became a memorial park complex for "the victims of 1944–1947 NKVD–KGB repressions," and in 2008 it was placed under the direction of the Genocide and Resistance Research Centre.[150] It is the location of the annual National Day of Remembrance for Lithuanian Victims of Communism and another material site that narrates the Soviet genocide of the Lithuanian nation. The complication, however, is that some of those buried here were Lithuanian Nazi collaborators, who were shot by the Soviets in summary executions after the war. So as not to disturb the narrative of a mass grave of unknown Lithuanian victims of communism, the bodies at Tuskulėnai have remained unidentified.[151]

These complications of memory are found in memorial sites across Lithuania. The large exhibition at the Ninth Fort in Kaunas—the site of the execution of thirty thousand Jews—provides a history of Nazi executions without mentioning Lithuanian participation at all. In fact, the Ninth Fort Museum very carefully dates the beginning of anti-Jewish violence to the arrival of Germans in Kaunas on June 25, 1941—especially Franz Walter Stahlecker, the commander of Einsatzgruppe A, who, in the museum's telling, "organized the destruction of the Jews and Communists."[152] The museum does not mention the earlier pogroms that were carried out by Lithuanians on the eve of the Holocaust. The most well-known of the June 1941 pogroms, at the Lietūkis garage in Kaunas, has been memorialized at the site since 2002, but with this inscription: "In this place, the former Lietūkis Garage, dozens of Jews from Kaunas were brutally murdered on June 27, 1941" (in Lithuanian

150. Genocide and Resistance Research Centre of Lithuania, The Memorial Complex of the Tuskulėnai Peace Park, accessed February 17, 2019, http://genocid.lt/tuskulenai/en.

151. James Mark, "What Remains? Anti-communism, Forensic Archaeology, and the Retelling of the National past in Lithuania and Romania," *Past and Present* 206, no. suppl_5 (2010): 276–300.

152. Kauno IX forto muziejus, "The Place of Mass Murder," accessed February 17, 2019, http://www.9fortomuziejus.lt/istorija/masiniu-zudyniu-vieta/?lang=en.

and Yiddish). Who carried out the massacre—clearly the critical part of the story—the inscription does not say.

Even more interesting than these historical omissions is the way in which the purpose of the Ninth Fort memorial site has changed since Lithuanian independence. The site today memorializes both the Nazi executions and the Soviet prison that existed at the location. It is also the site of a mass grave, with thirty thousand Jewish bodies lying underground, unmarked. The Holocaust, however, is presented as only one—and not even the most important—event to be commemorated at the Ninth Fort; it is one of four permanent exhibitions at the museum, the other three being *Soviet Occupation 1940–41; 1944–1990*, *Kaunas Hard Labor Prison 1924–1940*, and *Kaunas Fortress 1882–1915*.

The Ninth Fort is the second largest site of Holocaust mass murder in Lithuania after Ponary. By not giving the Holocaust pride of place as its central commemorative feature, the museum thus appears to be engaging in "Holocaust obfuscation," a particular type of Holocaust revisionism that does not deny the Holocaust and its central events but rather drowns it out by treating it as just one among many other atrocities, big and small, major and minor, related and unrelated, making the Holocaust appear as just another bad moment in time and not the core event of Lithuania's modern history.[153]

At a larger level, Lithuania's "authorized heritage discourse" —the official story about its cultural past—also curates historical memory in a way that abstracts the Holocaust away and focuses instead on Lithuanian victimization during the Soviet occupation—a coordinated representation that is remarkably coherent and uniform across multiple commemorative sites.[154] The consequence of these remembrance practices, this hegemonic domination of Lithuanian victimhood, is to silence Jewish voices and relegate them outside of Lithuania's mainstream history and outside of Lithuanian contemporary body politic.

Holocaust Remembrance at the Jewish Museum

To counter these hegemonic narratives of an abstract, passive Holocaust, narratives that dominate Lithuanian state institutions of memory, the

153. Dovid Katz, "On Three Definitions: Genocide, Holocaust Denial, Holocaust Obfuscation," in *A Litmus Test Case of Modernity: Examining Modern Sensibilities and the Public Domain in the Baltic States at the Turn of the Century*, ed. Leonidas Donskis (Bern: Peter Lang, 2009), 259–77.

154. Laurajane Smith, *Uses of Heritage* (London: Routledge, 2006).

Jewish Museum's Green House Holocaust exhibition acts as "a site of discursive resistance."[155] The Green House narrates the story of the Lithuanian Holocaust in detail, including a comprehensive if not particularly prominently displayed discussion of the issue of Lithuanian collaboration. It also ties the history of the Holocaust with the larger arc of Litvak life—the long history of the Jewish presence in Lithuania, the cultural significance of Vilna to the European Jewish, especially Yiddish, literary tradition, and the slow and difficult road to postwar reconstruction. It includes a few video testimonies from survivors as well as from perpetrators but it is mostly based on textual and photographic material—letters, diaries, German documents, reports, and surviving material from the ghettos. Its most emotionally affecting space is a room in the attic repurposed to represent a hiding place for Jewish children. It is unheated, sparse, with a wooden bench and a few ragged toys scattered on the floor. The visitor experiences the claustrophobic and frigidly cold room while listening to the narration of Yitzchak Rudashevski's Vilna ghetto diary.

The Green House Holocaust exhibition, however, is incredibly modest in both presentation and volume. It is located in a small, hard-to-find building on a side street, and even though it was renovated in 2009–10, in its aesthetic it is still very much a late 1980s cultural artifact, far removed from the advanced visual presentations of major contemporary Holocaust museums (in Washington, Jerusalem, Warsaw, or Berlin). It is staffed primarily by volunteers, some of them aging Holocaust survivors or their descendants, with few professional guides.[156] Its cultural and mnemonic impact is modest as well. It greets a fraction of the number of visitors that the Museum of Genocide/Occupation attracts, and the visitors that do come tend to be foreign tourists, not Lithuanians.[157]

In addition to the issue of the small and largely publicly invisible Green House, the visual narration of the Jewish Museum is also fragmented by the

155. Wight, "Lithuanian Genocide Heritage," 73.

156. This is not the case for its research wing, however, which is staffed by professional and prolific historians. This research group has created immensely valuable projects, such as the Holocaust Atlas of Lithuania, which identifies all known sites of murder in the Holocaust and provides basic information about the events and consequent memorialization (available in Lithuanian and English at http://www.holocaustatlas.lt), as well as the online database of Holocaust victims in Lithuania, "The Lithuanian Jewish Communities in the Face of the Holocaust: (Un)Forgotten Names and Fates" (available in Lithuanian and English at http://www.holocaustnames.lt).

157. Curatorial staff of the Green House, author interview, February 2, 2018. When I visited the Green House museum, its location was listed inaccurately on Google Maps and only a lonely street sign could point me in roughly the right direction. I arrived at 1 PM and was the first visitor that day. Even the volunteers were not Lithuanian—the extremely knowledgeable and enthusiastic volunteer who provided an ad hoc tour was part of the Austrian government exchange program.

existence of multiple museum sites. A separate exhibition on the Holocaust is housed in the Tolerance Center and yet another at Ponary, a location on the outskirts of Vilnius with difficult public transportation access and short opening hours—all practical hurdles that make visits, and therefore their pedagogical impact, difficult.[158]

The Ponary site itself remains in poor shape, with only a small exhibition on the premises. The exhibition was renovated in 2009, but it still remains a material, not a narrative, museum—it displays documents and reports by Nazi authorities and many personal belongings of victims found on the site in successive waves of archaeological excavations. What it does not provide, however, is a larger narrative arc linking the centrality of this site to the Holocaust in Lithuania—and, especially, to the Lithuanian perpetration of the genocide, a critical aspect of the killing that places the Ponary site at the core of Holocaust remembrance for the few surviving Lithuanian Jews.

The Tolerance Center, yet another museum site that is part of the Vilna Gaon Jewish Museum group of institutions, attempts to square the circle of Lithuania's memory wars. Its objective is to incorporate the history of the Litvaks into the national story of Lithuania—a difficult task and one that leads to much compromising. As an outreach to the Lithuanian majority, the Tolerance Center's permanent exhibition downplays Lithuanian responsibility for the Holocaust and attempts to tell the story of larger connections between the Jews and Lithuanians.

Describing the beginning of the Nazi occupation, the Tolerance Center provides an extremely vague narrative of the chaotic days in June 1941 when the first anti-Jewish pogroms occurred. The exhibition says, "There was an uprising against the former occupants as well as fighting against Red Army soldiers. Arrests, shootings and revenge attacks were directed against Communists, members of the Communist youth and those who collaborated with them. Many innocent people were caught up in the frenzy, Jews among them." This bland discussion avoids mentioning the purposeful targeting of the Jews, who were attacked either because local Lithuanians associated them with Soviet rule or because of anti-Semitism unrelated to the Soviets, or both. This particular sentence seemed to have been a cause of some internal discussion and disagreement among the Tolerance Center staff, and so the phrase "Jews among them" has been clumsily taped over with a loose post-it note that says "Jews in particular." Only a very close inspection of the

158. The Ponary exhibition is closed between October and May, and visits can be arranged by appointment only.

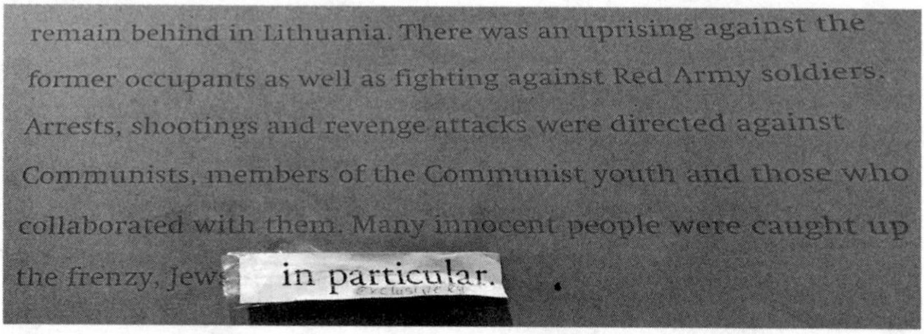
remain behind in Lithuania. There was an uprising against the
former occupants as well as fighting against Red Army soldiers.
Arrests, shootings and revenge attacks were directed against
Communists, members of the Communist youth and those who
collaborated with them. Many innocent people were caught up
the frenzy, Jews
in particular.

FIGURE 7. Display at the Tolerance Center Museum, Vilnius, Lithuania (photograph by author)

post-it note reveals that someone, mostly likely a visitor, has scribbled under "in particular," "exclusively."[159]

Prosecuting "Genocide"

In 2006, *Respublika*, one of the most popular Lithuanian newspapers, published a story with the title "The Expert with Blood on His Hands." The story alleged that the expert in question, Yitzhak Arad, the former director of Yad Vashem, a noted historian of the Holocaust in Lithuania, and a member of Lithuania's own International Commission for the Evaluation of the Crimes of the Nazi and Soviet Occupation Regimes in Lithuania, had committed grave crimes against humanity during WWII, including "ethnic cleansing of Lithuanians" as part of a broader "Soviet genocide." The *Respublika* article referred to Arad throughout as the "NKVD storm trooper"—a not so subtle cooptation of Nazi terminology for a Soviet partisan. The basis for these allegations was Arad's own memoir, *The Partisan*, which was published in English in 1979 but had become of sudden interest in Lithuania more than twenty-five years later. In his memoir, Arad described how his partisan unit carried out a "mopping-up operation" against armed Lithuanians in 1944 in the aftermath of Nazi withdrawal from the area.[160]

The article caused an initial stir and embarrassment for the Lithuanian establishment but could have been dismissed as a particularly egregious anti-Semitic account in a tabloid. The scandal, however, quickly became a full-blown international crisis when in 2007 Lithuanian prosecutors opened an investigation of Arad for war crimes, citing Arad's memoir as evidence.

159. Tolerance Center permanent exhibition, as observed by author, February 2018.
160. Brook, "Double Genocide."

In addition to Arad, the prosecution also requested to interview Rachel Margolis, another Vilna ghetto survivor and Jewish partisan, as well as Fania Brantsovskaya, another survivor, as witnesses in the case.

To Holocaust survivors, prosecuting resistance heroes like Arad was shocking and deeply insulting, as, in their view, fighting the Nazis was nothing short of commendable—then and now.[161] This is why Arad himself felt the need to reiterate: "I am proud that I fought the Nazi Germans and their Lithuanian collaborators. That fate made it possible for me to fight against the murderers of my family, the murderers of my people."[162]

But this context and this fight are simply not part of the main Lithuanian narrative of its past. What matters in terms of the dominant historical memory in Lithuania is that Jewish partisans were Soviet and communist; that they were fighting for their lives and in the process also helped rid Europe of Nazism is irrelevant to this narrative. To outside observers—and obviously to the Jews—this Lithuanian story looks at best incomplete and at worst cruel, but for Lithuanians it is the only way to make sense of their twentieth-century experience. These narratives are not just incompatible. They are incommensurable.

The Lithuanian judiciary, however, seemed to have overplayed its hand, and the international outrage at the Arad investigation was swift and consequential. Yad Vashem refused to participate in the workings of the Lithuanian historical commission, and other foreign experts also resigned in protest. A year into the investigation, the prosecution closed the case.

After almost five years of paralysis in the aftermath of the Arad investigation, in 2012, the Lithuanian president Dalia Grybauskaitė reinstated the commission and changed somewhat the description of its mandate in response to international criticism. The charge of the renewed commission was now to investigate "the distinct, unprecedented nature and scale of the Holocaust; other crimes of the Nazi regime, and the devastating consequences of the Soviet occupation regime for the people of Lithuania."[163] The Arad affair, however, tainted the work of the commission and presented a political and ethical obstacle that this institution never quite overcame.[164]

---

161. Some Jewish partisans, however, embrace a more critical account of Soviet partisans. In her memoir, Rachel Margolis accounts multiple instances of antisemitism and misogyny among Soviet partisans. Rachel Margolis, *A Partisan from Vilna* (Brighton: Academic Studies Press, 2010).

162. Interviewed in Brook, "Double Genocide."

163. Dovile Budryte, "Travelling Trauma: Lithuanian Transnational Memory after World War II," in *Memory and Trauma in International Relations: Theories, Cases, and Debates*, ed. Erica Resende and Dovile Budryte (London: Routledge, 2013), 168–82, here 176.

164. Karn, *Amending the Past*.

At the same time, Lithuania has continued to legislate its memory. In 2010 a law was passed criminalizing the minimization of Soviet crimes, a crime now punishable by up to two years in prison (the law mandates the same penalty for Holocaust denial). That the Soviets committed "genocide" in Lithuania is now the law of the land.[165]

And while Lithuania is aggressively prosecuting former communists for genocide against the Lithuanian nation, it has shown no effort at all in prosecuting Nazi collaborators. The high-profile case of Aleksandras Lileikis, the former head of the Lithuanian security police in Vilnius, was delayed in perpetuity until his death in 2000. Under international pressure, three Lithuanian collaborators were eventually sentenced, but were all declared unfit for prison due to their own or their spouses' ill health. This means that not a single Lithuanian Nazi collaborator has served a day in prison.[166] In the bitter words of a Holocaust survivor, "The government is waiting for witnesses to die."[167]

Lithuania, now safely in the EU, has created a political space for its memory laws that can withstand international pressure, and it has done so by spearheading the EU's own project of leveling the "two totalitarianisms" of the twentieth century. A big part of Lithuania's post-independence European project has been internationalizing Soviet-era remembrance. In 2000, a group of former political prisoners and Soviet deportees gathered in Vilnius to demand the establishment of an international court to prosecute "international communism and communist criminals."[168] This gathering became known as Nuremberg-2, as the purpose of this movement is to use the existing architecture of international justice developed to process the crimes of the Holocaust to now process the crimes of communism.

Lithuania has since been at the forefront of EU resolutions condemning the "two totalitarianisms." Leading Lithuanian politicians signed the Prague Declaration on European Conscience and Communism. The Lithuanian delegation also successfully proposed the Resolution on Divided Europe Reunited at the Vilnius meeting of the Organization for Economic Cooperation and Development (OECD) in 2009, which instituted August 23 as the Day of Remembrance of the Victims of Stalinism and Nazism across Europe. Far from being an aspiring EU candidate state, busily adopting European models and standards of commemorative practice, Lithuania today is a

165. English translation of the law available via Defending History, accessed February 17, 2019, http://www.holocaustinthebaltics.com/2010June29Red-BrownLawPassedBy%20Seimas.pdf.

166. Brook, "Double Genocide."

167. Gerdziunas, "Decades after Soviet Terror."

168. Budrytė, *Taming Nationalism?*, 183.

leader in European memory politics and has managed to successfully internationalize its vision of its past, which presents Eastern Europe as a site of Soviet genocide.

Memory Interventions

Lithuania, however, does not speak with one voice, and there have been a few important memory interventions into this hegemonic narrative that have come from unofficial sources—some Jewish, but also many Lithuanian.

In 2016, Marius Ivaškevičius, a popular Lithuanian playwright, published a powerful essay, "I Am Not Jewish," in which he lamented the indifference Lithuanians felt about the Holocaust, and called for more remembrance, especially in his hometown of Molėtai, where 1,200 Jews were killed in August 1941 by the Lithuanian "white armbanders" militia.[169] Ivaškevičius then organized—together with the Molėtai regional museum director and two children of Holocaust survivors—a massive march of remembrance in the town on August 29, 2016, in which four thousand people walked to mark seventy-five years since the destruction of Molėtai's Jews.[170]

Another unsettling memory intervention was the 2016 book *Mūsiškiai* (Our people) by the well-known Lithuanian author Rūta Vanagaitė, which presents a popular, non-scholarly account of Lithuanian perpetrators in the Holocaust, including members of Vanagaitė's own family. Written in an accessible style, the book reached a wide audience—it had three print runs—and caused quite a stir.

As the book grew in popularity, however, so did the backlash against the author. Vanagaitė was accused of playing fast and loose with facts and not presenting a scholarly account. The most pointed criticism, however, had to do with defamation of the nation, as for example in an angry rebuttal by a Lithuanian historian who said, "Your people are not our people."[171] As the media backlash against Vanagaitė intensified, the Lithuanian publisher decided to cut ties with her in 2017, pull the book, and recall it from bookstores.[172]

169. Vilna Gaon State Jewish Museum, *Holocaust Atlas of Lithuania.*

170. Davoliūtė and Budrytė, "Entangled History," 323.

171. Quoted in Davoliūtė and Budrytė, "Entangled History," 338.

172. Cnaan Liphshiz, "Lithuanian Publisher Recalls Books by Writer Who Triggered Holocaust Debate," *Times of Israel*, October 30, 2017. The book was pulled over Vanagaitė's contested interpretation of activities of a revered Lithuanian anti-Soviet partisan. Specifically, the issue was Vanagaitė's October 2017 statement suggesting that Adolfas Ramanauskas-Vanagas, a prominent leader of the Lithuanian anti-Soviet partisans, may have cooperated with the Soviet secret police and may have

And while the publisher's decision to pull the book initiated a series of international protests, including an official protest by PEN America, the Vanagaitė scandal also opened up political space for the Lithuanian government to further legislate Holocaust remembrance. In 2018, the economy minister submitted a bill to Parliament that would ban selling material that "distorted historical facts" about Lithuania—such as books discussing the culpability of Lithuanians in the Holocaust.[173]

In July 2018, another bombshell disturbed Lithuanian Holocaust memory: an article by Silvia Foti, the granddaughter of Jonas Noreika, a celebrated Lithuanian anti-Soviet resistant fighter and national hero executed by the Soviet police in 1947. Foti's article documents Noreika's direct and extensive participation in the Holocaust of Lithuanian Jews in the town of Plungė, in "the first week" of the Holocaust, before the Germans arrived. Her research led her to conclude that Noreika had ordered the murder of 2,000 Jews in Plungė, 5,500 Jews in Šiauliai and 7,000 in Telšiai.[174]

This revelation was critical for three reasons—first, it destabilized the Lithuanian hegemonic narrative that no pogroms occurred before the Germans came, and second, it questioned the reverence with which leaders of the anti-Soviet uprising like Noreika were seen in Lithuania. But perhaps most significantly, it put in serious doubt the scholarly legitimacy and authority of the Genocide and Resistance Research Centre, the main institution that set the parameters of Holocaust memory in Lithuania and the institution that was behind much of the national mythology construction around Noreika.[175] Using some evidence from Foti's research but also new detailed historical research conducted by independent historians, Grant Gochin, a Holocaust memory activist of Litvak descent based in the United States, placed a request with the Lithuanian prosecutor to begin pre-trial

---

even participated in the Holocaust. Dovilė Budrytė, "War Memories and Insecurities: The Politics of Memory in Lithuania," *Baltic Rim Economies*, December 2017.

173. Jewish Telegraphic Agency, April 3, 2018, https://www.jta.org/2018/04/03/news-opinion/lithuanian-bill-banning-published-material-critical-of-the-country-seen-as-response-to-holocaust-book. The bill has since been withdrawn.

174. Silvia Foti, "My Grandfather Wasn't a Nazi-Fighting War Hero—He Was a Brutal Collaborator," *Salon*, July 14, 2018, https://www.salon.com/2018/07/14/my-grandfather-didnt-fight-the-nazis-as-family-lore-told-it-he-was-a-brutal-collaborator.

175. Noreika is one of the Lithuanian national heroes most prominently portrayed in the Museum of Genocide/Occupation, which is managed by the Genocide and Resistance Research Centre, and the center has also published a major glowing biography of Noreika, *Generolas Vėtra* (General Storm) in 1997. The center has aggressively guarded Noreika's legacy. In 2015, in responding to a petition to remove the plaque honoring Noreika from a major Vilnius building, the center dismissed the petition by blaming it on Russian influence—"The contempt being shown for Lithuanian patriots is organized by neighbors from the East." Higgins, "Nazi Collaborator or National Hero?"

investigation into the director of the Genocide and Resistance Research Centre for Holocaust denial, on account of the center's continuing refusal to acknowledge Noreika's direct participation in the Holocaust. The Lithuanian prosecutor, however, has rejected the request.[176]

The Paradoxes of Jewish Life in Contemporary Lithuania

The Lithuanian Jewish community today is small, isolated, marginalized, and insecure. From a prewar population of one hundred eighty thousand Litvaks, today the Jewish community numbers no more than three thousand, most of whom are not originally Litvak but are instead Jewish immigrants from other parts of the Soviet Union who moved to Lithuania after the 1950s. Of the original Litvaks, completely decimated in the Holocaust, there are no more than three hundred families left today.[177]

The main organization representing Lithuanian Jews, the Lithuanian Jewish Community, pursues its mandate as a voice of this small minority with a sensitivity that sometimes comes at the cost of true historical remembrance. With its mission being "tolerance," the concern is that to point out Lithuanian complicity in the Holocaust too directly may make the Jews' position today more precarious. As the chairwoman of the Jewish association said, "My role is to make the best conditions for Jews living here"—and this has led to compromise.[178] This approach has created deep divisions among Lithuania's Jews. A different organization, the Vilnius Jewish Community, worries that the Jewish community is being used by the Lithuanian government for international public relations purposes in the lack of a serious change in Lithuanian attitudes toward the Jews, past and present.[179]

In the absence of state efforts, the Jewish community has taken over remembrance through its own projects. In an illustration of how far Holocaust remembrance has been from the center of Lithuanian public memory,

176. Gochin, the chief plaintiff in the case, lost a hundred family members in the Holocaust in Lithuania. His Notice to the Prosecutor is available at Lithuanian Jewish Community, "Lithuanian Prosecutor Rejects Holocaust Denial Case against Genocide Center," September 9, 2018, https://www.lzb.lt/en/2018/09/12/lithuanian-prosecutor-rejects-holocaust-denial-case-against-genocide-center. Also, author correspondence with Andrius Kulikauskas, lecturer at Vilnius Gediminas Technical University, and one of the historians who prepared the material for the brief, July 14, 2018.

177. Author interview with Monika Antanaitytė, chief of staff, Lithuanian Jewish Community, February 2, 2018, Vilnius.

178. Kukliansky, interview.

179. "Vilnius Jewish Community Releases Letter Signed by Twenty Elected Board Members Addressed to 'Good Will Foundation,'" *Defending History*, August 7, 2017, http://defendinghistory.com/vilnius-jewish-community-releases-letter-signed-by-20-elected-board-members-addressed-to-good-will-foundation/89289.

it took until 2018, forty-five years after its publication in English in Israel, for Yitzchak Rudashevski's Vilna ghetto diary to be published in Lithuanian—and only as a project of the Lithuanian Jewish community, not of Lithuanian state institutions of remembrance.

In 2016, the Jewish community partnered with the Lithuanian Centre for Human Rights to install nineteen *Stolpersteine* (stumbling stones), small memorial stones placed outside of the houses of Holocaust victims, a popular international remembrance project by German artist Gunter Demnig.[180] The *Stolpersteine* were installed in Vilnius, Kaunas, Šiauliai and Panėvėžys. One of them was placed in remembrance of Yitzchak Rudashevski.[181] While the *Stolpersteine* project was a nonstate effort, the Lithuanian government still took public relations credit for it, featuring it prominently on the website of the Lithuanian Ministry of National Minorities and promoting it on the government's Twitter feed.[182]

In 2016, a new monument was built at the site of the Seventh Fort in Kaunas, where the graveyard of five thousand killed Jews had been completely abandoned until 2011.[183] In 2018, the Šeduva Jewish Memorial Fund began construction on an ambitious Lost Shtetl Museum and Memorial Complex, which would include four monuments to the lost Jewish community of Šeduva (Shadeve), entirely annihilated in the shooting spree in August 1941. The big project also includes publications and documentary films and is billed as a major new institution of Holocaust remembrance in Lithuania.[184]

As was the case with the installment of the *Stolpersteine*, this nonstate project received top state attention, with President Grybauskaitė in attendance and, significantly, Lithuania's prime minister Saulius Skvernelis at the ground-breaking ceremony issuing an official apology for the role of Lithuanian perpetrators of the Holocaust.[185] But as if to starkly illustrate just how contradictory official Holocaust remembrance is in Lithuania, this

---

180. Gunther Demnig, *Stolpersteine: Hier wohnte 1933–1945*, accessed February 17, 2019, http://www.stolpersteine.eu.

181. Ellen Cassedy, "Stones Of Remembrance In Lithuania," *Huffington Post*, September 7, 2016, https://www.huffingtonpost.com/ellen-cassedy/stones-of-remembrance-in-_b_11882122.html.

182. Department of National Minorities, "Stolpersteine in Vilnius," August 3, 2016, http://tmde.lrv.lt/en/news/stolpersteine-in-vilnius.

183. "Paminklo žuvusiems VII forte atidengimo ceremonija" [The opening ceremony for the monument to those killed at the 7th fort], Kauno Tvirtovės VII Fortas, accessed March 15, 2019, http://www.septintasfortas.lt/renginys/paminklo-zuvusiems-vii-forte-atidengimo-ceremonija.

184. "Dingęs Štetlas / The Lost Stetl," accessed February 17, 2019, http://lostshtetl.com.

185. "High-Profile Ceremony for the Forthcoming Museum in Lithuania," *Jerusalem Connection Report*, May 9, 2018, http://thejerusalemconnection.us/blog/2018/05/09/high-profile-ceremony-for-the-forthcoming-museum-in-lithuania.

FIGURE 8. Memorial stone (*Stolperstein*) placed in memory of Yitzchak Rudashevski in 2016, Vilnius, Lithuania (photograph by author)

same prime minister also said that Lithuania did not need to review its attitude toward the role of Lithuanians during the Holocaust: "We have nothing to review. We have made all the steps as a state and we continue to have an excellent dialogue with the Lithuanian Jewish community and with the global (Jewish) community."[186]

The contradictions of outward respect for and pride in Jewish heritage coupled with continuing indifference and politicization is also evident in government plans to build a major convention center right on top of a five-hundred-year-old Jewish cemetery known as Piramónt, to the consternation

186. "Prime Minister Sees No Need for Lithuania to Review Its Stance on Lithuanians' Role in Holocaust," *Baltic Times*, November 2, 2017, https://www.baltictimes.com/prime_minister_sees_no_need_for_lithuania_to_review_its_stance_on_lithuanians__role_in_holocaust.

of local Jews and an international outcry.[187] Even more bizarre was the "Recovering Memory" announcement in 2017 by Vilnius University that it would posthumously award academic degrees to Jewish students killed in the Holocaust, unless they fought with Soviet partisans—as if their anti-Nazi resistance made them less worthy of respect and remembrance.[188]

In 2011 Lithuania passed a long overdue Restitution Law on Good Will Compensation for the Real Estate of Jewish Communities, which allocated thirty-seven million euros in compensation to the Jewish community; a small fraction of this—eight hundred seventy thousand euros—was dedicated for direct compensation to Holocaust survivors or their descendants who, again in official state parlance, "had been victims of occupying totalitarian regimes."[189] Because proving Lithuanian citizenship—a condition for eligibility that similar laws in Estonia and Latvia did not include—has been very difficult, restitution claims are often unsuccessful.[190] As most Lithuanian Holocaust survivors left Lithuania after the war and became citizens of other countries, the citizenship requirement makes them ineligible for property restitution claims. Instead of individual restitution, therefore, the government set up the Good Will Foundation, which allocates grants to various Jewish community projects. This process, however, has further exacerbated already deep divisions within the Jewish community. While the Good Will Foundation has supported large-scale cultural projects, such as visits by the Israeli Philharmonic Orchestra or international art workshops, many members of the Jewish community have complained about a lack of resources and social services for older, destitute Lithuanian Jews or for Orthodox religious and educational services.[191]

The absence of any legislation on heirless property—a key in Holocaust restitution legislation and a best practice of the EU Terezin restitution agreement—makes requests for compensation extremely difficult. The 2011 law allowed for a one-time, largely symbolic compensation to Holocaust victims' descendants, but it did nothing to tackle the large issue of massive property transfer from Jewish to non-Jewish families in the aftermath of the

187. Dovid Katz, "Lithuania's Liveliest Cemetery," *Times of Israel*, December 13, 2015, http://blogs.timesofisrael.com/lithuanias-liveliest-cemetery.

188. JTA, "Vilnius University to Honor Jewish Students Killed in Holocaust—Unless They Fought the Nazis," *Haaretz*, April 14, 2017.

189. Good Will Foundation, "About Us," accessed February 17, 2019, https://gvf.lt/en/about-us.

190. Kukliansky, interview.

191. "Defending History's 2017 People of the Year," January 1, 2017, http://defendinghistory.com/defending-historys-2017-people-of-the-year/85592.

Holocaust.[192] This has made life for Lithuanian Jews often precarious and uncomfortable. Many Jews still feel resentment over their looted property, some expressing anxiousness about buying antiques; in the words of Faina Kukliansky, "I don't know if these things are mine."[193]

In this political environment of mixed messages, the daily experience of living as a Jew in Lithuania is complicated. Across Lithuania there are street names and memorials to Lithuanian heroes who have participated in the Holocaust, either as officials giving orders to dispossess and isolate the Jews or as actual henchmen in Lithuanian anti-Soviet militias, such as Kazys Škirpa streets in Kaunas and Vilnius, Juozas Krikštaponis square in Ukmergė, or the Jonas Noreika plaque at the Library of the National Academy of Sciences in Vilnius.[194] So extremely different is the narrative of Lithuania's twentieth century for the Lithuanian majority that June 23 is celebrated as a national day of remembrance of the anti-Soviet June 1941 uprising, and "June 23" streets are common in Lithuanian cities, including in Vilnius. This memorialization is seemingly completely oblivious or indifferent to the fact that the Soviet occupation ended on June 23rd only because the Soviets were run out by the Nazis who occupied Lithuania and put in place a systematic effort to exterminate the Jews. That Lithuania was the deadliest place in Europe to be a Jew, that it was ground zero for the Holocaust—are not part of this public memory.

It is therefore not surprising that public anti-Semitic incidents, publications, and vandalism have been met with slow and inadequate government response.[195] A particularly painful incident was the defacing of the Ponary monument in 2011, when a graffiti "Hitler was right" in Russian was painted on a memorial stone, while another profanity was sprayed on a nearby monument, in apparent reference to the Lithuanian government's decision to begin restitution to Holocaust survivors.[196] The Ninth Fort memorial in Kaunas was also vandalized that same year—swastikas were drawn on memorial plates and a granite marker with a Star of David stolen.[197]

---

192. ESLI Restorative Justice and Post-Holocaust Immovable Property Restitution Study Team, "Overview of Immovable Property Restitution/Compensation Regime—Lithuania," in *Immovable Property Restitution Study* (Prague: European Shoah Legacy Institute, 2016), 225–39.

193. Kukliansky, interview.

194. "Memorials to Holocaust Collaborators in Public Spaces and State Sponsored Institutions in Lithuania," *Defending History*, http://defendinghistory.com/memorials-to-holocaust-collaborators-in-public-spaces-and-state-sponsored-institutions-in-lithuania.

195. Sužiedėlis and Liekis, "Conflicting Memories," 338–39.

196. Snyder, "Neglecting the Lithuanian Holocaust."

197. Orlando Radice, "Lithuania Holocaust Memorial Vandalised," *Jewish Chronicle*, April 14, 2011, https://www.thejc.com/news/world/lithuania-holocaust-memorial-vandalised-1.22491.

Anti-Semitic cartoons have appeared in major newspapers, while a local court declared that the swastika predated the Nazis and could be displayed in public with impunity.[198] A prominent Lithuanian photographer claimed in a much-publicized article that the iconic photographs of the Lietūkis garage pogrom in Kaunas—some of the most well-known images of pogroms anywhere during the Holocaust—were unreliable and doctored by the Nazis to impute responsibility on the Lithuanians.[199]

In 2010, a historian and advisor to the Lithuanian Interior Ministry wrote in a column for a popular weekly magazine that the Holocaust was a "legend" and the Nuremberg trial "the biggest legal farce in history."[200] A particularly virulent display of anti-Semitism occurred during the annual celebration of Lithuania's independence in 2011, when not only youth participants but also members of Lithuanian parliament and a staff member of the Genocide and Resistance Research Centre proudly wore swastika armbands.[201]

Paradoxically, though, Jewish heritage has been officially appropriated as Lithuanian legacy, especially for international eyes. Yiddish heritage has been especially showcased, as Vilnius now houses the Yiddish Institute, a Yiddish library, and the International Yiddish Center of the World Jewish Congress, as well as a research center affiliated with YIVO. In Vilnius Old Town, the historically Jewish quarter, street signs were put up with original Yiddish names and there are plaques designating the houses of Vilnius's Yiddish writers.[202] Lithuanian government has insisted that the newly discovered literary artifacts from Vilna ghetto's Paper Brigade remain in Lithuania, and not be taken to YIVO in New York where most of the original documents are kept, because it wants to showcase them as part of its national heritage.[203] It is in this international context that the government declared 2019 "The Year of the Jew."[204]

What makes Lithuania's relationship to the Holocaust even more complex is the renewed interest in learning Yiddish and Hebrew, especially

198. Violeta Davoliūtė, "The Prague Declaration of 2008 and its Repercussions in Lithuania," *Lituanus* 57, no. 3 (2011): 49–62, here 60.

199. Rimantas Varnauskas, "Lietūkio garažas—klastočių pinklėse?" [Lietūkis garage: A forged trap?], *Delfi*, April 2, 2007, https://www.delfi.lt/news/daily/lithuania/lietukio-garazas-klastociu-pinklese.d?id=12723652.

200. "Lithuanian Holocaust Denial Sparks European Outrage," *Baltic Times*, November 26, 2010, https://www.baltictimes.com/news/articles/27422.

201. Davoliūtė, "Prague Declaration," 60. The staffer was dismissed.

202. Adam Asher, "Vilna without Vilna," *Oxford Review of Books*, March 30, 2018, http://the-orb.org/2018/03/30/vilna-without-vilna.

203. Berger, "Trove of Yiddish Artifacts."

204. Nordland, "Where the Genocide Museum."

among the younger Lithuanian generation.[205] Being interested in Lithuania's Jewish past has become a sign of a hipster cultural trend for some Lithuanian youth.[206] The small but active Lithuanian Union of Jewish Students organizes popular walking tours of Jewish Vilnius.[207] The Jewish community generally sees this interest as a favorable, if somewhat superficial, development.[208] The larger problem, however, is that this trendy Jewish revival can distract from a serious inquiry into Lithuanians' culpability for the Holocaust, and relegate Lithuania's Jewish past to the realm of rich folklore, disconnected from any historical accountability, address, or acknowledgment.[209]

There are three fundamental challenges to deep Holocaust memorialization in Lithuania: the lack of recognition of Jewish life and culture as integral to Lithuania's history and identity; a national narrative that does not see the Holocaust as the critical event in all of Lithuania's history; and the almost complete absence of accounting for massive Lithuanian complicity in the destruction of its Jews.[210] Specifically, the official Lithuanian narrative builds on a very narrow understanding of the Holocaust in Lithuania that sees the actions of anti-Soviet partisans in 1941 as completely distinct from their crimes against the Jews; that sees all responsibility for anti-Jewish crimes as resting with the Nazis; that views Lithuanian collaborators as having had no other choice; and that holds only Lithuanians who directly killed the Jews as responsible.[211]

The full significance, scale, and importance of the Holocaust in Lithuania has not permeated to the general public and is not part of the larger Lithuanian national imagination. This is not by accident. Instead, it is the natural consequence of the way in which postindependence Lithuania has constructed its identity and placed its own victimization at the hands of the Soviets, front and center.

---

205. Author interview with Ruth Reches, Hebrew teacher, February 2, 2018, Vilnius.

206. As evidence of this growing interest in the Jewish past among Lithuania's youth, in 2018 a group of young alternative filmmakers crowdsourced the production of *Izaokas* (Isaac), the first ever Lithuanian feature film about Lithuanian participation in the Holocaust that explores the Lietūkis garage massacre in 1941. Lithuanian Jewish Community, "First Lithuanian Dramatic Film about Mass Murder of Jews in Production," June 22, 2018, https://www.lzb.lt/en/2018/06/22/first-lithuanian-dramatic-film-about-mass-murder-of-jews-in-production.

207. Ellen Cassedy, "Keeping the Faith in Vilnius," *Hadassah Magazine*, August, 2016.

208. Antanaitytė, interview.

209. Asher, "Vilna without Vilna."

210. Sužiedėlis and Liekis, "Conflicting Memories," 344.

211. Kulikauskas, correspondence.

Not only is the Holocaust not the central feature in Lithuanian memory politics, but it is used instrumentally through everyday remembrance practices to further bolster the narrative about the real genocide Lithuania lived through. The political point of the "double genocide" narrative, as Yitzhak Arad has noted, was to bring the histories of the two occupations together, in order "to establish the theory of a Holocaust suffered by the Lithuanian people."[212] Lithuanian collaboration in the extermination of their fellow citizens—extensive, deep, and carried out across multiple sites and years—is only narrated to the extent that it can be quickly counteracted with stories of either Lithuanian righteousness and assistance to the Jews or, more perniciously, with continuing arguments about Jewish pro-Soviet allegiances that can be used to justify their elimination as political enemies of the Lithuanian nation. History has become a field of negotiation, where the price for truth-telling on some aspects of collaboration is the watering down or obfuscation of the critical junctures in Lithuania's Holocaust history—such as, most painfully, "the first week" of Lithuanian anti-Jewish pogroms.[213]

At the same time, Lithuania has instrumentalized its Jewish heritage to reposition itself as a responsible European state. It has used its historical multiculturalism for international representation—including, not insignificantly, as a way to attract tourists—while at the same time deflecting calls for a true reckoning of how, exactly, this multiculturalism is no more and who is to blame. The memory of Lithuanian Jews, and especially the memory of the Holocaust, is threatening to the ontological security of the new Lithuania because it questions the roots of contemporary Lithuanian ethnic homogeneity, which is the glue that holds the contemporary Lithuanian body politic together but is itself the result of genocide.

But most important, the story of the Holocaust is narrated in Lithuania as a foil, a backboard to the story of *the genocide*—that of Soviet occupation. The Holocaust is here just a backdrop, a canvas of horrors, a visual repertoire of atrocity, terror, and death that is then used to make sense of what is at the core of Lithuanian national memory—the fifty years of communism. One hundred ninety-five thousand murdered Jews of Lithuania, across the ghettos and the death pits, the attics and the sewers, are providing a theatrical stage for the story Lithuania really wants to tell. It is not a story about them.

212. Yitzhak Arad, "The Holocaust in Lithuania, and Its Obfuscation, in Lithuanian Sources," *Defending History*, December 1, 2012, http://defendinghistory.com/yitzhak-arad-on-the-holocaust-in-lithuania-and-its-obfuscation-in-lithuanian-sources/46252#conclusion.

213. Katz, correspondence.

The Stakes of Holocaust Remembrance in the Twenty-First Century

In February 2018, the Polish president Andrzej Duda signed into law a bill that criminalized any implication that some Poles committed crimes during the Holocaust.[1] After months of hesitation, Duda signed the bill amid much domestic political pressure and demonstrations from the far right that included slogans such as "Take off your yarmulke and sign the bill."[2] During the high-octane domestic controversy that the Holocaust bill generated in Poland, the staff of the Auschwitz Memorial Museum in Oświęcim reported a wave of online and in-person abuse, including physical and verbal attacks on the museum's guides. The Polish nationalist complaint against the museum was that it presented foreign, rather than Polish, narratives of the Holocaust.[3] As part of the international public relations blitz following the passage of the law, Polish companies sent trucks across Western Europe with a message and a readymade social media hashtag, "#RespectUs—During WW2 Poles saved over 100,000 Jews" plastered on the side.[4]

1. The law was amended in June 2018 to make the offense civil and not criminal.

2. Wojciech Moskwa and Maciej Martewicz, "President Signs Law to Outlaw Linking Poland With Holocaust," *Bloomberg News*, February 6, 2018, https://www.bloomberg.com/news/articles/2018-02-06/far-right-groups-demand-polish-president-sign-holocaust-bill.

3. Christian Davies, "Poland's Holocaust Law Triggers Tide of Abuse against Auschwitz Museum," *Guardian*, May 7, 2018.

4. Alice Cuddy, "Polish #RespectUs Campaign Sends Trucks across Europe to Spread Message on Nazi Crimes," *Euronews*, February 28, 2018, http://www.euronews.com/2018/02/28/polish-respectus-campaign-sends-trucks-across-europe-to-spread-message-on-nazi-crimes.

The bill is part of a long-term effort by Polish nationalists to rid Poland of what they call *pedagogika wstydu* (the education of shame), the "alleged subservience and subjugation of the Polish elites to the dominant European narrative."[5] Initially introduced as a limited measure that would criminalize the use of the misnomer "Polish death camps" to refer to Nazi death camps on the territory of occupied Poland, the 2018 law was in fact a much more expansive, almost comprehensive disciplining of political memory in Poland. It eliminated any discussion of Polish complicity in the Holocaust, including the deeply researched and well established Polish anti-Jewish pogroms before, during, and after the Holocaust; the myriad ways in which some Poles harmed their Jewish neighbors through blackmail, theft, and denunciation; and the extensive anti-Semitism that has continued after the war, raising its ugly head in the 1968 anti-Semitic purges and making a loud revival today. Instead of discussing Polish complicity in the Holocaust, Polish lawmakers argued, what should be the focus of everyone's attention is Polish suffering in WWII—what they coined, with no apparent sense of irony or hesitation, Polocaust.[6] And while Israel and the United States were quick to condemn the Polish law, Germany refrained. "We as Germans are responsible for what happened during the Holocaust, the Shoah, under National Socialism," Germany's chancellor Angela Merkel said.[7]

The question that motivated this book is simple: how did we get here? What explains the apparent need of so many postcommunist Eastern European states to revisit the Holocaust now, seventy-five years after the war has ended, and control the way in which the Holocaust is remembered, understood, and interpreted? The argument I have made in the book is that these developments can best be understood as actions of profoundly ontologically insecure states. While scholars have analyzed domestic political machinations of various political structures—right-wing and populist parties in particular—and ways in which they have instrumentalized Holocaust remembrance to make very specific domestic political gains (expanding the voter base, delegitimizing liberal opponents, and mobilizing nationalism), this book has taken a broader view.[8] It has explored how states have reacted when their

5. Jan Grabowski, "The Holocaust and Poland's 'History Policy,'" *Israel Journal of Foreign Affairs* 10, no. 3 (2016): 481–86, here 483.

6. Konstanty Gebert, "Projecting Poland and Its Past: Poland Wants You to Talk about the 'Polocaust'," *Index on Censorship* 47, no. 1 (2018): 35–37.

7. "Merkel Reiterates German Guilt as Polish Holocaust Bill Spat Rages," *Deutche Welle*, February 10, 2018, https://www.dw.com/en/merkel-reiterates-german-guilt-as-polish-holocaust-bill-spat-rages/a-42533935.

8. Volha Charnysh and Evgeny Finkel, "Rewriting History in Eastern Europe: Poland's New Holocaust Law and the Politics of the Past," *Foreign Affairs*, February 14, 2018, https://www.foreignaffairs.com/articles/hungary/2018-02-14/rewriting-history-eastern-europe.

sense of self, their identity, is threatened by external political narratives that undermine the very basis of that identity. As the case studies in the book have shown, as they pursued their new postcommunist, European identities, these states encountered a solidified and codified political memory of the Holocaust, a memory that did not fit with their own understanding of WWII. The desire to become European, to finally (re)join "the West," then produced a particular type of Holocaust remembrance that nominally followed the Western canon—memorial days were instituted, museums were opened, memorials were built, textbooks were adapted—but that, in doing so, used the existing narrative and visual imagery of the Holocaust to fight the real mnemonic battle of delegitimizing and criminalizing communism.[9]

Holocaust Remembrance beyond the Balkans and the Baltics

The Holocaust remembrance practices described and analyzed in the book have focused on two regions—the (Western) Balkans and the Baltics. But Holocaust appropriation—inversion, divergence, and conflation—is ubiquitous across postcommunist Eastern and Central Europe. These practices, however, vary depending on the way in which the Holocaust itself played out in each country, the country's unique experience of communism, and the domestic and international environment that the country has experienced since the postcommunist transition. To illustrate this diversity, I next briefly sketch Holocaust remembrance practices in two additional states—Slovakia and Ukraine—and discuss ways in which contemporary Russia is acting as a memory entrepreneur, influencing narratives of Holocaust remembrance across the post-Soviet space.

Slovakia

In the immediate aftermath of WWII in what was then Czechoslovakia, there was more space available to discuss the Holocaust than in much of the rest of communist Europe. This is because the particularly clear example of WWII-era Slovakia, a clerical-fascist Nazi puppet state that deported almost all of Slovakia's Jews to death camps, was a useful narrative foil for the communist regime. Czechoslovak communists built the legitimacy of the

9. Maria Mälksoo, "Criminalizing Communism: Transnational Mnemopolitics in Europe," *International Political Sociology* 8, no. 1 (2014): 82–99.

communist state on full delegitimation of WWII fascism, and the horrors of the Holocaust were helpful evidence of the precommunist criminal past.[10]

This opening closed in the late 1950s as the relationship between the Soviet Union and Israel soured, and it had an immediate effect on the remembrance of Jewish suffering in Czechoslovak representations of WWII. For example, when Czechoslovakia was preparing its first national exhibition at the Auschwitz-Birkenau Memorial Museum in 1960, a decision was made to exclude the names of Czechoslovak Jews deported to Auschwitz, as "such groups passively and without any resistance went into gas chambers."[11] The only room for memorialization—just as was the case in the Yugoslav national exhibition at Auschwitz—was for heroic resistance.

After the collapse of the communist regime, Czechoslovakia split in 1993, and both newly independent states began pursuing European Union membership. Holocaust remembrance was made an explicit condition for EU accession.[12] Slovakia, like Lithuania, joined the EU in the first wave of Eastern enlargement in 2004.

The new postcommunist Slovakia began to construct its new identity along strikingly similar lines to Croatia. As was the case in Croatia, Slovakia had to deal with the problem that its only pre-1993 experience with independence was as a puppet Nazi state that operated according to Nazi racial laws and carried out a full-scale deportation of its Jews. A particularly problematic fact is that between 1939 and 1944 Slovakia functioned as one of Germany's closest allies but was not occupied by Germany, which meant it had territorial sovereignty and independence to carry out deportations on its own using its own state apparatus of terror. It is during this time that fifty-seven thousand Slovak Jews were first interned in Slovakian camps, and then deported to death camps in occupied Poland, where almost all of them were killed.[13] Once Nazi Germany occupied Slovakia, starting in 1944, a further twelve thousand Slovak Jews were deported and killed in Auschwitz and other camps.[14]

10. Nina Paulovičová, "Holocaust Memory and Antisemitism in Slovakia: The Postwar Era to the Present," *Antisemitism Studies* 2, no. 1 (2018): 4–34.

11. Tomas Sniegon, *Vanished History: The Holocaust in Czech and Slovak Historical Culture* (New York: Berghahn Books, 2014), 62.

12. Paulovičová, "Holocaust Memory."

13. According to the same agreement the Independent State of Croatia had with Germany, Slovakia also paid 500 Reichsmarks for each Jew deported to Germany. James Mace Ward, *Priest, Politician, Collaborator: Jozef Tiso and the Making of Fascist Slovakia* (Ithaca, NY: Cornell University Press, 2013).

14. United States Holocaust Memorial Museum, "The Holocaust in Slovakia," accessed February 18, 2019, https://www.ushmm.org/wlc/en/article.php?ModuleId=10007324.

And as did Croatia, Slovakia largely ignored this inconvenient past. Nationalist elites contextualized Slovakia's WWII behavior by either downplaying it, referring to Jewish deportations as "evacuations," or by clinging to the notion that Slovak authorities only followed German orders and had no autonomy of their own. The Slovak Catholic Church was one of the main purveyors of these revisionist narratives, including a strong effort to rehabilitate the priest and Slovak WWII leader Jozef Tiso.[15]

In preparation for EU accession, Slovakia made a number of gestures to indicate its seriousness regarding Holocausts remembrance. Already in 1990, the new Slovak parliament officially apologized for the role Slovakia played in the Holocaust in the Declaration on the Deportation of Jews from Slovakia to Concentration Camps in 1942 and 1944. The Museum of Jewish Culture in Bratislava opened in 1994. More than a hundred Holocaust memorials were unveiled across the country, including in 1997 the prominent Central Memorial to the Holocaust of Jews in Slovakia, which opened in Bratislava.[16] In 2001, the Slovak Parliament declared September 9 Memorial Day to the Victims of the Holocaust and Racial Violence.

In 2002, Slovakia established the Nation's Memory Institute, a state institution tasked with investigating the country's past. The commission was clearly established with Slovakia's European Union ambitions front and center. Ján Langoš, the institute's first director, wrote an open letter to the then chairman of the European Commission, the European Union's chief executive body, in which he said, "The truth about the European past is our common heritage and it should be accessible to us as well as to people from the West."[17] The director then asked the European Commission to elevate the work of the institute to the level of the EU. This appeal served two purposes: to educate the West on "the European past"—by which the director meant that the crimes of communism committed against Slovakia should be added to Europe's existing memory repertoire—and to present Slovakia as a country ready for EU membership on account of its serious dedication to dealing with its totalitarian past.[18]

15. Paulovičová, "Holocaust Memory."

16. Nina Paulovičová, "The 'Unmasterable Past'? The Reception of the Holocaust in Postcommunist Slovakia," in *Bringing the Dark Past to Light: The Reception of the Holocaust in Postcommunist Europe*, ed. Joanna Beata Michlic and John-Paul Himka (Lincoln: University of Nebraska Press, 2013), 549–90, here 574.

17. Quoted in Tomas Sniegon, "Implementing Post-communist National Memory in the Czech Republic and Slovakia," *European Studies*, no. 30 (2013): 97–124, here 119.

18. Barbara Lášticová and Andrej Findor, "From Regime Legitimation to Democratic Museum Pedagogy? Studying Europeanization at the Museum of the Slovak National Uprising," in *Politics of*

Adopting a historical interpretation of the twentieth century that was prominent in the Lithuanian case, the Slovak government mandated the institute explore the "period of repression, 1939–1989." This approach, however, conflated the Nazi occupation and the communist era into one long timeline of terror, flattening both the radically different experiences of various Slovak populations during WWII and its immediate aftermath and the different time periods and types of repression between 1945 and 1989.

In addition to using this broad timeline, which the law establishing the institute simply called the period of *nesloboda* (nonfreedom), the institute's mandate distinguished the study of the "Slovak nation" from that of the "members of nationalities living in Slovakia," thus clearly separating ethnic Slovaks from all "others"—most directly, from the Jews and Roma.[19] In a patriotic nod, the institute's establishing legal document praised "a tradition of the Slovak's nation's fight against the occupiers, fascism, and communism."[20]

While the activities of the institute's first director seem to indicate a genuine interest in historical research, including research on collaboration, after his death in 2006 the institute took a different turn and became a more direct instrument of Slovakia's selective view of its own history.[21] The institute's main goal became the delegitimization of Slovakia's communist regime, achieved by grouping it together with fascism while making a case that communist dictatorship was, in fact, worse.[22] For example, the institute mandated that its own board members (thus presumably the writers of Slovakia's official national memory) must not ever have belonged to the Communist Party—but there was no such requirement for those who belonged to Hlinka's Slovak People's Party, which was the de facto ruling regime of Slovakia's WWII-era fascist state.[23] The consequence of this was that the institute's leadership became packed with apologists of Tiso's Slovakia, and this was reflected in the institute's scholarly output. While the institute published a number of publications of serious scholarly value, quite a number were also clearly revisionist, purposefully downplaying the overt anti-Semitism of Slovak WWII-era public figures.[24]

Collective Memory: Cultural Patterns of Commemorative Practices in Post-war Europe, ed. Sophie Wahnich, Barbara Lášticová, and Andrej Findor (Vienna: Lit Verlag, 2008), 237–58.

19. Sniegon, "Implementing Post-communist National Memory," 103–4.

20. Sniegon, "Implementing Post-communist National Memory," 104.

21. I thank Nadya Nedelsky for clarifying these points.

22. Nadya Nedelsky, "'The Struggle for the Memory of the Nation': Post-Communist Slovakia and its World War II Past," *Human Rights Quarterly* 38, no. 4 (2016): 969–92.

23. Sniegon, "Implementing Post-communist National Memory."

24. Nedelsky, "Struggle for the Memory."

Even though Slovakia joined the EU in 2004, "securing EU membership had less the effect of bringing Slovakia into line with the European Holocaust consensus, and more of lowering the costs of challenging it," as Nadya Nedelsky has demonstrated.[25] Slovakia joined the IHRA in 2005 and since then has worked on revamping its educational curriculum to more accurately and deeply reflect the scholarship on the Holocaust. However, a comprehensive study of the treatment of the Holocaust in Slovak secondary school textbooks has demonstrated patterns of omission, obfuscation, and downplaying of the Holocaust, especially the Slovak state role in extermination of its own citizens.[26]

Slovak remembrance, therefore, is full of contradictions. While there are many revisionist efforts, a big step in a country with still high rates of anti-Roma prejudice and almost no knowledge of the Roma Holocaust was the unveiling of the memorial to Roma victims of the Holocaust in Dunajská Streda in 2006.[27] In 2016, a comprehensive new Holocaust Museum opened at the site of the former concentration camp in Sereď, which documents the fate of Slovak Jews as well as Slovak collaboration in the Holocaust.[28]

In Slovakia, like in Croatia, the fundamental memory knot is the fact that the contemporary Slovak state is rooting its sovereignty—if not legally, then certainly discursively—in the First Slovak Republic, the fascist state during WWII. It is this original sin of establishing statehood as a fascist state that makes Slovakia's state biography so uncomfortable. This has presented a paradox for postcommunist Slovakia's identity construction. If the First Slovak Republic was truly independent and sovereign, then it acted independently in the Holocaust. If, however, WWII Slovakia was a puppet statelet and had to take orders from Germany, that diminishes the argument that it was a sovereign state to which contemporary Slovakia should look in its search for state legitimacy.[29] It is this tension between the concept of Slovak national sovereignty and the contested source of state legitimacy that shapes the contradictions of Holocaust remembrance in Slovakia today.

---

25. Nedelsky, "Struggle for the Memory," 990.

26. Deborah L. Michaels, "Holocaust Education in the 'Black Hole of Europe': Slovakia's Identity Politics and History Textbooks Pre-and Post-1989," *Intercultural Education* 24, no. 1–2 (2013): 19–40.

27. "Slovakia Commemorates Roma Holocaust Victims," *Slovak Spectator*, August 12, 2013, https://spectator.sme.sk/c/20047854/slovakia-commemorates-roma-holocaust-victims.html.

28. Slovak National Museum, Sereď Holocaust Museum, accessed February 18, 2019, http://www.snm.sk/?permanent-exhibitions-8&clanok=sered-holocaust-museum.

29. Michaels, "Holocaust Education."

Ukraine

The contours of the Holocaust in Ukraine are broadly similar to those described in the case of Lithuania. There is the circumstance of the "double occupation"—first by the Soviet Union, then by Nazi Germany—then the reincorporation of Ukraine into the USSR in 1945. The machinery of extermination was also similar; rooted in the broadly shared trope of "Judeo-communism," the Holocaust began with massive anti-Jewish pogroms, many by the Ukrainian militia, which was then—again, like in Lithuania—incorporated into the Nazi apparatus of murder. Most Ukrainian Jews were killed by shooting (the most well-known mass execution site is Babi Yar in Kyiv, where some thirty-three thousand Jews were killed in just two days); those who survived 1941 were sent to death camps.

Holocaust remembrance in Ukraine has been largely marginal since the end of communism and has, if anything, gotten more contested, becoming instrumentalized and appropriated, after the Maidan revolution in 2014. Squeezed between hostile Russia and the increasingly disinterested EU, Ukraine was not subjected to expectations and demands for Holocaust remembrance as part of the EU accession package. In the deeply divided Ukrainian society, the memory of the Holocaust has been equally split between the largely pro-Russian narrative, which relies on the old Soviet-era communist understanding of the Great Patriotic War and the Soviet Union's principal role in defeating Nazism, and the ever more aggressive nationalist revisionism, which glorifies anti-Soviet partisans and the right-wing militias of the Ukrainian Insurgent Army (UPA) and the Organization of Ukrainian Nationalists (OUN).[30] Both of these narratives, each for its own ideological reasons, marginalize if not outright ignore the Holocaust of Ukrainian Jews and the massive local participation of the Ukrainian militias in it.[31] The Ukrainian state Institute of National Memory, established in 2008, as well as the country's top state officials, including the president, have been active promoters of the rehabilitation of Ukrainian WWII nationalists and have ignored their involvement in the Holocaust.[32]

30. Sarah Fainberg, "Memory at the Margins: The Shoah in Ukraine (1991–2011)," in *History, Memory and Politics in Central and Eastern Europe: Memory Games*, ed. Georges Mink and Laure Neumayer (Houndmills: Springer, 2013), 86–102.

31. Andrii Portnov, "The Holocaust in the Public Discourse of Post-Soviet Ukraine," in *War and Memory in Russia, Ukraine and Belarus*, ed. Julie Fedor et al. (Cham: Springer, 2017), 347–70.

32. Jared McBride, "How Ukraine's New Memory Commissar Is Controlling the Nation's Past," *Nation*, August 13, 2015, https://www.thenation.com/article/how-ukraines-new-memory-commissar-is-controlling-the-nations-past.

Particularly visible has been the nationalist rallying around the legacies of Stepan Bandera, the leader of the radical and often anti-Semitic wing of the WWII-era OUN, and Roman Shukhevych, the military leader of the UPA.[33] This rallying was notable during the 2013–14 Euromaidan revolution, motivated in part by Ukraine's European ambitions but also even more by a strong desire of much of its population to get out from under Russian control. It is here that Holocaust remembrance meets state ontological security. Ukraine is a state uncertain of its identity—divided between Russian and ethnic Ukrainian populations, priorities and symbols, a state without a clear prior, fully independent pre-Soviet Ukrainian statehood to draw inspiration from. In its longing to construct its own, non-Russian, post-Soviet identity, Ukraine embraced Bandera and Shukhevych, bestowing upon them honors as Heroes of Ukraine in 2010 and 2007, respectively, and in the process it ignored (and some nationalists fully embraced) evidence of their anti-Semitism and history of Nazi collaboration.[34] This embrace has also caused increasing problems in relations with Poland, as UPA and OUN killed between them one hundred thousand Poles in a series of massacres in 1943 and 1944 in Volhynia and eastern Galicia, atrocities Poland often refers to as "genocide."[35]

The appropriation of the Holocaust to mean different things and, most significant, different victims—a dynamic evident in Serbia, Croatia, and Lithuania—was present in Ukraine as well.[36] Members of the Ukrainian diaspora routinely referred to the Great Famine of 1932–33 (Holodomor) as the Ukrainian Holocaust, and the former Ukrainian president Viktor Yushchenko made a big international push to recognize Holodomor as an international crime of genocide by the Soviet Union against the Ukrainian nation. Holodomor—and not the Holocaust—became a critical element in the construction of a new, post-Soviet Ukrainian identity, which conceptualized the Ukrainian nation as a post-genocide survivor, a collective victim of communism.[37] Again similar to the Lithuanian case, a strong undercurrent

33. Bandera's actions during WWII are difficult to neatly unravel because he collaborated with the Nazis in some periods but was imprisoned by them in others.

34. John-Paul Himka, "The Lviv Pogrom of 1941: The Germans, Ukrainian Nationalists, and the Carnival Crowd," *Canadian Slavonic Papers* 53, nos. 2–4 (2011): 209–43.

35. Jared McBride, "Peasants into Perpetrators: The OUN-UPA and the Ethnic Cleansing of Volhynia, 1943–1944," *Slavic Review* 75, no. 3 (2016): 630–54, here 639.

36. For a direct comparison of Ukraine and Lithuania along these lines, see Dovilė Budrytė, "Memory, War, and Mnemonical In/Security: A Comparison of Lithuania and Ukraine," in *Crisis and Change in Post-Cold War Global Politics*, ed. Erica Resende, Dovilė Budrytė, and Didem Buhari-Gulmez (Cham: Springer, 2018), 155–77.

37. Tatiana Zhurzhenko, "'Capital of Despair:' Holodomor Memory and Political Conflicts in Kharkiv after the Orange Revolution," *East European Politics and Societies* 25, no. 3 (2011): 597–639.

of this memory was the "Judeo-communism" narrative, which held Ukrainian Jews partly responsible for Holodomor on account of their membership in the Communist Party.[38]

In 2006, Ukraine legalized the memory of the Great Famine by passing a law criminalizing denial of Holodomor as a genocide against the Ukrainian people. A big part of "Holocausting" Holodomor involved inflating the number of Great Famine victims to more than the Holocaust's six million—this is why the former Ukrainian president Viktor Yushchenko insisted that the number of Holodomor's victims was seven to ten million.[39]

At the same time, Ukrainian Jews have tried to become more assertive while still being deeply divided about whether to support the Ukrainian nationalist government. In 2012, a huge Jewish community center complex—the largest of its kind in Eastern Europe—was erected in Dnipropetrovsk. It includes a Holocaust museum, the only one in Ukraine. Old Soviet-era inscriptions on Holocaust memorials have been replaced with more complete ones that specified the nature of Jewish victimization. But the site at Babi Yar, one of the largest execution sites anywhere in the former Soviet Union, where some one hundred thousand Jews were killed over a few months—continues to be a site of contested memory. There remains a 1976 Soviet memorial and a newer 1989 memorial that describes the killing of the Jews, but there are also more than twenty other memorials on the site, most with no connection to the Holocaust and some memorializing the OUN militia—itself implicated in the Holocaust.[40] The government of the president Petro Poroshenko has further tried to integrate Holocaust remembrance with OUN remembrance by, for example, appointing two high-profile supporters of OUN to a special committee to oversee the long-term development of the Babi Yar site, creating "a very awkward situation where Jewish leaders have to sit together in the Babi Yar committee with those who praise and glorify anti-Semites and murderers of Jews."[41]

As Omer Bartov has documented, almost all traces of a Jewish presence in Western Ukraine (Eastern Galicia) have been completely eradicated. Instead, in what was once a thriving center of Jewish life in the region, memorials to

38. Portnov, "Holocaust in the Public Discourse."

39. Fainberg, "Memory at the Margins," 98. The scholarly consensus puts the number of deaths in Holodomor between 2.5 and 3.5 million. John-Paul Himka, "How Many Perished in the Famine and Why Does It Matter?," *BRAMA*, February 2, 2008, http://www.brama.com/news/press/2008/02/080202himka_famine.html.

40. Portnov, "Holocaust in the Public Discourse," 360.

41. Eduard Dolinsky, Ukrainian Jewish Committee, quoted in Sam Sokol, "Anxiety over Far-right Role in Ukraine's Plans to Mark Babi Yar Anniversary," *Jewish Chronicle*, February 25, 2018.

Ukrainian nationals have been built over Holocaust memorials, synagogues have been turned into restaurants and sport halls, and death pits and ghettos remain unmarked. A monument to Stepan Bandera was erected on the physical site of the former ghetto in Drochobych.[42] Across Ukraine, there are former execution sites that now memorialize Ukrainian killers instead of their victims.[43] Pro-European Ukraine, however, is aware that the open embrace of anti-Semitic historical figures is problematic, which is why there has been a renewed effort to create a "multicultural" appeal for Ukrainian WWII nationalists—an effort that has included inventing, out of full cloth, narratives about Jews voluntarily joining the ranks of the UPA.[44]

In 2015 Ukraine passed a series of memory laws legislating how its contentious past was to be remembered and specifically rehabilitating WWII right-wing militias, which the Soviet Union had criminalized. The Law on the Legal Status and Honoring of Fighters for Ukraine's Independence in the 20th Century states that "the public denial of . . . the just cause of the fighters for Ukrainian independence in the 20th century insults the dignity of the Ukrainian people and is illegal."[45] That same year, the Ukrainian parliament passed a law making the UPA eligible for official government commemoration.[46]

On their face, these decommunization laws fit within the transitional justice paradigm of making a clean break from the communist past, without which, much scholarship on Eastern European transitions has warned us, postcommunist countries could not move on. Similar laws have also been passed in various forms in the Baltic states and in Hungary, the Czech Republic, Poland, and Moldova.[47] But in fact, it is clear that these laws have nothing to do with transitional justice and were driven instead by Ukraine's security concerns, especially its anxiety in the aftermath of Russia's annexation of Crimea and the conflict in Donbass. The post-Maidan Ukrainian government

42. Omer Bartov, *Erased: Vanishing Traces of Jewish Galicia in Present-day Ukraine* (Princeton, NJ: Princeton University Press, 2007), 41.

43. Jared McBride, "Ukrainian Holocaust Perpetrators Are Being Honored in Place of Their Victims," *Tablet*, July 20, 2016, http://www.tabletmag.com/jewish-news-and-politics/208439/holocaust-perpetrators-honored.

44. Jared McBride, "Ukraine's Invented a 'Jewish-Ukrainian Nationalist' to Whitewash Its Nazi-era Past," *Haaretz*, November 9, 2017.

45. Quoted in McBride, "Ukraine's New Memory Commissar."

46. Sam Sokol, "Ukrainian Parliament Recognizes Militia that Collaborated with the Nazis," *Jerusalem Post*, April 13, 2015.

47. Michael Shafir, "Ideology, Memory and Religion in Post-communist East Central Europe: A Comparative Study Focused on Post-Holocaust," *Journal for the Study of Religions and Ideologies* 15, no. 44 (2016): 52–110; also, Nikolay Koposov, *Memory Laws, Memory Wars: The Politics of the Past in Europe and Russia* (Cambridge: Cambridge University Press, 2017).

made this argument explicitly when it claimed that conflict in Ukraine is "hot" where the Soviet narrative of the past still reigns.[48] The Holocaust in Ukraine, therefore, remains a marginal memory that is understood through the prism of Ukraine's divisions, the expansionist role of Russia, and the extreme precariousness of Ukraine as a sovereign state.

Russia as a Memory Entrepreneur

World War II remembrance practices in postcommunist Europe, especially in the countries of the former Soviet Union, cannot be properly understood without taking into consideration the role Russia continues to play as a memory entrepreneur in the region. In its own memory routines, Russia has by and large continued with the Soviet "antifascist" narrative of WWII, which allows for very limited if any space for the Holocaust. When the Holocaust does appear in public life, its story remains one of Soviet heroism. For example, the popular 2018 Russian film *Escape from Sobibor*, while reminding Russians of the Jewish fate in death camps, still narrates the story of passive Jewish victims who needed a Soviet hero—a Red Army officer interned in the camp as a POW—to organize the prisoners' escape.[49]

Russia, however, has aggressively weaponized the memory of WWII—and the Holocaust memory embedded in it—to portray anti-Russian nationalists, especially in the Baltics and Ukraine, as "fascists." The reaction to this has sometimes been a blanket dismissal of the accusation as absurd; other times, the accusation by Russia has resulted in the celebration of WWII-era fascist movements, Russian accusations giving them a sort of renewed contemporary legitimacy.[50] From the perspective of the Baltic and Ukrainian governments and elite nationalists (including establishment historians), Russian accusations of fascism immediately delegitimize calls coming from elsewhere—from the West or from progressive voices within these states themselves—to reevaluate their past. Serious attempts to provide an honest historical account of WWII behavior in these countries, including their complicity in the Holocaust, are instantly dismissed as being pro-Russian. This has created a complete narrative stalemate where any

48. Ilya Nuzov, "The Dynamics of Collective Memory in the Ukraine Crisis: A Transitional Justice Perspective," *International Journal of Transitional Justice* 11, no. 1 (2016): 132–53.

49. I thank Elizaveta Gaufman for bringing this to my attention. Also, Isabel Sawkins, "Russia's Nationalist Mobilisation of the Holocaust on the Screen: Khabensky's film *Sobibor* (2018)," paper presented at the conference "A Crisis in 'Coming to Terms with the Past'? At the Crossroads of Translation and Memory," London, February 1–2, 2019.

50. Andrii Portnov, "Bandera Mythologies and their Traps for Ukraine," *Open Democracy*, June 22, 2016, https://www.opendemocracy.net/od-russia/andrii-portnov/bandera-mythologies-and-their-traps-for-ukraine.

criticism of right-wing historiography and memory politics is interpreted as a "Russian narrative" and not an independent scholarly pursuit.

Meanwhile, Russia has invoked its ossified narrative of the Great Patriotic War and the role the USSR played in ridding Europe of Nazism to justify its territorial expansion into Ukraine as a renewed fight against Ukrainian fascists, a continuation of a fight from seventy-five years ago.[51] In fact, the way in which WWII is memorialized in Russia provided direct narrative context for Russia's invasion of Crimea in 2014, as evidenced in the Russian president Vladimir Putin's justification of the annexation as "a legitimate reaction to Ukraine's persistent attempts to deprive Russians in Crimea of their 'historical memory,' subjecting them to 'forced assimilation.'"[52] Russian media framed the conflict as a fight against Western-sponsored Ukrainian fascists whose aim was to carry out a "genocide" against Russians in Ukraine.[53]

Russia has also institutionalized its view of WWII in its own memory law in 2014, which introduced criminal responsibility for "dissemination of knowingly false information about the activities of the USSR during the Second World War."[54] Putin directly weaponized this law by arguing, quite cynically, that it supported pro-Russian forces in Ukraine who were protecting ethnic Russians from "a rampage of Nazi, nationalist, and anti-Semitic forces."[55] Of course, the Russian commitment to antifascism and Russia's accusations of fascism do not signify genuine interest in antifascism and certainly not a genuine interest in the Holocaust, which is still largely lacking.[56] In fact, Russia has made direct overtures to openly fascist parties and movements in the West.[57]

The Russian foundational myth of the Great Patriotic War, however, is significant not only for how Russia views others, but also for how it views itself, as it is the building block of a self-identity that sees itself as a "historically

51. Marco Siddi, "The Ukraine Crisis and European Memory Politics of the Second World War," *European Politics and Society* 18, no. 4 (2017): 465–79.

52. Nuzov, "Dynamics of Collective Memory," 134.

53. Elizaveta Gaufman, "Memory, Media and Securitization: Russian Media Framing of the Ukrainian Crisis," *Journal of Soviet and Post-Soviet Politics and Society* 1, no. 1 (2015): 141–74.

54. Gleb Bogush and Ilya Nuzov, "Russia's Supreme Court Rewrites History of the Second World War," *EJIL: Talk!*, October 28, 2016, https://www.ejiltalk.org/russias-supreme-court-rewrites-history-of-the-second-world-war.

55. Vladimir Putin, press conference, March 4, 2014, quoted in Nuzov, "Dynamics of Collective Memory," 144.

56. Klas-Göran Karlsson, "The Reception of the Holocaust in Russia: Silence, Conspiracy, and Glimpses of Light," in *Bringing the Dark Past to Light: The Reception of the Holocaust in Postcommunist Europe*, ed. John-Paul Himka and Joanna B. Michlic (Lincoln: University of Nebraska Press, 2013), 487–515.

57. Marlene Laruelle, "Dangerous Liaisons: Eurasianism, the European Far Right, and Putin's Russia," in *Eurasianism and the European Far Right: Reshaping the Europe–Russia Relationship*, ed. Marlene Laruelle (Lanham: Lexington, 2015), 1–32.

great power on a distinct civilizational mission."[58] By accusing Ukraine and the Baltic states of neofascism, Russia presents itself internationally as the one "true defender of European values" and relives its moment of "geopolitical triumph."[59]

As Russia has asserted itself and acted on its territorial expansionist desires, there has been obvious reluctance by the West to criticize anti-Russian narratives—such as those in Ukraine and the Baltics—even if they clearly distort the past.[60] This decision not to confront the historical revisionism—including clear Holocaust revisionism—of anti-Russian governments in postcommunist Eastern Europe has then further provided these governments international cover to solidify and legislate the way Holocaust memory is produced and diffused across the post-Soviet space.[61]

Political Implications of Postcommunist Holocaust Remembrance

While most of this book has focused on Holocaust representation and appropriation—in museums, memorials, laws, and history textbooks—the political consequences of Holocaust appropriation, especially the rehabilitation of fascist movements that supported and often directly participated in the Holocaust, have been evident in the stunning rise of the far right across postcommunist Europe, part of a much broader, global far-right resurgence that has also critically destabilized politics in the West. The precise determination of causal factors that link Holocaust remembrance and the rise of the far right is beyond the scope and methodology of this book. What I want to showcase, however, are some examples of the ways in which Holocaust remembrance features in the far right's increasing assertiveness in postcommunist Europe.

---

58. Nuzov, "Dynamics of Collective Memory," 135.

59. Tatiana Zhurzhenko, "The Geopolitics of Memory," *Eurozine*, May 10, 2007, http://www.eurozine.com/the-geopolitics-of-memory/.

60. For an example of a Western pro-Ukrainian narrative of WWII in this vein, see Anne Applebaum, *Red Famine: Stalin's War on Ukraine* (New York: Doubleday, 2017).

61. It is worth pointing out that Israel has played a similar role in this dynamic by staying largely silent on the question of increasing Holocaust revisionism across Eastern Europe. In the attempt to shore up alliances across the postcommunist world, Israel's government has made a calculated judgment that securing diplomatic support in the face of international political isolation regarding its ongoing policies of occupation is more important than setting the record straight on the Holocaust. Michael Barnett, "The Real Reason Netanyahu Gave Cover To Holocaust Deniers," *Forward*, July 5, 2018, https://forward.com/opinion/404834/the-real-reason-netanyahu-gave-cover-to-holocaust-deniers.

In Poland, the two major far-right groups, All-Polish Youth and the National-Radical Camp, organized a massive (sixty thousand participants) rally in November 2017 in Warsaw that welcomed neo-Nazis and carried banners asserting that "only white Christians belonged in Europe."[62] The Polish government supported the rally, and while it condemned the racist and anti-Semitic banners, the government still called the rally "a great celebration of Poles" and "a beautiful sight."[63] Indeed, extreme xenophobia of the kind demonstrated in this rally is not only the provenance of the far-right movement—the mainstream Polish PiS (Law and Justice) party has become radicalized and moved further to the right. A PiS member of parliament wondered in 2018 why there were "so many Jews among the abortionists, despite the Holocaust."[64] A PiS senator shared on his Facebook page a Nazi propaganda film that depicted the Jews as controlling and cruelly abusing those confined in the Warsaw Ghetto. This narrative about "Jewish perpetrators" of the Holocaust is prevalent and was repeated in the Polish prime minister Mateusz Morawiecki's defense of the 2018 Holocaust bill.[65] While PiS as a party may not be openly anti-Semitic, it is careful not to risk losing the seemingly deep reservoir of anti-Semitic votes.

In Ukraine, there was a wave of anti-Semitic and anti-Roma incidents in 2018, including a call by a far-right politician to "cleans[e] Ukraine of zhidi [Jews]," the destruction of a Holocaust memorial in Ternopil, a neo-Nazi march in honor of an SS unit in Lviv, and an especially violent attack on a Roma encampment in Kyiv—all in the span of a few weeks.[66] Members of the far-right National Squad militia marched along the streets of Ukrainian cities dressed in black, promising to "establish order in Ukraine" and fight the "alcoholic genocide of the Ukrainian people." A smoke grenade was thrown at a bookshop in Lviv during a lecture on the Holocaust.[67] These incidents may be isolated and marginalized,

---

62. Volha Charnysh, "The Rise of Poland's Far Right: How Extremism Is Going Mainstream," *Foreign Affairs*, December 18, 2017, https://www.foreignaffairs.com/articles/poland/2017-12-18/rise-polands-far-right.

63. Rick Noack, "How Poland Became a Breeding Bround for Europe's Far Right," *Washington Post*, November 14, 2017.

64. Charnysh, "Rise of Poland's Far Right."

65. Leonid Bershidsky, "Why Polish Jews Are Growing Uneasy," *Bloomberg News*, February 27, 2018, https://www.bloomberg.com/view/articles/2018-02-27/polish-jews-are-growing-worried-about-anti-semitism.

66. Lev Golinkin, "Violent Anti-Semitism Is Gripping Ukraine—And The Government Is Standing Idly By," *Forward*, May 20, 2018, https://forward.com/opinion/401518/violent-anti-semitism-is-gripping-ukraine-and-the-government-is-standing.

67. Anna Nemtsova, "The Frightening Far-Right Militia That's Marching in Ukraine's Streets, Promising to Bring 'Order,'" *Daily Beast*, February 5, 2018, https://www.thedailybeast.com/the-frightening-far-right-militia-thats-marching-in-ukraines-streets-promising-to-bring-order.

but they have caused Ukrainian Jews to note a "disturbing correlation between Holocaust revisionism and violence against living Jews."[68]

In Hungary in 2010, the far-right party Jobbik, in language that could be easily replaced with that in any Nazi document, called for those members of the Roma community the government deemed "antisocial" to be removed from their homes and placed in concentration camps.[69] Jobbik has since only gained in strength and has become the second strongest party in Hungary. Fidesz, the party of the current Hungarian prime minister, Viktor Orbán, has in many ways copied Jobbik's platform, especially on issues of immigration and refugees.[70] Under Orbán, Hungary has placed Middle Eastern refugees in "container camps" and most of Orbán's continuing popularity is based on his extreme views on immigration and his increasingly unveiled anti-Semitism.[71] At a March 2018 election rally in Budapest, Orbán reached into the well of the oldest anti-Semitic tropes and made them the centerpiece of his popular appeal when he attacked the Hungarian-American philanthropist George Soros: "We are fighting an enemy that is different from us. Not open, but hiding; not straightforward but crafty; not honest but base; not national but international; does not believe in working but speculates with money; does not have its own homeland but feels it owns the whole world."[72]

Philo-Semitism and Jewish Cultural Appropriation

A parallel development to the rise of the far right and spike in overt anti-Semitism has been the cultural appropriation of Jewishness as a form of philo-Semitism in various countries in the region. This has been most manifest in Poland, where scholars have been tracking the so-called "Jewish cultural turn" in which young people, mostly on the left, have been showing a strong interest in all thing Jewish, past and present. Polish Jewish community organizations have noted an increased interest in conversion to Judaism, both

68. Lev Golinkin, "How the Holocaust Haunts Eastern Europe," *New York Times*, January 26, 2018.

69. Daniel McLaughlin, "Far-Right Party Calls for Camps for Hungary's Roma," *Irish Times*, September 3, 2010.

70. Emily Schultheis, "How Hungary's Far-Right Extremists Became Warm and Fuzzy," *Foreign Policy*, April 6, 2018, http://foreignpolicy.com/2018/04/06/how-hungarys-far-right-extremists-became-warm-and-fuzzy.

71. Patrick Wintour, "Hungary to Detain All Asylum Seekers in Container Camps," *Guardian*, March 7, 2017; Michael Colborne, "Orbán Blamed All of Hungary's Problems on a Jew—and Won, Big Time," *Haaretz*, April 9, 2018.

72. Shaun Walker, "Hungarian Leader Says Europe is Now 'Under Invasion' by Migrants," *Guardian*, March 15, 2018.

from Poles who are discovering their Jewish roots and from non-Jewish Poles who are simply attracted to Judaism and Jewish culture.[73] This manifestation of philo-Semitism in Poland, while often clearly well intentioned, can also be interpreted as at times self-serving. Its motivation may not always be just respecting the Jews (dead or living); philo-Semitism may also act as a form of virtue signaling for a segment of cosmopolitan-leaning Poles who appropriate Jewishness as a way to expand the boundaries of what it means to be Polish and to move Polish identity from ethnic to multicultural, from Catholic to secular.[74] These non-Jewish Poles are, in another reading, appropriating Jewishness as a form of "redemptive cosmopolitanism."[75] The website Virtual Shtetl, run by the POLIN Museum of the History of Polish Jews, performs a similar function by making a connection between the Polish history of diversity—as manifested in the historic numbers and diversity of Jewish shtetls—and the contemporary multicultural world to which this new, progressive Poland wants to belong.[76]

Other Jewish revival projects are more clearly directed at the international audience and as such can coexist with the otherwise hostile official narrative. These are projects of public diplomacy that advertise Polish multiculturalism and European values, in an attempt to deflect international criticism.[77] Rather than philo-Semitic, these projects better fit the practice of "remembering to benefit," which takes the form of praising the lost multiethnic and multicultural past and remembering the Holocaust in order to obtain international legitimacy and respectability and to signal the adoption of European norms and values.[78] As I have described in the case of Lithuania embracing its Yiddish heritage and presenting it is a major tourist draw, Holocaust remembrance here is instrumentalized for very specific political purposes—elevating the state's international status, diffusing the criticisms about ethnic homogeneity, and inventing a multicultural world that, in reality, simply does not exist. The profound consequence of a total absence of

---

73. Geneviève Zubrzycki, "Nationalism, 'Philosemitism,' and Symbolic Boundary-Making in Contemporary Poland," *Comparative Studies in Society and History* 58, no. 1 (2016): 66–98.

74. Zubrzycki, "Nationalism, 'Philosemitism.'"

75. Michael Meng, *Shattered Spaces: Encountering Jewish Ruins in Postwar Germany and Poland* (Cambridge: Harvard University Press, 2011).

76. Museum of the History of Polish Jews POLIN, Virtual Shtetl, accessed February 18, 2019, https://sztetl.org.pl/en.

77. Thomas Just, "Public Diplomacy and Domestic Engagement: The Jewish Revival in Poland," *Place Branding and Public Diplomacy* 11, no. 4 (2015): 263–75.

78. Joanna Beata Michlic, "'Remembering to Remember,' 'Remembering to Benefit,' 'Remembering to Forget': The Variety of Memories of Jews and the Holocaust in Postcommunist Poland," *Post-Holocaust and Anti-Semitism*, no. 113 (Jerusalem: Jerusalem Center for Public Affairs, 2012).

real, living Jews, and of any discussion of local complicity in that absence, is then covered up by performances of multiculturalism for international audiences.[79] The murdered Jews of Europe serve to retroactively impart an image of multiculturalism and diversity onto countries that have neither.[80]

Much of this retrofitted multiculturalism is also of a commercial variety, such as the somewhat Jewish-theme-park quality of Krakow's Kazimierz neighborhood, the pre-WWII Jewish quarter decimated in the war but then reconstructed by Steven Spielberg in 1993 as a filming location for *Schindler's List*.[81] Since then, the Kazimierz neighborhood has become a place of commercial tourism, with Jewish food restaurants and souvenir shops lining the streets, catering both to curious tourists (many of whom are no doubt not aware that what they are experiencing is a Hollywood reconstruction and not anything authentic to Krakow's Jewish experience) and to Krakow's young hipster crowd, for whom all things Jewish have become attractive as a symbol of cultured status.[82]

The remembrance of Jewish life and death has also served very direct political purposes for governments across the region. In 2018, a magnificent synagogue in Subotica, northern Serbia, was finally reopened after years of painstaking reconstruction, financed mostly by the European Union. It is the second largest synagogue in Europe (after the Great Synagogue in Budapest), and an architectural jewel in the art nouveau style. Subotica, a city with a substantial pre-WWII Jewish population—almost all transported to and killed in Auschwitz—today has a Hungarian plurality (33 percent) and so was of interest to Hungarian prime minister Viktor Orbán. At the official opening of the renovated synagogue, Orbán used the opportunity to claim common cause with Jews against Muslim immigrants: "[It is] our moral duty to stand up for a Hungary and a Europe in which Jews and Christians can live and practice their religions without fear." Arguing that it is

79. Karen C Underhill, "Next Year in Drohobych: On the Uses of Jewish Absence," *East European Politics and Societies* 25, no. 3 (2011): 581–96; Meng, *Shattered Spaces*; Ruth Ellen Gruber, *Virtually Jewish: Reinventing Jewish Culture in Europe* (Berkeley: University of California Press, 2002).

80. Alejandro Baer and Natan Sznaider, *Memory and Forgetting in the Post-Holocaust Era: The Ethics of Never Again* (Milton Park: Routledge, 2017), 14.

81. A much more offensive version of this commercial fake Jewishness can be found in "Jewish themed" restaurants like the "Pid Zolotoju Rozoju" (At the golden rose) in Lviv, Ukraine, which does not have fixed prices "because Jews like to haggle"; its waiters are dressed in fake Jewish garb, complete with the fake peyot sidelocks, and its staff entertain customers with anti-Semitic jokes. Cnaan Liphshiz, "A Queasy Dinner at Lviv's Controversial Jewish Themed Restaurant," *Haaretz*, April 4, 2016.

82. Eleonora Narvselius, "Spicing Up Memories and Serving Nostalgias: Thematic Restaurants and Transnational Memories in East-Central European Borderland Cities," *Journal of Contemporary European Studies* 23, no. 3 (2015): 417–32.

not his government but rather Muslim immigrants who are responsible for the increase in anti-Semitism in Hungary, Orbán also warned the somewhat shocked Jews who gathered for this important ceremonial occasion, "Our migrant policies serve the interests of European Jewish communities, even if they don't stand up for their own interests."[83]

Orbán was not the only Eastern European leader who used the Subotica synagogue opening as a political rally. The Serbian president Aleksandar Vučić, another high-profile leader at the event, used the occasion for two separate purposes. The first was to signal to the European Union Serbia's continuing support for the Jewish community. The second was to make a big show of Serbian-Hungarian unity in a continuing bid for Hungarian support for Serbia's delayed EU accession. Vučić gratefully stood next to Orbán as the Hungarian prime minister, in the midst of his overtly anti-Semitic electoral campaign, declared in the Subotica Synagogue, "Respect for the Jewish community is what we have in common."[84]

Exclusionary Nation-Building

Much of the scholarship on postcommunist Eastern Europe is built on the premise that these states need to make a complete, clean break with the communist past in order to transition to the world of European liberal democracies. In fact, much of the literature on postcommunist transitions has been devoted to measuring obstacles to democratization and liberalization based on enduring communist legacies and suggesting ways to overcome them.[85]

My book, however, has taken a different approach. It has traced the process of not an institutional but rather a narrative break with the communist past to explore its consequences for contemporary state identity politics. The findings of this book demonstrate ways in which postcommunist states have constructed a narrative about the past that bolsters their identity and self-esteem in the present. The practices of Holocaust remembrance I have described are important for contemporary politics because they indicate that the basis of nation-building after communism was ethnic and exclusionary. While this new identity construction may not be about the Jews or about the Holocaust at all, it comes from a place of exclusion of others, the

83. Colborne, "Orbán Blamed."

84. Ana Milosevic, "Serbia and Hungary Play Cynical Games With Past," *Balkan Insight*, April 6, 2018, http://www.balkaninsight.com/en/article/feature-04-05-2018.

85. For an attempt to empirically measure the effect of legacies of communism, see Grigore Pop-Eleches and Joshua A. Tucker, *Communism's Shadow: Historical Legacies and Contemporary Political Attitudes* (Princeton, NJ: Princeton University Press, 2017).

non-existent Jews but also the existent new others—refugees, migrants, or other ethnic minorities such as the Roma or Muslims.

This exclusionary concept of nationhood has come into sharp focus since the 2015 refugee crisis, when politics became intensely ethnic and old anti-Semitic tropes morphed easily into new prejudices—the already existing, deep anti-Romism and the newer and increasingly mainstreamed Islamophobia. It is within this context of old prejudices being used against different groups of people that we can understand how even left-of-center politicians such as the Slovak prime minister Robert Fico can publicly declare that, "Islam has no place in Slovakia," and not "a single Muslim" migrant is welcome in his country.[86] The prime minister did not speak out of turn. His is the view completely in line with public opinion—70 percent of respondents surveyed in 2015 expressed concern about the arrival of refugees in Slovakia, a country that has accepted almost no refugees in this wave.[87] Similarly, in Poland, 74 percent of respondents in 2017 opposed accepting refugees from the Middle East and Africa.[88] The Slovak far-right party Kotleba–People's Party Our Slovakia originally built its support on nostalgia for the WWII Slovak fascist state and displayed open anti-Semitism. Once they won seats in the parliament for the first time in 2016, their rhetoric shifted from anti-Semitism to attacks against immigrants and the Roma.[89] The targets may be shifting, but the sentiment remains the same.

But I want to be very clear—the problems of Holocaust appropriation, revision, indifference, or conflation are evident everywhere, not just in Eastern Europe. There are patterns of Holocaust remembrance in Western Europe that are just as problematic as those described in this book, if in different ways. France, the Netherlands, Italy, and Belgium have nurtured a narrative of heroic resistance to Nazism even though evidence increasingly indicates that collaboration was much more prevalent than these narratives allow.[90] The United Kingdom has built its entire post-WWII identity on its national bravery in the face of German might and its status as a haven for Jewish refugees. But the UK in

86. Paulovičová, "Holocaust Memory," 24.

87. Paulovičová, "Holocaust Memory," 24.

88. Charnysh, "Rise of Poland's Far Right."

89. Rick Lyman, "After Years in the Shadows, Europe's Neo-Fascists Are Stepping Back Out," *New York Times*, March 20, 2017.

90. Rebecca Clifford, *Commemorating the Holocaust: The Dilemmas of Remembrance in France and Italy* (Oxford: Oxford University Press, 2013); Roni Stauber, *Collaboration with the Nazis: Public Discourse after the Holocaust* (London: Routledge, 2010). On the removal of Holocaust memorials in the Netherlands and an increasing opposition to the memorialization of Jewish suffering and Dutch complicity, see Cnaan Liphshiz, "Why Are People Protesting Holocaust Memorials in Holland and Belgium?," *Jewish Telegraphic Agency*, October 23, 2018.

fact refused entry to many more Jews than it accepted, and it has never fully acknowledged that it allowed the Holocaust on its own soil when Jews from the Channel Islands were deported to Nazi death camps, from which almost none returned.[91] The state of Holocaust education in the UK remains wanting.[92] In the United States, there is little awareness of the cruelty with which the US government refused entry to Jewish refugees, most famously on the *St. Louis* ship in 1939, when none of the 937 Jewish passengers on board were allowed to enter the country, and of how much the US public in fact knew about the fate of the Jews but overwhelmingly opposed their immigration.[93]

The increase in anti-Semitism, the rise of the far right, and the Islamophobic refusal to allow in Middle Eastern refugees fleeing civil war and destitution are also central features of contemporary politics in the West, including the prominent example of the United States under the administration of the US president Donald Trump.[94] In Italy, the minister of the interior proposed creating a registry of Italian Roma in an effort to expel them from the country. This is not the only contemporary move reminiscent of Italy's fascist past—the Italian government has also routinely refused to allow ships with Middle Eastern migrants to dock in Italy.[95] And in Denmark, the country that has built its own state biography as the rare safe haven for Jews during the Holocaust, the government has proposed a new law that would designate immigrant communities as ghettos, and, starting at age one, separate ghetto children from their parents for twenty-five hours a week for mandatory instruction in "Danish values."[96]

These actions have caused great anxiety among European Jews, as, in the words of a Hungarian Jewish human rights activist, "When a Roma person is targeted, I feel less safe because I know they will come for me next."[97] All of these are examples of contemporary policies that are rooted in an understanding of national identity in exclusively ethnic terms. The consequences of these policies can be catastrophic.

---

91. Gilly Carr, *On British Soil: Nazi Persecution in the Channel Islands* (Cambridge: McDonald Institute for Archaeological Research, 2017).

92. Rosie Whitehouse, "The Failure of Holocaust Education in Britain," *Tablet*, October 16, 2018, https://www.tabletmag.com/jewish-arts-and-culture/272237/holocaust-education-britain.

93. United States Holocaust Memorial Museum, "Voyage of the St. Louis," accessed February 18, 2019, https://www.ushmm.org/wlc/en/article.php?ModuleId=10005267.

94. Faiza Patel and Rachel Levinson-Waldman, "The Islamophobic Administration," April 19 (New York: Brennan Center for Justice, 2017).

95. Stephanie Kirchgaessner, "Far-Right Italy Minister Vows 'Action' To Expel Thousands of Roma," *Guardian*, June 19, 2018.

96. Ellen Barry and Martin Selsoe Sorensen, "In Denmark, Harsh New Laws for Immigrant 'Ghettos,'" *New York Times*, July 1, 2018.

97. Jewish Telegraphic Agency and Cnaan Liphshiz, "European Jews Watch on in Fear as Italy Targets Roma People," *Haaretz*, June 24, 2018.

What the findings of my book imply is that not dealing with historical exclusion, marginalization, dispossession, and brutality; not understanding, working through, and acknowledging the pernicious consequences of conceptualizing the nation in an exclusionary way leads to contemporary exclusion, marginalization, dispossession, and brutality.[98] The practices of Holocaust remembrance I have described are in different countries practices of indifference, inversion, appropriation, or conflation, but in all cases they are patterns of exclusion and not belonging. The Holocaust, to the extent that it is remembered and memorialized at all, is remembered and memorialized as a "Jewish issue," a "Jewish thing" that even if dutifully acknowledged has not much, if anything, to do with the contemporary nation. And because it is difficult to integrate the Holocaust into a memory that is centered on a particular nation, the Holocaust may be commemorated through official state practices, but it has not become a national memory.[99]

While there is much need for work on Holocaust remembrance practices in the West and ways in which they may be changing to fit the political needs of contemporary Western societies, my book has explored the role of communism as an intervening memory and system of meaning in Eastern Europe, the principal site of the Holocaust, the space where millions were murdered, often by people they knew, and where their graves remain unmarked; their houses, businesses, small intimate objects taken, also often by people they knew; their absence morphing into the social and economic fabric of new ethnic nation-states.

It is here, in Eastern Europe, that postcommunist states have used the Holocaust to search for their own genocides, in which they are the victims, never the perpetrators.[100] In so doing, they have removed Jews from the history of Eastern Europe's twentieth century and thus also from the history of the Holocaust, replacing them with stories of their Righteous Gentile saviors—Poles, Lithuanians, Slovaks, or Serbs, who, in this narrative, were the true victims of the twentieth century.[101] The Jews become the background to either displaced victimhood or stories about heroism of the non-Jewish majority. The postcommunist interest in the past, I have argued, was

98. Swaan van Iterson and Maja Nenadović, "The Danger of Not Facing History: Exploring the Link between Education about the Past and Present-Day Anti-Semitism and Racism in Hungary," *Intercultural Education* 24, nos. 1–2 (2013): 93–102.

99. Sławomir Kapralski, "The Holocaust: Commemorated but Not Remembered? Post-colonial and Post-traumatic Perspectives on the Reception of the Holocaust Memory Discourse in Poland," *Journal of Historical Sociology* 31, no. 1 (2018): e48–e65.

100. Evgeny Finkel, "In Search of Lost Genocide: Historical Policy and International Politics in Post-1989 Eastern Europe," *Global Society* 24, no. 1 (2010): 51–70.

101. Grabowski, "The Holocaust."

motivated not by a search for an honest account of history but rather by the desire to further strengthen national identity and a sense of the nation's valor as existing continuously in time.[102]

A Plea for Memory Solidarity

The question that I want to end this book with is: why is memory solidarity so difficult? There is a tacit understanding in scholarship as well as in popular writing that admitting responsibility for past acts is difficult, asking too much, painful, traumatic. But why, exactly, do we take this absence of societal self-reflection as a normal state of affairs? What would it take away from the postcommunist successes of Eastern Europe to admit the role some of their countrymen played in the destruction of their fellow citizens, to be honest about history and to make amends? This is not an issue of a lack of empathy or lack of knowledge; it is an issue of how postcommunist states have organized their politics and of how some groups have never much mattered to a national sense of self—not in 1941 and not today.

The problem here is one of what Michael Rothberg called "competitive memory," where "the boundaries of memory parallel the boundaries of group identity."[103] Social groups fail to recognize the trauma of others because they are consumed by their own trauma, even sometimes projecting the responsibility for it onto those others.[104] And this is what explains the violent reaction against calls for a serious reckoning with the crimes of the Holocaust and for accepting a degree of culpability—including culpability for the economic and social benefit from the Jewish absence—across the postcommunist space.[105] The Jews of Eastern Europe are again inconvenient, their demands for remembrance raining on the parade of postcommunist independence and ruining the moment that was supposed to be triumphant, liberating, and hopeful.

My plea, following Rothberg, is for true memory solidarity, where groups feel invested in and empathetic for histories that include *all* of their fellow

102. Kapralski, "The Holocaust," e48.

103. Michael Rothberg, *Multidirectional Memory: Remembering the Holocaust in the Age of Decolonization* (Stanford: Stanford University Press, 2009), 5.

104. Jeffrey C. Alexander, "Toward a Theory of Cultural Trauma," in *Cultural Trauma and Collective Identity*, ed. Jeffrey C. Alexander et al. (Berkeley: University of California Press, 2004), 1–30, here 1.

105. The Polish documentary film *The Legacy of Jedwabne* (2005) shows incredibly uncomfortable scenes of Holocaust survivors and their children and grandchildren visiting Jedwabne in the early 2000s to see the site of murder. Polish villagers—who have generations ago moved into the murdered Jews' homes—refuse to talk to them out of fear that they have come to take their houses back.

citizens, majorities and minorities alike—histories that recognize that the unimaginable violence that was committed against their former neighbors was a betrayal of their own citizens and, in that sense, was also a betrayal of them. Feeling and expressing accountability for all of this violent history makes our histories more balanced and complete and our societies more just. Memory solidarity is politically difficult. Avoiding it may be pragmatic, but it is morally indefensible. This is why Holocaust remembrance is of continued importance—ethical and political. The Holocaust is not just in the Eastern European past. It continues to be a part of its present.

INDEX